JAZZ TEXT

JAZZ TEXT

VOICE AND IMPROVISATION
IN POETRY, JAZZ, AND SONG

Charles O. Hartman

PRINCETON UNIVERSITY PRESS   PRINCETON, NEW JERSEY

Library of Congress Cataloging-in-Publication Data
Hartman, Charles O., 1949–
Jazz text : voice and improvisation in poetry, jazz, and song /
Charles O. Hartman.
p. cm.
Includes bibliographical references (p.) and index.
Discography: p.
ISBN 0-691-06817-8
1. Jazz—History and criticism. 2. Music and literature. 3. Improvisation
(Music) I. Title.
ML3506.H38   1991   781.65—dc20   90–47773

This book has been composed in Linotron Times Roman

Princeton University Press books are printed
on acid-free paper, and meet the guidelines
for permanence and durability of the Committee
on Production Guidelines for Book Longevity
of the Council on Library Resources

Printed in the United States of America by
Princeton University Press,
Princeton, New Jersey

10 9 8 7 6 5 4 3 2 1

''All the Things You Are.'' Music by Jerome Kern and lyrics by Oscar
Hammerstein II. Copyright © 1939 T. B. Harms Company (c/o The Welk
Music Group, Santa Monica, CA 90401). Copyright renewed. International
copyright secured. All rights reserved. Used by permission.

Excerpts from the following are reprinted by permission of New Directions
Publishing Corp.: William Carlos Williams, *Collected Poems, 1909–1939*;
copyright 1938 by New Directions Publishing Corp. William Carlos
Williams, *Imaginations*; copyright © 1970 by Florence H. Williams. David
Antin, *talking at the boundaries*; copyright © 1976 by Daniel Allman.

Excerpts from *Sin* by Ai are reprinted by permission of Houghton Mifflin
Company. Copyright © 1986 by Ai.

''I Know a Man,'' ''The Immoral Proposition,'' and the third section of ''I
cannot see you,'' by Robert Creeley, from the *Collected Poems, 1945–
1975* (University of California Press, 1984), are reprinted by permission of
the author.

(*permissions continued at back of book*)

For Carl F. Hartman

Contents

Acknowledgments ————————————————————————————

SUPPORT for the writing of this book has come less from institutions than from individuals. Meredith Steinbach got me to write it by asking at the right moment what I really wanted to write about; through the years it has taken, she has been companion, soundboard, goad, guide, and always friend. James McCalla not only read the musical sections with a professional exactitude that forestalled many solecisms, but brought to the book as a whole his considerable and scrupulous literary intelligence. Without the generous and frequent help of Don Bialostosky, I would still be floundering or despairing at one or another intermediate point; every chapter bears his mark, and at few points can I readily distinguish what I originally thought from the results of our discussions. Robert Brown, a wise and diligent editor of my *Free Verse*, has been even more indispensable to the task this time.

I am also very grateful to Ed Brunner for his detailed and penetrating comments at the crucial beginning stage; to Lee Konitz, Larry Coryell, David Antin, Philip Levine, and Jackson Mac Low for their first-hand wisdom; to Michael Harper for some key words and a key recording; to Dan Morgenstern of the Institute for Jazz Studies at Rutgers University for a letter clarifying several historical points about vocalese; to Paul Mariani for expert help with William Carlos Williams; to David Smalover of the National Guitar Summer Workshop for logistical help; and to Don Berger and Cindy Moss for the room in which the beginning of chapter 2 was to be found.

Parts of chapter 2 were delivered at a special session of the Modern Language Association on Robert Creeley's work in December 1984, and some material is adapted from "Cognitive Metaphor," *New Literary History* 13, no. 2 (Winter 1982).

Some of the material in chapter 5 on "Michael from Mountains" was originally published in different form in "Analysis of a Song: Joni Mitchell's 'Michael from Mountains,' " *Centennial Review* 21, no. 4 (Fall 1977).

Part of chapter 7 was published as "Essay Ending with Six Reasons to Read Jackson Mac Low," *Prairie Schooner*, Spring 1988.

Chapter 6 was published in *Southwest Review*, Spring 1988.

JAZZ TEXT

Introduction

HUMAN voices speak volumes to us. In a song, for instance: We understand that when

> eleven moons played across the rainbow

there were eleven not because Jimi Hendrix is appealing to some mystical tradition, but because of a personal visionary excitement. Though we deduce this partly from the more obviously arbitrary "a thousand stars" in a previous line, our real conviction comes from the tone of his singing voice. His voice rises emphatically on both "eleven" and "moons," daring anyone's doubt. Without thinking about any of this, we know.

This profound knack underlies many human interactions besides the situations of talk and song. Various arts extend it, or count on an audience being able to extend it, in various directions, none more evidently than poetry and jazz. The speaking voice through its tone tells us far more than the words that one could transcribe onto a page; yet poets have techniques (which we summarize under the heading of *prosody*) for recreating that tonal supplement in a written medium. So we habitually speak of the "voice" of a poem, or of the poet in a poem. Going in the other direction—subtracting from the speaking voice the words and the information they convey—musicians can transfer the eloquent remainder to an instrument; so that we can also speak of the "voice" of a musician who might be physically mute.

The different modes of the voice (singing, talking, reciting) and its different extensions (a printed poem, an instrumental solo) are the mysterious phenomena on which this book dwells.

Discussions of the arts, particularly poetry and jazz, use the term *voice* constantly, always with some claim on its thick implicit knot of meanings, but we seldom tease out any of the strands. Puzzles abound. "Voice," for example, includes the physical medium of identification; in "voice" an abstract idea of selfhood (Martin Luther King as a voice in American political history) and the vibrations of air in a particular throat (Martin Luther King's unmistakable voice) are not metaphorically juxtaposed, but interwoven. Again, though my voice is the truest sign of my self, yet voice is detachable from self, so that one person can serve as another's voice (an *advocate*), the *Village Voice* can speak for Greenwich Village, and so on. Voice seems to be not self but the going outward of the self, a going that can be indirect or redirected. In the Old Testament "voice" is the axis between man and God; the word occurs most often as a synonym for either "command" or "prayer" (as in "lifted up his voice"). Sometimes it epitomizes life; II Kings 4:31 says, as a periphrasis for death, "There was neither voice, nor hearing."

The varied relations among different uses of the word ask to be explored through some complementary variety of material. Roland Barthes has remarked that for all the books on metaphor, there are few on metonymy. My first chapters deal with "voice" as metaphor—not far from the normal usage of the word in literary criticism, but here applied to both (silent) poems and (unspeaking) jazz. The adaptations this requires also help illuminate what critics usually mean by "voice." The later chapters explore more metonymic senses of "voice," first by taking in the further complications of song, and then by examining some uses and limits of voice. Still, these are not opposed or even constantly distinguishable aspects of the continuous idea of "voice"; the metaphor never disappears, and the metonymy is there from the beginning.

My first four chapters alternate between jazz and poetry, and the last chapters move more freely between them. Though some connection between these two arts in postwar America is frequently intuited, even inevitable, the pair rarely confront each other in criticism. Yet contemporary American poetry is vitally interested—as many poets are personally interested—in two of the central principles of the jazz art: improvisation, and that emphasis on personalized sound which again we often call the player's "voice." For the whole poetry that derives from Williams's modernism rather than Eliot's, the logic of poetic authority runs almost this directly:

improvisation →
            spontaneity →
                    genuineness →
                            authenticity →
                                    authority

Tenuous as this oversimplified chain must be, it points toward yearnings in poetry—often yearnings away from the printed page—that make jazz the land of heart's desire.

If voice and improvisation constitute a common ground for jazz and poetry, the position of the two arts within our cultural moment also sets them side by side. Though both are commercially negligible (romance novels and rock music sell better by perhaps two orders of magnitude), they have a central place in American culture and in the role of the U.S. in world culture. That jazz is America's only major original artistic invention is a commonplace that may call for footnotes but needs no defense. On the other hand, the fight to create a truly American poetry (Whitman's fight, Williams's fight against Eliot, Olson's belated obsession) has been won; it is no longer an issue. And American poetry is of world importance at least in the same way that Roman poetry at the time of Augustus was more significant than that of the Goths.

Because much of the material treated here is music, it is urgent to point out that the reader must *hear* it to make sense of my argument. I have no foolish ambition to replace jazz with descriptions of jazz; and the reduction of a song to its printed lyrics is a pernicious fallacy scrutinized in chapter 5. Therefore I have made a particular effort to discuss works that are readily available. Recorded jazz performances come and go with the whims of a recording industry whose motives are even less archival than book publishers'; I have second-guessed as well as I can. The ideal solution—to include recordings of all the music discussed—is economic fantasy.

It should surely be obvious that this book is not a survey of its field or fields. Such a survey would deal with the history of explicit links between jazz and poetry (Beat readings with jazz accompaniment; the constant interaction between African-American poetry and music; recent settings of Robert Creeley's poems by Steve Lacy and Steve Swallow, and so on). It would attend to poetry by Langston Hughes, Michael Harper, Hayden Carruth, Gwendolyn Brooks, Sterling Hayden, Quincy Troupe, and others; the music of Charlie Parker, Miles Davis, John Coltrane, and others; the songs of Bob Dylan. As a glance at the table of contents reveals, my choices have been governed by other principles. Some are works whose grip originally led me to the questions the book came to pose. Most were chosen for their purity as examples, though the purity may be a matter only of uniqueness—not that they prove anything clearly, but that they muddy the waters in a promising way. My aim has been not to cover the ground, but to interrogate landmarks; less to build a wall than weave a net.

We who deal with poems in classrooms usually know where to begin. A century of English Studies, consolidating the preceding millennia of scrutiny, perfection, and classification, has given us a toolkit adequate to the parsing of a great mass of literature. Yet classroom criticism may well be stumped by poetry like the opening stanza of Michael Harper's "Brother John":

Black man:
I'm a black man;
I'm black; I am—
A black man; black—
I'm a black man;
I'm a black man;
I'm a man; black—
I am[1]

One way to emphasize the complexities within this poem's apparently monolithic language would be to classify its repetitions into kinds. Traditional Greek and Latin rhetorical terms excel at this task. Perhaps little is added to our understanding if we label the general method of this passage as *commoratio* ("emphasizing a strong point by repeating it several times in different words").[2] On the other hand, to pin down the "different or contrary sense" which repetition uncovers in some of the words, it might help to isolate that particular technique by giving it its traditional name, *antistasis*. The apparatus of rhetorical terminology may even lead us to new questions: Does *diaphora* ("repetition of a common word rather than a proper name to signify qualities of the person as well as naming him") here work differently than in the exemplary passage Lanham quotes from *Othello*, Desdemona's "My lord is not my lord," or the one he might have adduced from Iago, "I am not what I am"?

Following the grain the knife has found, we might go on cataloguing the rhetorical wealth of the lines. Thus *anaphora* (repetition of a word at the beginnings of successive clauses or lines) is here joined by the complementary figure, *antistrophe* (repetition at the ends). The combination is traditionally called *symploce*.[3] So overwhelming is this *conduplicatio* (repetition of words in succeeding clauses) or *diacope* (repetition with a few words intervening) that one might not notice how, within the refrain (*epimone*) itself, not only whole words but smaller units of sound are also linked, as in the *assonance* of "black" and "man." Identification of *agnominatio* (altered repetition of a word) in "I'm" and "I am" seems merely pedantic; but *epanalepsis* (repetition of a word at beginning and end of a unit) here significantly involves not the syntactical unit but rather, as so often in modern free verse, the line:

A black man; black—

This approach has the advantage of not slighting (or allowing our students to slight) the rich patterning Harper has woven into a few word sounds. But the labeling degenerates into an absurdity that not only demeans the analytical method and the poem, but belies our experience of reading it.

Yet we must be quite precise about what mistake is being made here, or what is not. The analysis does not go astray because it is analysis, because the flower is too delicate for such fumbling gloves. The rhetorical classifications attempt to distinguish the poem's parts and sort them, not an unreasonable project. Indeed the poem depends on differences within sameness. For instance, the passage can be read as a gradual transformation from one to another ellipsis ("omission of a word easily understood"): "I'm a black man" is reduced first to "I'm black" and later to "I'm a man." "I'm black" is ambiguously a projected racist reduction of the man's whole being to a single superficial characteristic, or a prideful abstraction that treats blackness as a flag. "I'm a man" restores the individual's wholeness, returning us to the ground on which he stands firmest and at the same time most resembles others; while that penultimate line adds "black" as the most urgent of all secondary qualities. And "man" hovers between its two senses, "male" and "human," evoking a turmoil of dignity, machismo, individuality, sexual and social identification. "Black" and "am" undergo similar changes. A method that promised to sort out these complex figurations might legitimately be welcomed.

Part of the problem lies in the inherent tendency of rhetoric to treat repetitions as ornaments. "Brother John" would seem to present an ultimate reduction of that principle—a poem consisting entirely of ornament. But the poem's impassioned directness of statement tends all the other way. The sense of absurdity is inspired partly by this disparity.

More profoundly, the problem can be traced to my treating the poem as if it were most centrally a printed object. Print (as Walter Ong has noted) encourages study, and study encourages dissection and categorization. But our critical problem in confronting "Brother John" arises exactly from the way the poem resists our impulse to study it and insists instead on being said or heard. There are no allusions to track down while one finger marks our place in the text; no Miltonian syntax to untangle; no patterns of imagery for us to develop and fix through slow, darkroom meditation. This is a poem for mouth and ear. While the rest of the poem after this introductory stanza varies slightly more in language, its larger structure follows a similarly formulaic pattern, with a stanza each on Charlie Parker, Miles Davis, John Coltrane, and a Brother John who "plays no instrument." The poem remains well outside normal poetic limits of repetition: a poem on the other side of poetry from discursive prose.

Yet we need more than a declaration that poetry is a species of music. Poetry is, as I will suggest and often say, language working in ways that uniquely preserve the priority of the ear, and in general a poem not heard (at least by the mind's ear) is a poem unread. But "Brother John" is not poetry as music in a simple, Sitwellian mode. If Harper's words insist on being said or heard, they are also intent on *saying something* in a direct verbal sense. If the reiterated words were "I'm a white man," it would be not just an opposite poem, but an utterly different kind of poem.

In summary, what characterizes the poem is a tension between music and statement. This tension—which might serve as a gnomic definition for "voice"—is why the poem sloughs off thematic and rhetorical criticism with equal disdain. In still shorter summary, "Brother John" is a jazz poem.

For anyone for whom that phrase functions as description—for whom it implies how the rhythm of the words plays against both the lineation and the beat implied by the words' own repetition, how insistence has become music—it replaces much of the preceding discussion. But my aim is to sketch part of the framework within which such a category, the ''jazz poem,'' takes on a special life, and a life with special importance to contemporary American poetry and culture.

Particularly for readers whose home ground is poetry, the place to begin will be with jazz.

One

Lee Konitz: All the Things "All the Things You Are" Is

JAZZ—everyone realizes—combines essential elements of West African music and European concert music. The elements usually picked out are African rhythm and European harmony, but the blend is richer than these stereotypes suggest. In jazz the improvised nature of African music adapts to and transforms a European framework of more or less elaborate prior composition.[1]

And jazz holds in relation—sometimes uneasy relation—the very different social situations that African music and European music underwrite. In an African village, the villagers often are the musicians;[2] while the European salon or stage divides professionalized performers from silent auditors. The very word *concert*, which originally suggested how the musicians cooperate, now implies at least as strongly what separates them from an audience of ticketholders. As for jazz, we can equally readily think of it being made at an after-hours jam session in a room full of musicians playing and musicians listening, or in Carnegie Hall, with the Modern Jazz Quartet in white tie and tails.

The communal music of African peoples from the Shona to the Arabs, with its ties to both mystical trance and tribal conviviality, often goes on for hours without interruption; it does not comprise "pieces."[3] Individual musicians pass into and out of the musical ensemble as molecules pass through and constitute a candle flame. The continuousness of the music—linked to a worldview in which historical process means less than cyclical stability—reduces the status of beginnings and endings. Where beginnings and endings claim importance, temporal limits contribute to a consciousness of temporal structure, whether in sacred history or in narrative plot.[4] European music, like European art in general, has emphasized this kind of structure since around the time writing became important, in classical Greek culture.[5] Aristotle's premise that a work must have a beginning, middle, and end, which can seem trivially obvious to us, was not obvious before his time; and in the remaining oral cultures even today, this kind of closure does not possess the same hegemony we suppose it to have. *Music as a state of being*, as in the day-long or week-long festivals held by the Berbers and other tribes, exercises a quite different power over its listeners, *means* in a quite different way, from (in Susanne Langer's phrase) *music as symbolic form*.

The standard structure of a small-group jazz performance brings these different ontologies of music to a truce or compromise—ideally, a synthesis. Though players vary this structure endlessly and historical developments complicate the picture, the "typical" performance goes like this: The musicians agree on a "tune"—a melodic and/or harmonic pattern of set length—which they may inherit as a generalized communal property like the twelve-bar blues, or adapt from a popular show tune, or write themselves as a specialized jazz composition. They repeat a series of "choruses" of this tune. The performance usually begins and ends with a "melody chorus," in which one or more "front line" players (conventionally the wind instrumentalists) play through the set melody in unison or harmony, while the "rhythm section" (drums, bass, perhaps piano or guitar) iterates the rhythmic/harmonic infrastructure of the tune. In between the relatively formal beginning and ending, the various players take turns improvising for one or many choruses each. This string of solos can go on so long that it reduces the melody choruses at both ends almost to pro forma punctuation, making it clear that the performers feel less concern for structure than for continuation. This is not a fault but an aesthetic, though not a modern European one. The jazz player's prowess is measured, in part, by how long he or she can keep inventing compelling variations.

This basic structure of *melody/string of solos/melody* may be elaborated or subverted in the "arrangements" (often written ones) used by large bands and bands that work together steadily. In the pure form described here, it appears most frequently as a common ground for players who do not usually play together and have no repertoire of arranged pieces. It makes the jam session possible—a structure tight enough to keep everyone together at the start and finish, and to keep the soloist in synchronization with the rhythm section, but loose enough to accommodate any combination of players.

Even the casual situation of a jam session allows for some conventional variations. One familiar way jazz players spark and jostle each other is to "trade fours"; instead of improvising singly for entire choruses, they exchange phrases four measures long, still over the continuing basis of the tune. Often a chorus of fours will follow a sequence of more extended solos by each player, just before the return of the melody. The new, quicker rhythm of interaction brings a natural heightening of excitement; sometimes, to sharpen the sense of climactic arrangement, the fours become twos or even ones. But fours seem the natural unit, especially at faster tempos. A four-measure phrase leaves the player enough room (say, three to six seconds) to develop one idea, to make one statement; yet there is no mistaking the dialogue within which each statement takes its place, and often the musicians answer each other directly. The resemblance to conversation can be uncanny. With two or four soloists, the system works neatly, because of the powers-of-two structure of almost all popular tunes, including most jazz standards.

"All the Things You Are" is a standard, built of standard four-bar units. It is unusually athletic in its modulations; and the shifting keys give each part of the tune a slightly different character as a context for improvisation. This makes the variety and exchange of traded phrases especially inviting. But "All the Things You Are" is thirty-six measures long, not the usual thirty-two. Yet so naturally is the tune constructed, that it can baffle an unwary pair of players: Trumpeter B expects to answer each question, cap each brag, comment on each statement by saxophonist A; but A's last say comes at the chorus's end; and if B feels strongly enough the impulse to answer, they find themselves unexpectedly embarking on another chorus of fours.

Where do the "extra" four measures intrude? The most common structure in popular songs comprises four strains, related as AABA:

(A) an eight-measure melody in one key;
(A) repeated;
(B) followed by a "bridge" in a new but related key;
(A) completed by a reprise of the first eight measures.

(Think of "Five Foot Two," or "In a Sentimental Mood," or "I Saw Her Standing There.") In "All the Things You Are," the first two groups of eight bars mirror each other closely, though in different keys; their relation to each other is only a little more complicated than the relation between the identical opening strains of a more conventional tune. The third eight-measure segment divides into two four-bar sequences, part of whose function is to return, tortuously, to the original key. This exaggerates the standard pattern of a bridge that follows the doubled first strain and returns to its reprise. Up to this point, "All the Things You Are" offers harmonic meta-variations on the standard AABA structure: The A sections are linked by similar (rather than identical) harmonic structures; the B section is distinguished by a new structure (not just a new tonality).

Here is the chord structure of "All the Things You Are." Its measures are numbered for guidance; and for readers whose familiarity with the song depends on its lyrics, they are interlineated with the chords:[6]

First strain (measures 1–8):

Fm	B♭m	E♭7	A♭	
You	are the	promised kiss of	springtime That	

D♭		G7	C	C
makes the lonely		winter seem	long	

Second strain (measures 9–16):

Cm	Fm	B♭7		E♭	
You	are the	breathless hush of		evening That	

A♭		D7		G	G
trembles on the		brink of a lovely		song	You are the

Bridge (measures 17–24):

Am		D7		G	G	
angel glow		that lights a		star	The dearest	

F♯m7(−5)		B7		E	C+7	
things I know		are what you		are		

Last strain (measures 25–36):

Fm	B♭m	E♭7		A♭	
Some	day my	happy arms will		hold you And	

D♭	D♭m	Cm		Bdim	
some	day I'll	know that moment di-		-vine when	

B♭m		E♭7	A♭	A♭
all the things you		are are	mine	

By examining some details of this harmonic structure, we can see what materials the jazz improviser begins with. The first strain (measures 1 through 8) commences with the relative minor of A♭, and establishes that key. But then it modulates to the mediant (C major) by way of a downward chromatic shift to a G7 chord that becomes the new dominant. This modulation is a fairly sharp and unexpected one; it leads us to anticipate a certain amount of slippery chromaticism in the overall structure of the tune. When the second strain begins by shifting into the parallel minor, it confirms that expectation. The second strain goes on to repeat exactly the pattern of the first, in the new key. For the improviser, each of these key-stable areas suggests a lexicon of appropriate notes, basically a major scale (first in A♭, then in C)—though absolutely any other note can be domesticated by the right local elaborations of context. Between the stable areas, ambiguities enrich (or beset) the choice of appropriate notes.

The two four-measure halves of the bridge (like the first two strains) each use the ordinary ii-V-I progression to confirm a key. The first half continues the key of G major with which the second strain has just ended—the first sign of stability that the tune displays, though the key stands an odd half-step away from the original tonic of A♭. The second half of the bridge, by sliding down-

ward chromatically again (from G to a half-diminished F♯), arrives momentarily at E major, very far indeed from A♭. The very next measure, however
(measure 24), augments the E major chord and treats it as its enharmonic twin,
C augmented; newly perceived as an altered dominant, this chord prepares for
a return to the original F minor, from which the basic key of A♭ once more
establishes itself. This enharmonic modulation by way of an ambiguous chord
acts as a sort of musical pun, startling and witty. The tune suddenly seems to
recollect or discover a purpose. Literary parallels might be the repetition of
the word ''Forlorn'' across a stanza break near the end of ''Ode to a Nightin-
gale''; or the syllepsis in certain lines of Pope (''Or stain her honor, or her
new brocade''). Closest of all might be Marcel's father's revelation, near the
beginning of *A la Recherche du temps perdu*, that the mysterious corner at
which the family has arrived after their winding walk is in fact their own back
gate.

The symmetry of these eight-bar and four-bar pairs makes it clear that the
''extra'' four measures come into the structure in the last section. Considerations of dramatic development would lead to the same conclusion. The last
section of the tune begins by recapitulating the beginning: measures 25
through 29 duplicate measures one through five. The next measure introduces
a new harmonic element (the minor of the subdominant), matched with an
expressively dissonant note, which is also the highest one in the tune. The
whole melody tends to drift very steadily downward (though the upward step
of a fourth acts as a kind of signature); so the sudden leap up a seventh to this
high E♭ strikes the ear with a special poignancy. The remainder of the chorus
devotes itself to settling the melody back down, and neatly tying up the harmonic package.

In short, the structural manipulation of the tune takes part in a consistent
technique that also embraces the melody—and indeed the lyrics, since the
repetition of ''Some day'' reveals the upward seventh as an apotheosis of the
preceding upward fourths. All these resources are channeled toward effecting
the maximum possible climax at this point, measure 30, near the end of the
chorus.

I have been speaking of ''the tune'' as though it were anonymous. In one
sense, this reflects a reality. ''Standards'' are to jazz what *loci communes*,
commonplaces, are to oratory: the common property from which the speaker
selects and on which he or she constructs the particular argument. They are
like folk tales, ready to be retold. But some materials serve better than others.
''All the Things You Are'' was written by Jerome Kern, whose show tunes
owe part of their favored status among jazz players to the kind of fruitful complexity this one exhibits. The enharmonic shift at the end of the bridge exem-
plifies Kern's usual ingenuity.[7] He used a similar technique in ''The Song Is
You,'' whose bridge winds through improbable modulations to a point where

the return to the melody requires an abrupt, exhilarating shift upward by a half-step. The main-strain melody of "Smoke Gets in Your Eyes" takes almost maddeningly symmetrical units (measures containing a half note followed by four eighth notes) and phrases them into an expanding dramatic progression; in the bridge melody, by contrast, Kern constructs out of highly asymmetrical rhythms a coherence almost like that of recitative. Kern, then, is no anonymous contributor to a folklore; and the relation between his art and that of the improviser, as we examine a rendition of his tune, will help to illuminate the special intricacies of social and aesthetic dialogue in jazz.

In the 1950s, Lee Konitz emerged as one of the first original alto saxophonists since Charlie Parker. His light, steely sound and intricate sense of timing, both encouraged by his apprenticeship with Lennie Tristano's groups, still distinguish him from other players so thoroughly that a few measures suffice to identify him. Paul Desmond picked up Konitz's lightness of sound; but while Desmond's wit ran from wry quotation toward lyricism,[8] Konitz has always seemed more acerbic. Those who prefer to think of jazz as expressing raw emotion distrust his intellectualism. His relation to the material on which he improvises is dispassionate—not the opposite of passionate, but never enthralled. Leading us far into the center of a tune, yet always glancing outside and through it, he seems to act as a critic of the tune as he plays it.[9]

Konitz recorded "All the Things You Are" as a guest with Gerry Mulligan's quartet in the mid-fifties.[10] The quartet gained renown for its adventurous abnegation of any chordal instrument (piano or guitar). This instrumentation went along with an interest in contrapuntal improvisation—two players inventing independent but related melodies simultaneously, in a quasi-fugato style.[11] A guest-artist recording encourages an even sparser texture than the basic instrumentation requires: Here, the bass and drums keep unobtrusive track of the beat and sketch the harmonic progress of the tune; Mulligan's baritone saxophone and Chet Baker's trumpet provide a background that, even after it has built up a little volume and rhythmic intensity over the full six choruses, remains barely audible. Konitz later made at least one record with no accompaniment at all (*Lone-Lee*)—a rare venture for a horn player[12]—and here he approaches that austere extreme.

Later in this chapter I will give a complete transcription of Konitz's solo. But to begin with, it will be most useful to compare his first chorus in detail with the melody against which he is improvising. Like any jazz player, particularly since the Bebop revolution of the mid-forties, Konitz personalizes his opening statement of the tune. Anyone who knows the tune will recognize the melody, but will also hear how Konitz has distorted it. Here is the first strain, as published, in parallel with Konitz's revision:[13]

Ex. 1.1. Melody and solo: first strain

(The speed is about ♩ = 160.) The recording begins with no introduction at all: The bass and drums play the first three beats, and Konitz comes in on the fourth with two notes—the same two with which the melody begins, but reduced from whole to eighth notes. The entire first two measures are thus summarized by one beat, placed in the middle of the time allotted for them.

Konitz plays the third measure as written. And so the fourth, with minor variations; but an effect of those variations is to anticipate the melody by one beat. The anticipation then increases: By eliminating repetitions, Konitz condenses the second four bars of the melody into his fifth and sixth measures, completing the whole first strain nine beats early. To this melody, he adds a three-note flourish, an arpeggio that underscores the new key (C major) toward which the strain has modulated. Almost two measures—static in the melody, silent in the improvisation—remain in the regulation eight-bar strain. Compared with the original tune, Konitz's version is distinctly laconic.

In the second eight measures, Konitz does the same sort of thing, but even more consistently:

Ex. 1.2. Melody and solo: second strain

The principle here is to anticipate almost everything by two beats. Again, one effect is to leave a longish space between phrases of the tune. This sparseness, emphasized by the minimal accompaniment, helps to intensify the individuality of each bounded phrase.

The next section of the melody, the bridge (combined, in example 3 below, with the last strain), embodies a different structure, which repeats in four bars rather than eight. Further compounding the symmetry, Kern builds each of the four-bar groups from two similar two-bar phrases:

Ex. 1.3. Melody and solo: bridge and last strain

At the beginning of the bridge, the isolating silences with which Konitz punctuated phrases in the first sixteen measures start to invade the phrases themselves. Kern's melody simply double-times the rhythm of repetition; the four-bar phrases act like the two rhymed dimeters in the middle of a limerick, sandwiched between longer lines. Konitz dissects the structure more radically. Minimizing the importance of the rising pickups that introduce each phrase, he builds a new pattern on repetitions of a high D at intervals of four, two, three, and six beats. This irregular rhythm combines with the much increased fragmentation of phrases to heighten the sense of fast time, of events crowding together. Rhythmic displacement, which the listener felt previously only in relation to the unheard, remembered melody, here comes more directly into our awareness—less an idea, more an immediate sensation.

Furthermore, Konitz's much more continuous second phrase (beginning in measure 22; see example 1.3) does not end with the bridge, where the melody's phrase ends, but continues well into the next section. This complements the fragmentation he introduced in the phrase centered on the recurring high D. If one way to counterpoint a structure is to insert new divisions, the other way is to override the old ones.

The point where Konitz begins this long fast phrase, straddling the bridge and last strain, approximates the point where Kern's melody stays still to allow the harmony to make its clever transition back to the original key. Kern has written one eight-beat note which changes its spelling from G♯ (the third of the E major tonic) to A♭ (here serving as the flat sixth or augmented fifth of the dominant seventh chord in the key of F minor). Konitz fills up this transition with notes, disallowing the gap which Kern built into the melody's structure. That gap was meant to prepare for a recapitulation of the tune's beginning. But Konitz does not repeat the original tune at all. Instead, his phrase of quick eighth notes, almost six measures long, builds toward a rising arpeggio that finishes on the highest note of his chorus—the second highest in his whole solo.

Obviously, in all of this Konitz is preparing and then realizing a climax. He might be expected to follow this with some little pause to delimit the climactic phrase. But the empty space Konitz keeps clear extends for a total of five measures—a quite extraordinary time for a soloist to remain silent. And these long measures coincide exactly with the climactic part of the original tune which I discussed earlier. When Kern's melody is just preparing to rise to its highest dramatic point, Konitz has already made his statement. Having nothing further to say after this point, he says nothing. The confidence is authoritative; he has rewritten the tune.

When Konitz does continue, his phrases owe very little to the original melody. He is through with the "melody chorus," and what he plays next belongs unmistakably to the following chorus, officially still four measures away. So clear does he make the juncture between his choruses (that five-bar silence) that the listener may have difficulty hearing where the second chorus formally does begin.

The remainder of Konitz's solo, six choruses in total, is improvised at a greater distance from the original melody. What kinds of coherence we can expect or find in such an instantaneous production, and what other sources of energy, are questions vital to our understanding of jazz and its relation to poetry, and I will return to them. But questions equally intriguing arise if we reconsider this first, expository chorus once more from a different point of view.

In classical Western music, as our century has received it from the two or three preceding, sharply defined roles distinguish the composer and the performer. In the paradigmatic case, the performer serves as a skilled interpreter, a scholar of one or more genres and periods of the musical repertoire, and a stage personality and presence. Ideally, he or she is there for the audience to watch—even in the technicalities of recording, the engineers pursue the goal of maximum "presence." The performer may or may not participate in a carefully rehearsed group.[14] The composer, on the other hand, is absent and perhaps dead; his work or hers (we are just starting to realize how much women composers have contributed) was completed at some remove in time, in private, and at length: The piece on which a typical composer labors for some months lasts for some minutes. Composers produce works; musicians—even severely classical musicians—play. In that Calvinist opposition we indicate our sense of the difference between tenacious construction and the immediate engagement of performance.

In almost any imaginable music, some such distinction can be drawn between the materials on the one hand, and their treatment or interpretation or presentation on the other; it may or may not entail a distinction between the composer of the material, and the performer who treats or interprets or presents it. (The choice of verbs sketches part of the range of possible relations; the performer may function as spokesman, critic, translator, messenger, preacher with a text.) We can adduce a surprisingly concise and orderly history of jazz by attending to changes in what materials are seen as *given* before the performer starts.

Most jazz history has involved reducing the given. In the ragtime that immediately preceded jazz,[15] the given was a score, usually for piano, which the player performed with appropriate feeling. The ragtime feeling was distinctive, of course (the term *syncopation* covers many of its important features); but the player stood in a relation to the composed music that closely resembled the European musician's. At an extreme, the score might be frozen into a roll for player piano—the duties of the performer being trivialized to footwork, recalling the bellows-boys who assisted Bach at the organ. (But Duke Ellington did learn to play by following piano rolls.)

In early jazz through Louis Armstrong, the player stepped progressively to the fore. Armstrong completed this movement, being not simply a great jazz musician but the first of the three or four greatest jazz soloists. The improvised solo came to the center of jazz during this time. The soloist's given material for improvisation was not a whole composition, but a melody, repeated with variations through multiple choruses.

Melody is the most superficial aspect of a tune, in the sense that it presents itself most availably on the surface, is easiest for the listener to recognize, and resides closest to the singing voice. The human voice sounds through any jazz performance—directly in Armstrong, who was nearly as great a singer as trumpeter, indirectly later in more stringently instrumental Bebop and cool jazz; and it is melody that responds most warmly to the needs of the voice. The improvisations of jazz players of the twenties and early thirties are variations on melodic themes.

Armstrong also initiated a shift from improvisation on the melody to improvisation on the harmonic structure underlying the melody. In the latter style, the player bases variations not on a pattern of notes, but on a pattern of chords.[16] Coleman Hawkins's recording of "Body and Soul" (which just passed its fiftieth anniversary) carried this new reduction of the given to its logical conclusion: The opening strain of his first chorus states the melody, more or less, but the whole remaining solo is devoted to working out the melodic implications in the chords of the tune—a series of arpeggios.[17]

This 1939 recording by Hawkins popularized but did not invent the method of "playing the changes," which grew steadily in earlier jazz and characterized late-thirties Swing. And the hegemony of the method lasted long afterwards. Konitz in the eighties (and certainly in the 1953 recording) is still playing variations on an underlying harmonic structure, without seeming old-fashioned.

Historians conventionally divide jazz history into pre-bop and post-bop halves; the Charlie Parker–Dizzy Gillespie experiments of the forties radically altered both the tone and the vital rhythmic basis of the music. But Bebop players also intensified and elaborated the principle of harmonic variation which had already been established. They altered the tradition of an opening "melody chorus" in a relevant way. Many of Parker's most important compositions were new tunes constructed on old harmonic foundations: "Donna Lee" is based on "Back Home in Indiana," "Ko Ko" on "Cherokee," and so on. Such a composition bears the same relation to its predecessor as an improvisation would. (In Parker's incredibly inventive case, it usually *was* an improvisation that he or someone else then wrote down.) This practice resulted not only from a desire to avoid royalty payments, but also from the new aesthetics of melody and rhythm. Bebop employs much faster and more complex

tunes than most earlier jazz; yet the old chord structures (the "changes") re-
mained the essential foundation for improvisation. Therefore, the new melody
in the opening chorus announced the revolutionary virtuosic style; and then
the players constructed their new solos on the familiar harmonic pattern.[18]

The more recent history of jazz suggests that the path of development might
run through—and not merely to its end in—this rich style of harmonic variation, of "playing the changes." Two further developments represent forays
toward a yet greater reduction of the given. The solos on Miles Davis's 1959
album *Kind of Blue*—a single recording session in which some of the key
players of the next decade's jazz participated[19]—are built not on melodies
(though the tunes have melodies), nor on chords (though simultaneous notes
inevitably form chords), but on different scales or modes. In modal jazz the
material which the performer treats or uses is abstracted as a *selection of
notes*—a melodic diction, not a melody. The sense of revelatory liberation this
created at first (all reductions in constraint are at first liberations)[20] probably
accounts in part for the amazing beauty of the album's music.

Modalism became one among several available styles in the sixties. Another, the next logical step in the progression, was first tried by Ornette Coleman on an album called *Free Jazz*; John Coltrane repeated the experiment on
Ascension.[21] These recordings reduce the given almost to nothing. A group of
players is assembled; an order of soloing—or at least of stepping forward—is
assigned; a signal is given to begin; thirty or forty minutes later, the music
stops. Passive voice seems appropriate in this description. The leader has reduced his role to that of master of ceremonies, and there is no composer at all.
The musical given, by now, is simply a block of time. (In the Coltrane piece,
another given is a home pitch, B♭, to which players may return and which
recurs intermittently as a pedal point. The associations of B♭—it is the most
"classic" key for the blues, for instance, and the note to which jazz players
tune their instruments[22]—connect the performance's material at least in a minimal way with a tradition of such material.) To put it in a different way, the
given has become social, an order of solos and a general relation of soloist to
players in the background; the emphasis shifts to the immediate interaction of
the group, largely excluding interactions with any pre-existing material. The
given pertains to the performance alone; as far as possible, the tension between
improvisation and prior composition is dissolved in absolute presentness.

The style of harmonic variation continues as a living tradition; we think of
it now as "mainstream jazz." The modal style remains an alternative, border-
ing and sometimes blending with the mainstream. Free jazz has more or less
disappeared, for reasons worth speculating about. Another alternative, the
Third Stream experiment of the sixties, a series of attempts to combine jazz
and European classical music, required some movement back toward composed material. It never made much headway. But the more commercially
dynamic development of the seventies, "fusion" (of jazz and rock), went be-

yond Third Stream music in increasing the given again. A fusion performance reabsorbs solos into complex, virtuosic ensemble playing.

Despite complications and uncertainties, most of which I have ignored in this thumbnail sketch, behind jazz history we can discern a spectrum in the givenness of materials and in stances toward the given. Leaving aside our diachronic view of the historical progression, we can abstract this spectrum synchronically as a theoretical range of possibilities for the art. (Since jazz history is so dizzyingly brief, the lifetimes of most styles have in fact overlapped a great deal.) At one end, the performance of composed music defines its own goal, however complexly, as fidelity. At the other end, the performers completely abandon any constraining (or supporting) framework of prior arrangement. Some linguistic parallels to this spectrum will engage us in later chapters.

Most jazz, of course, lies between these extremes. Anywhere between, the performance is bound to be in a certain sense impure. It embraces neither pure reduplication nor pure invention. It desires neither the pure resurrection of the stilled voice of the composer—which a performance of Beethoven might think of itself as striving toward—nor the soloist's voice sounding in pure isolation. Inevitably, it resounds with a mixture of voices. We can call this mixture a "dialogue"—remaining aware of a possible confusion, since the relation among players within the group performance also accepts the same metaphor. Nor does the mixture confine itself to two voices, the composer's and the soloist's. Many voices may speak together in oblique relation to each other, and at a wide range of volumes. I have suggested how intricately a listener might hear Jerome Kern's tune through Lee Konitz's recomposition of it in his first chorus. All the dozens of other performances of the same tune that we may have heard (and that Konitz has both heard and played) also join in. Some solos directly quote other tunes or other performances. And entirely aside from the tune, in the instrumental "voice" of Konitz we may hear some of Parker's sharpness, some of Lester Young's lightness, and one part of Richie Cole's style in the making.

How can the idea of *a voice* be defined at all? In any performance, we confront not Tradition and the Individual Talent, but many voices of tradition and many constituents of individual talent. And how individual—that is, single and indivisible—can the talent be? To find a voice may be truly to find a place among voices.

We will return to these questions, because they concern both contemporary American music and poetry. But already the potential multiple richness of "voice" hints that the jazz improviser's art, though instantaneous, is not in any simple way immediate. The solo is unplanned, but not entirely unprepared. Some of the mediating influences on it favor a highly organized, even rigorously architectonic sense of structure. We should go back to see what becomes of Lee Konitz's solo after his most direct opening dialogue with Kern.

A transcription of Konitz's whole solo (the six choruses marked A through F) begins on the following page. One's first impression of the solo, as of most Bebop and post-bop improvisations, is that it contains an awful lot of notes. Not until we examine the barrage for some principle of selection do we begin to imagine any real order in all this.

One principle of selection, turned up by our theoretical history of jazz, requires that the notes at each point be either chord-tones or appoggiaturas: They either belong to the chord that governs that measure, or prepare for other notes that belong to the chord. Jazz players spend years learning to play the changes, to move quickly from the field of one chord to the field of the next. A tune like Coltrane's "Giant Steps," whose chords shift in nonobvious ways approximately twice each second, often serves as a shibboleth in competitive situations. Simply to get through these complexities, without making actual *mistakes*, constitutes a kind of final exam. The uninspired (that is, inattentive) moments in run-of-the-mill jazz solos may display no further ordering principle than this negative and mechanical one of avoiding wrong notes. But we demand more for real interest.[23]

A further possibility is that the chosen notes should make up a new and interesting melody—whatever constitutes a melody and interest in a melody. Armstrong's solos achieve this over and over; and some of the more lyrical players of recent decades have revived the principle. But it is a principle that does not coexist easily with the density of notes that Parker and Gillespie and later Bebop players like Konitz generate. Lyric moments occur in Konitz's solo (the end of the C chorus and, inevitably, scattered phrases in the two "melody" choruses); but they serve more to provide a depth of contrast than as simple centers of thought or feeling. The foundation of order in this solo lies elsewhere.

For a listener to discover further ordering principles requires analysis, conscious or unconscious, though even the most careful listeners may not think of themselves as analyzing the music. This analysis can be considered more casually as reflection on the particular tone or character of the solo: What makes one melody (composed or improvised) different from another? Tunes make characteristic gestures. "All the Things You Are" emphasizes long notes, quarter-note repetitions, the melodic interval of an upward fourth (perfect or augmented), and downward modulations that feel chromatic. These features do not constitute a recipe for the tune; but they distinguish it from, say, "Darn That Dream" (extended upward chromaticism, reversed in the

All the Things You Are

Solo by Lee Konitz
with Mulligan Quartet

Concert Key

"All the Things You Are": solo by Lee Konitz, with Mulligan Quartet

second half of the tune) or ''I Loves You Porgy'' (sequences of rising thirds with a root descending by thirds).

These gestures can act like rhetorical tropes: a finite but ample set of categorized or conventional ways in which the atoms of a medium (words, notes) are grouped and excerpted from ''common'' (that is, unnoticed) use, for special emphasis or meaning.[24] Different tropes in music verge on each other as indefinitely as those in literature. (Is metonymy a species of metaphor, or its opposite?) But away from the boundaries they are quite recognizable.

Konitz bases his solo on such elements as once-repeated notes, sequences, long silences, and a ''teetering'' pattern related to a trill or a mordant. One can pick out instances of these gestures fairly easily from the printed page or—after seeing them there, where they hold still, or after some practice at listening—in the solo itself. The long silences, for instance, occupy measures A–29/33 (that is, the twenty-ninth through thirty-third measures of the A chorus), B–33/36, and F–8/10. We have already seen some of the implications of the first one, the five-bar rest that replaces the climax of the original tune; and others produce similar effects, beyond the punctuation of shorter pauses. They resemble moments when conversation dissolves into thought. The other tropes I have named can be recognized locally in much the same way as these silences, and plainly tabulated.[25]

Recognizing recurring patterns like these is the very stuff of our musical hearing. In a nonreferential medium like music, such recurrences are in a sense the only things that can ever happen; the patterns themselves are constituted by recurrent relationships among single notes.[26] And various half-recognitions and interconnections between patterns have still more telling effects within our attention to the music. Here is a passage from the second chorus containing typical repeated notes:

Ex. 1.4. Chorus B, measures 8–11

Do the following measures, from the fourth chorus, exhibit the same pattern?

Ex. 1.5. Chorus D, measures 26–31

The answer depends on what limits we place on sameness. This ambiguity in the relation of theme to variation crops up in every aspect of music, perhaps never trivially. At the least it mimics the linguistic action of puns; more powerfully, it may underlie the musical equivalent of patterns of imagery in poems. In Frost's ''After Apple-Picking,'' the opening declaration that his ladder points ''Toward heaven still'' sensitizes us to eschatological diction and thought throughout the poem, though the uncapitalized ''heaven'' *could* simply mean ''sky.'' Does a later word like ''sleep'' associate with ''heaven''? Yes or no, or yes and no at once, depending on how one listens. Similarly, the first hint of a ''teetering'' pattern in measures like these

Ex. 1.6. Chorus B, measures 1 and 21–22

returns, confirmed and solidified, in the next chorus:

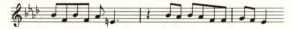

Ex. 1.7. Chorus C, measures 29–30

This and further instances allow us to hear a more distant echo near the end:

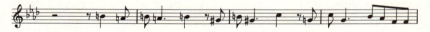

Ex. 1.8. Chorus F, measures 21–23

Compounds of two tropes similarly alert us and enrich our recognition. Here is a repeating *and* teetering phrase:

Ex. 1.9. Chorus E, measures 27–28

And here a sequence (marked by the long slurs) in which we may or may not hear a teetering pattern:

Ex. 1.10. Chorus C, measures 13–15

Such uncertainties should interest the psychologist of musical perception. They half arouse and half satisfy our expectations, and so bring them into especially sharp relief. As natural test points for the amount of *information* we are receiving from the music, they help keep us aware.

Beyond these local details, Konitz uses such tropes to build up larger statements. Consider the structure of the third chorus. One of its themes is anticipated by a sequence in the B chorus:

Ex. 1.11. Chorus B, measures 24–28

Almost the first gesture in the C chorus is this sequential inversion of the earlier phrase:

Ex. 1.12. Chorus C, measures 2–4

Here as earlier (and almost everywhere in the solo), Konitz builds the sequence from two-beat units, as marked in the example. But later in the chorus comes another sequence built from three-beat units, countering the four-beat measure:

Ex. 1.13. Chorus C, measures 13–14

Almost immediately, Konitz develops this into the most elaborate sequence in the solo, a repeated eight-beat pattern whose center (a two-beat syncopated rising arpeggio) he anticipates in a distinct but interlocking sequence:

Ex. 1.14. Chorus C, measures 15–20

By contrast with C's study in sequences, the D chorus is characterized by shifts in accent within a highly chromaticized melodic stream. For instance:

Ex. 1.15. Chorus D, measures 9–15

The D chorus includes only one sequence (the little run at the end of example 1.15). On the other hand, D abounds in passages of repeated notes, while C offers only one. The two choruses exhibit quite different personalities. The succeeding E chorus further develops both the chromaticism of D and its repetitions of notes. At the same time, Konitz links C and D in several ways, over and above the common ground of the tune's harmony and his general syncopated-stream-of-eighth-notes style. The shifting accents on D contribute to the overall sense of syncopation—of rhythmic energy and surprise—in a way that complements the shifting asymmetries of the sequences in C. Both choruses use appoggiaturas heavily (see the opening of C, and measures D–9/11, for instance).

So beyond the local sense of purpose given by tropic patterns, and beyond the generalized sense that all these four minutes of phrases somehow belong in the same performance and in the same improvisation, Konitz spins a richer continuity from the coherence of larger sections. Yet one could still wonder how inevitably the outermost boundaries of the performance are determined. Why these six choruses, rather than four or forty?

This is not necessarily a legitimate question. (Nor, incidentally, would it be a useful question to ask of all poems.) As I remarked earlier, there is nothing universally compelling about the idea of musical structure as closed, as temporal rather than eternal.

Yet Konitz's solo does offer quite strict closure. The last chorus combines and summarizes almost every feature offered to our attention by earlier choruses. It restates sections of the melody at the two points where harmony is reestablishing the original key: He repeats the first strain almost completely (and, reminding us of the A chorus's most striking characteristic, anticipates the melody by two beats); and by reiterating the melody's basic gesture once more at the return after the bridge (F–25/28) emphasizes the reprise. The chorus includes one sequence (F–16/18), one long silence (F–8/10), and, somewhat obliquely as we saw before, one "teetering" phrase (F-21/22).

The repeated-note trope gets the last chorus's most elaborate recapitulation. Two instances remember the tune's own repetitions:

Ex. 1.16. Chorus F, measures 1–4

Ex. 1.17. Chorus F, measures 26–27

Another reviews the standard pattern from earlier choruses:

Ex. 1.18. Chorus F, measures 12–13

Still others represent the two variations that have appeared earlier: augmentation to quarter notes,

Ex. 1.19. Chorus F, measures 19–20

and isolation of a single pair

Ex. 1.20. Chorus F, measures 24–25

like the pair that terminates the elaborated "teetering" phrase noted earlier (example 1.8).

One result of all this recapitulation is that, in retrospect, the *first* chorus of the solo takes on a different kind of life. It had seemed, as the standard "melody chorus," to be the improviser's lip service to the songwriter, the mere point of departure. So Konitz's rhythmic distortions had a tone of rebellion or flippancy. Now we understand that the first chorus also adumbrated Konitz's own themes, much as the last chorus reaffirms them. The A chorus, too, offers long silence, doubled notes, and a sequence. (Not Konitz, but Carson Smith on bass anticipates the "teetering" figure at the very end of the chorus.) The rest of the solo mines this material.[27]

It becomes easiest at some point to think of Konitz as a kind of composer whose work begins from Kern's but insists on being seen as a creation of a partly different, partly parallel kind.[28] As compared with a previously composed set of variations on a theme, this performance is reduced in scope and in the rigor with which the thematic materials are exfoliated. These relaxations are the least one would expect in the way of adjustment to the improviser's situation. Konitz cannot revise, cannot stop to consider, but must make up this present chorus, this present measure, while it is here, right now. We can think of the achievement as *instantaneous* composition, or as instantaneous *composition*. Either way, it must amaze.

On Bands _____

In writing programs all over the country young poets are asked to ''find their own voice.'' Fortunately the odds against them are not as great as those against, say, Toshiko Akiyoshi. Aside from the struggle a Japanese woman faced in the American man's world of jazz when she arrived here in the fifties, she is a musician (like Duke Ellington) whose main ''voice'' is not her instrument (piano) but her orchestra. Most poets do not have to locate and schedule sixteen constituents of their aesthetic self, just to get their work done.

A band extends the metaphor of instrumental ''voice'' one step further. The extension emphasizes the possible multiplicity of voice. What it does not demonstrate, though at first it seems to, is social or communal multiplicity. The band is Akiyoshi's voice because of the precision with which its members cooperate; they give up most of their individuality for the sake of hers. They take solos (especially her husband Lew Tabackin, who co-leads the band), but these improvised solos contrast with the rest of the musical texture even more sharply than solos with ripieno sections in a concerto grosso. Playing an intricate written part in a trumpet section is not like playing trumpet in the simultaneous group improvisations of a Dixieland septet. If we hear Akiyoshi's third trombonist as ''speaking,'' we hear him quoting her. Apparently voice, in jazz, has something quite directly to do with improvisation.

Two ⎯⎯⎯⎯⎯⎯⎯⎯⎯⎯⎯⎯⎯⎯⎯⎯⎯⎯⎯⎯⎯⎯⎯⎯⎯⎯⎯⎯⎯⎯⎯

Robert Creeley: "Because I Am Always Talking," or "The Passage of an Unexpected Thing"

REMEMBER the scene from *The Band Wagon*: Fred Astaire the old hoofer and Cyd Charisse the young ballerina, cast together against their will as the stars of a stage musical, have finally quarreled and then broken through to mutual liking. "But," says Charisse, "can we really dance together?"

Toward the answer, a horse cab carries them through the Central Park evening; they relax after weeks of frustrating rehearsals (the play is being badly directed). While the horse drinks from a fountain and the hack rolls a cigarette, the two amble down steps to an open piazza with an orchestra and dancing couples. They keep strolling slowly, exactly out of step, self-conscious, not touching, not joining the other dancers. They are wearing casual white. As they pass between high shrubberies to another, empty terrace, the music fades (what was that catchy, unmemorable tune?), and up comes "Dancing in the Dark." They are in step now. She pirouettes once; he gives a complementary turn; and they dance.

The development of the scene is erotic, magical, representative of the best the mature (1953) American musical can offer. The magic depends heavily on our conviction that the dance is spontaneous. What could we think, otherwise? That they are running through a number from the show they have been rehearsing? (But why could they not do that on stage as well? And where is the correct music coming from, by chance?) That they have worked up a special test piece for themselves—or worse, that someone else has? (But then the shyness of their beginning seems coy—an imputation that destroys the innocence and enthusiasm of the scene, and so of the whole movie.) No; of course we believe in this improvisation.

Yet of course we do not. The dance has been exquisitely constructed, in the somewhat baroque style of rhetoric at which musicals had arrived by the early fifties, when the brash exuberance of youth was tempered by a more far-seeing sophistication. (If this sounds like a bit of plot from a musical, that corresponds to a relevant self-consciousness in the genre.) At one point, Charisse comes to a momentary pose on a marble bench, extending the right leg along it; Astaire glides behind her, takes her hand in passing, and suddenly rises to one pointed foot on the end of the bench in front of her; toe to toe, as smoothly as the hinge of a door, he lifts her all the way up to her foot and then down to the ground. Again: They whirl together halfway up a flight of steps, pause, back down by two steps, then whirl back up to the top—their pauses timed with rests that punctuate the song's climactic thick brass chords. At the closing bars, the dance culminates in the stroll that began it and has shaped its course. The last note coincides with their final step into the cab to which they have exactly returned; they lounge back as it starts away.

These congruences of motion do not resemble our experience of the physical world any more than dancing resembles walking. We know they are choreographed.

When we speak of political "moves" as "choreographed," we speak cynically. But only those unfamiliar with musical theater would object to the duplicity of this scene, or to the way people suddenly burst into song—like the rube who complains about Shakespeare that folks do not really talk iambic pentameter. The proper audience of an art does not confuse its conventions with insincerities.

A musical of this vintage goes farther, however; it is *about* stage and movie musicals. Astaire plays a film dancer trying out the stage to redeem a stalled career; Charisse's ballerina is essaying the popular stage to expand her career's horizons.[1] The movie worries about the relation between entertainment, which it insists that it is ("That's Entertainment" serves as the big theme number), and Art, which it insists that it is not. It burlesques the misguided cultural pretensions of the director (Jack Buchanan) who wants to inflate the play into "a modern version of Faust." ("Faust by Marlowe; Faust by Gounod; Faust by Berlioz—I tell you everybody who's touched it has turned it into a gold mine.")[2] The film pays lip service to the heroine's world of balletic high art: After elaborate build-up, we first see Charisse in a ballet scene, intimidating Astaire in the audience. In fact it is quite insipid ballet; and for a moment that naiveté jolts us out of the movie's spell. Yet the scene may not be the *faux pas* it appears. Ultimately, the hero's song-and-dance world will absorb her; she abandons her highfalutin world of ballet like a maiden name.

The movie gives us a bouquet of dances: Against Charisse's pointe work at the beginning, it sets "Triplets," with Astaire and Buchanan and Nanette Fabray dancing on costume baby feet attached to their knees and singing about Baden Baden Baden and Walla Walla Walla. The two men do a classic white-tie-and-tails routine on "I Guess I'll Have to Change My Plan," perfecting debonair melancholy; we are meant to recognize it as classic.[3] But the "Dancing in the Dark" scene stands out; all the others are ostensibly, as well as actually, rehearsed and performed.

Consider the dancing couples in Central Park among whom the professional dancers walk. Their movements cannot be strictly categorized as either prearranged or impromptu. Their collaborations hardly approach Busby Berkeley's mechanizations; but these people perform identifiable dances, fox trot or waltz, unlike their children a decade later. The activity somewhat resembles

that of the oral storyteller: They combine known pieces, formulas, "steps,"
into a continuity that never quite repeats.

The centrality of time in certain arts—dance, music, at least some kinds of
poetry—makes possible the distinction between what is improvised and what
is composed. But if we try to draw this line with perfect sharpness, we will
often find ourselves baffled; and we would finally succeed only by blinding
ourselves to all or part of the richness that many works offer. Someone who
glorifies "concert music" at the expense of jazz falls into one blatant version
of this blindness. More subtly, the effect of various works in various media
depends strongly on the intricate way in which spontaneous and prearranged
elements interact. The audience's comprehension of pretended spontaneity in-
forms their awareness that they are witnessing a fictive work, a work of art. In
this direction lies the classical and neoclassical doctrine of *ars celare artem*,
artistry directed toward the concealment of artifice, dear to poets like Pope and
Horace. In an age that knows both Homer and Louis Armstrong as improvisers, the riddle of spontaneous art and artful spontaneity takes on a new acuity.
It bears particularly on a main strand of American poetry in this century.

Calling some poem "improvisational" in character may elicit intuitive agree-
ment among readers, but it does not cast much light on the basis of that intui-
tion. Poems in their most familiar guise are written artifacts, which need to be
reconstituted by the addition of a living voice. Simply speaking of a poem as
"spontaneous" could entail vacuous speculation about the circumstances of
its production, a trap from which the New Criticism laboriously rescued us
decades ago.

We cannot rest content in this safety; we necessarily ask about the provenance of a passage of language in coming to understand it. But a different
angle of approach may help. Mikhail Bakhtin, the Russian literary theorist,
describes novels as "dialogic." The term implies not just dialogue between
characters, but rather what Bakhtin calls "heteroglossia": the bickering of one
language with another in the novelist's prose. "Language" might include national languages and regional dialects, but it more tellingly embraces and distinguishes the characteristic speech of different classes, age groups, trades,
literary traditions, and perhaps states of mind.

Bakhtin develops this idea by opposing novels to poems: "The poet is a
poet insofar as he accepts the idea of a unitary and singular language and a
unitary, monologically sealed-off utterance. These ideas are immanent in the
poetic genres with which he works. . . . The meaning must emerge from language as a single intentional whole: none of its stratification, its speech diversity, to say nothing of its language diversity, may be reflected in any fundamental way in his poetic work."[4] This opposition would rule the dialogic out

of bounds for our purposes if we took it seriously. But this image of the poet reflects exactly the dismaying condition which early modernists like Pound and Williams set out to overthrow. (Under Bakhtin's definition, not only *Paterson* and *The Cantos* but also "The Love Song of J. Alfred Prufrock" would have been impossible to write.) The passage reads like a reverse manifesto of modern American poetry. We can claim historical as well as heuristic grounds for taking over Bakhtin's terminology while rejecting the scaffolding he employed to build it.

Robert Creeley's "I Know a Man" is clearly and richly dialogic. Indeed, the poem records an explicit exchange, since a second speaker answers in the last stanza.

I Know a Man

As I sd to my
friend, because I am
always talking,—John, I

sd, which was not his
name, the darkness sur-
rounds us, what

can we do against
it, or else, shall we &
why not, buy a goddamn big car,

drive, he sd, for
christ's sake, look
out where yr going.[5]

This is dialogue in the most straightforward, nonsimultaneous sense: two speakers conversing consecutively. But the main speaker also conducts dialogues internal to his own speech. He stops and starts, digresses, anticipates objections. "Or else" is his signature. He continually imagines alternatives to his situation. The impulse to "buy a goddamn big car" promises the most conventional alternative. We learn in the next line that he is already driving a car (bought or not), which underscores the parodic naiveté of this simplest yearning. The passage, "John, I sd, which was not his name," suggests— unless it shows a speaker forgetfully preoccupied—the subtler alternative of fictions, aliases, the movies. Such a movie might show literally how "the darkness surrounds us," and might also propose it melodramatically. This speaker, in other words, is conscious of himself in a way that recalls Emma Bovary or the characters in *Dubliners*.[6] Though more consciously, more experimentally than they, he too tells himself stories about what he is doing, constantly reworking and heightening his awareness of it. He has a period kinship with the fifties image of the jazz man (like Pynchon's McClintic

Sphere, who owes something to Kerouac's Dean Moriarty), living on the edge, making up his life by moments as he speeds toward destruction.

The second speaker urges a different dialogue, a regime of soberer transactions with the surrounding traffic—an alternative to "always talking." Yet that disarming "because I am always talking" has invoked for us the void that words fill. By the end of the poem, we are recognizing how language, *talk*, constitutes the world we most dynamically inhabit. We cannot take the second speaker as simply as he would like. Whether practically or not, through the play of his imagination the compulsive talker is exactly looking out where he is or might be going. The second speaker, then, enters unwillingly into a dialogue with a different scale of priorities. Within the consecutive dialogue of two speakers, a dialogic interplay of attitudes unfolds.

And who reports the exchange between these speakers? In telling the story, the first speaker takes on a new function. Now, as narrator, rather than projecting himself into alternative presents and futures, he speaks in past tense, characterizing himself ("because I am always talking") and his passenger ("my friend") from some distance. He takes a new kind of responsibility for the interest and significance of what he says; his speech is a declaration that the speeches he reports tell us something important—about him, about the other, about their opportunity or plight.

Nor can we quite stop there. We perceive still another "I," hovering behind both the narrator who says "I" in past tense and the speaker who says it in present tense. The "I" of the title—in present tense, yet formally outside the stanzas—may represent the single explicit appearance of this final participant in the poem. Adding to the cast of characters does not mean multiplying entities, but attending to the printed facts: Leaving aside the conventional transparency of speech transcription, we still ask who makes the line and stanza breaks, who abbreviates "said" and "you're." Abbreviation is a device of spelling, not of speech. Departures from orthographic conventions, like "sd" and "&" and "yr," call attention to themselves, and so ask to be assigned to someone. They belong to what we can call a voice—the best word we have for a sentience, even a mute one, developed in the language of a poem. In this case, the voice holds a special position: not a voice in the poem, but the voice of the poem. We as readers conveniently label the mouth of this voice "the poet."

Perhaps it is the narrator, inside the poem, who retrospectively selects and arranges the two speeches so as to build a dramatic situation out of a brief collage of talk by ensuring that various nouns begin as abstract ("darkness") or hypothetical ("car") and become concrete; perhaps it is he who decides to use just these two speeches, excluding descriptive stage directions. But it can only be the poet, in charge of the poem's typographical resources, who chooses to include both speeches in one fast, itinerant sentence. A printed poem only pretends to the spontaneity of talk.

Traditionally, the voice of the poem is privileged over others in the poem. The poet alone speaks to what is outside the poem, for instance to poetic history. Yet the poet of "I Know a Man" renders his stance toward other, more *authorized* kinds of poetry dialogic. He defies scriptural decorum to scrutinize actual speech. The abbreviations, for instance, signify speed—both to let speech be captured, and to confirm its rhythmic priorities. Fragmenting syntax yields a still more lively impression that we are hearing what someone really said. The poet, these devices say, has no time for the leisures of writing; he is after bigger game. Of course he uses writing, and the attention his devices call to it, to make this point. But such a poem insists on the priority of speech; it presents speech not as the lowest common denominator of language, but as generative—as producing (when heard and transmitted correctly) all the riches that literature would mine from it.

This poet's relation to the other voices is authorial but not exactly authoritative. He does not strive for "a unitary and singular language." His function depends on the others; their speech ostensibly precedes his, just as the narrator's act follows and embeds the speakers'; and his allegiance to speech appears to be as great as theirs. Where, then, does the poem get its authority? Bakhtin helps again, with his opposition between "the authoritative word" and "the internally persuasive word." The former he links with "reciting by heart"; religious and nationalistic creeds exemplify it, as do parroted opinions and received ideas. On the other hand, not recitation but "retelling in one's own words" characterizes internally persuasive discourse. In fact, it is a struggle among various authoritative words that engenders one's "own" word: "One's own discourse," he says, "is gradually and slowly wrought out of others' words that have been acknowledged and assimilated, and the boundaries between the two are at first scarcely perceptible" (p. 345n.). "The ideological becoming of a human being, in this view, is the process of selectively assimilating the words of others" (p. 341).

The poem brings into confrontation—and therefore into question—various versions of reality, various "words" or *logoi*, each of which seeks to impose itself as vision and to govern action. Driving, we should maintain a healthy paranoia about the real traffic around us; or see ourselves as being on the run from the law or the universe; or wish for a grander car. This conflict within the arena of the poem mimes the ideological struggle to which Bakhtin attributes the "becoming" of the individual mind. The poem itself could (as in the hands of a bad pedagogue) become externally authoritative; but properly attended to, it seeks to enact the process of internal persuasion: not to replace old authority, but to display an effort of assimilation. The poet refuses authority so as to insist that it be shared; it falls to us to revive the poem in our reading. It offers to engage us, not to enlist or instruct.

So the poem becomes an occasion of action, not an object. From a more traditional critical point of view, the reader's response to a poem is mimetic,

characterized by an aesthetic distance or gap of metaphor that must be leapt
rather than closed up or erased.[7] That analogical relation of poem to reader
has several advantages over the more fluid dialogic model, especially for the
explicative critic; it makes the poem a more stationary target. But Creeley
exacts our participation in a less classically stable exchange. He is, as Bakhtin
says of the novelist, "experimenting by turning persuasive discourse into
speaking persons" (p. 348).

If, as I said earlier, the first speaker's imaginative manipulation of his present is likewise experimental, then this "I" bears an important likeness to the
"I" we call the poet. The character and narrator and author do not adhere
strictly to the division of their roles, and attempting to demark every speaker's
province within the poem's language comes to seem futile and irrelevant. Indeed, we tend to assume that the first speaker and narrator and perhaps poet
are in some sense "the same person," at different times and in different situations. We have seen that the voice of the poem claims as little scriptural
privilege as possible over the voice in the poem. We might save the dichotomy
by calling the first speaker the *hero* of the poem, as Dean Moriarty is the hero
of *On the Road*, an ideal emulated by the narrator. But more is at stake. This
democratization of voices minimizes the division between art and life that underlies most European aesthetic thought. Without confusing the artist and his
artifact—we still need know nothing about Robert Creeley's biography—we
can hear how the talker in the poem speaks for the poet. The point the poem
makes concerns the stuff of which poetry is made: speech as continuous invention, spontaneous fabrication.

This reduced dichotomy between poem and poet would have disturbed the
New Critics, who in fact rarely dealt well with William Carlos Williams or
those who followed him. For them, the poem tended to be an object, whose
power to signify derived from its self-containment. Its closure as an object
enabled the one important openness, that of interpretation.[8] The closure of the
poem's form substantiated its ideal authority.

The form of "I Know a Man," in the simplest sense, mimics straightforward closure: The twelve lines fall into four three-line stanzas on the page.
From a great enough distance, the text of the poem looks like a Cavalier or
Romantic or even Greek lyric. But Creeley dialogizes this form, in part undermines it, by sharply counterpointing the stanzas (and lines) and the speech
sentence thrown as if carelessly across that formal armature. A more logical
division into stanzas would break the linguistic stream at other points, where
the topic shifts direction; and if the lines too were rationalized with respect to
syntax, the result could sound quite single-minded:

> As I sd to my friend,
> because I am always talking,

John, I sd,
which was not his name,

the darkness surrounds us,
what can we do against it, . . .

Compared with this travesty, Creeley's poem is both—and inseparably—more unpredictable and more alive.

What we cannot predict, we cannot provide for; what is unforeseen is, literally, improvised. The etymology, though at the expense of confusing our point of view with the artist's, reminds us why a jazz solo keeps us so alert. We know the tune; but we cannot know what we will hear about it. "I Know a Man" belongs, for us in reading it, as much in the category of the improvised as Astaire's and Charisse's dance. It seems natural to project our condition of moment-by-moment ignorance back onto the poet; and we do not essentially wrong the poem in doing so, no matter what the facts of its actual composition. We feel accompanied through such a poem, not guided.

Language, which we all use all the time to manipulate our surroundings, in this sense diverges utterly from music. But the poem leads a double existence. The lines embed its form in the page; the form releases the poem into time. Once we turn to the form of a poem, its extension in the structure of time, the analogy between poet and musician springs back to life. In the preface to the book in which "I Know a Man" originally appeared, Creeley remarks that "line-wise, the most complementary sense I have found is that of musicians like Charlie Parker, and Miles Davis. I am interested in how that is done, how 'time' there is held to a measure peculiarly an evidence (a hand) of the emotion which prompts (drives) the poem in the first place. If this seems hopeful, let me point to the 'line' of Miles Davis' chorus in BUT NOT FOR ME."[9] By putting his apparently nonce lineation and stanza divisions into play with the continuity of talk, Creeley manifests his interest "in how that is done"—how the musician invents phrases without depending directly on prior composition.

Creeley's poem does not randomly collect interesting bits of speech any more than a Parker solo randomly strings together a flurry of notes and arpeggios—though either may seem that way to an unaccustomed audience.[10] Creeley's measure, here as in other early poems, locates its shaping principle in reversing the standard shape of the English line. Though English speech strongly favors trochaic-dactylic rhythms—consider any list of place or surnames, or simply of bisyllabic words—in English verse iambic and anapestic meters dominate overwhelmingly. This subordination of falling rhythms to rising ones extends from the metrical foot to the line. Even most free verse makes the end of the line the point of maximum emphasis. In metrical contexts, the counterpoint which this encourages between meter and speech rhythm provides ubiquitous linguistic energy; and on the level of the line,

rhetorical considerations (as in the structure of periodic sentences) reinforce
the tendency toward climactic organization. By contrast, Creeley's lines get
much of their uncanny force—especially when read aloud—from his thrusting
emphasis toward the beginning.

Like Konitz, Creeley displaces accents to mark out a distinctive shape in
time. He establishes his unusual accentuation partly by pushing the last word
of a phrase over to start the next line:

>   . . . to my
> friend, . . .

>   . . . which was not his
> name, . . .

or most tellingly,

>   . . . the darkness sur-
> rounds us, . . .

So thoroughly does he suspend our rhythmic habits that the few nearly regular
trochaic-dactylic lines seem the norm:

> /   x   /   x   /   x
> always talking,—John, I

>   . . .

>   /   x   /   x   x
> name, the darkness sur-

>   . . .

>   /   x   x / x
> out where yr going.

The one stretch of rising rhythm stands apart as a moment of confusion, a
wavering of the speaker's fervor, from which he rescues himself by means of
a new impulse:

>   . . . what

>   x   x / x   /
> can we do against

> x x /   / x x
> it, or else, shall we &

>   /   x
> why not, . . .

The return of impetus at "shall we" is reinforced by a line almost all stresses, but basically trochaic:

```
  /   \    / x /   \   /   \
why not, buy a goddamn big car
```

These careful adjustments of rhythm, these syncopations, characterize the speaker for us as pervasively as the phrases themselves do. At the same time, they help Creeley to renew ("Make It New," said Pound) the traditional contention between verse form and speech rhythm. His prosodic form, insisting on both the page and speech (while most literature pretends to unite them), enacts the same commitment to dialogue we have seen in all his handling of the poem's voices. Like the main speaker, or like most jazz players in the heat of performance, the poet seems more intent on momentum than on accomplishment. Yet no careful reading could miss the deliberation with which the lines are constructed, or the satisfaction of the poem's ending.[11] If the form is contingent, rather than closed, it is not haphazard. Unless we are made uncomfortable by the rush and tangle of language, we are not listening intently enough; but what brings us back to this little speech over and over is the sense that each syllable falls just as it has to in its line, that the disorder betokens not chaos but complexity of attention.

Behind Creeley stands William Carlos Williams—as behind Robert Duncan, Denise Levertov, Charles Olson, and dozens of other recent American poets. Williams's modernism was eclipsed by Eliot's for half a century; and even now, the struggle between the two seems unlikely to subside before it is replaced by other preoccupations. The conflict, from various points of view, has divided America and England, the people and the academy, speech and literature, literature and philosophy, sensation and memory.

In a sense it is true of all modernism that its chief ethical ideal is authenticity. In the history that Lionel Trilling traces in *Sincerity and Authenticity*, the latter is a bitter virtue, achieved through violent resistance to the social definition of the self. But the American version can perhaps be distinguished by Whitman's inversion of this antagonism: The self is made to define others. "What I assume you shall assume," says the self that "contains multitudes." Compare his heartiness with the *nausée* of Sartre (who supplies Trilling's culminating example): "The commonplace belongs to everybody and it belongs to me; in me, it belongs to everybody; it is the presence of everybody in me"[12]—like a conspiracy of parasites. In Whitman, rather, joy becomes a victory for authenticity: The ecstatic speaker has literally stepped aside from the mask of his or her personality.

Whitman's exuberance could hardly carry undeterred through all the work of American poets in the twentieth century. And often, the compulsion toward authenticity is still put in defiantly isolationist terms, as in the bold bland declaration by one early writer that "every man's free verse is different."[13] In fact, this echoes Whitman's own demand for absolute rhythmic spontaneity from every poet.[14] This is a trap into which Eliot never fell. For him, the "Individual Talent" always stood in significant relation to a "Tradition" which he saw as a community (though rather of poems than of poets): "We shall often find that not only the best, but the most individual parts of [a poet's] work may be those in which the dead poets, his ancestors, assert their immortality most vigorously."[15] Williams did not always see or say this side of the matter so clearly. Yet his sometimes hysterical rebellions against Eliot's academicism, allusive classicism, and Anglicization should not be taken as proving that he failed to comprehend the subtleties of authenticity. Behind his occasional incoherence, we sense his shrewd conviction of another way to authenticate poetry, and another resource to enrich it.

Williams had three main ideas about the technique of poetry, and one of them was "no ideas but in things." In this he maintained the Imagist origins from which the branches of modernism can be seen to grow.[16] His other two ideas concerned diction and rhythm, and his names for them congregate in the title of a sequence of poems: "Some Simple Measures in the American Idiom and the Variable Foot." The "variable foot" and "measure" remain (despite the efforts of followers and the magnitude of his example) more or less opaque prosodic terms; yet it was clearly his search for what Marianne Moore called "a place for the genuine" that drove him to make and remake his idiosyncratic line and stanza until he found the three-staggered-line form that enlivens "Of Asphodel, That Greeny Flower" and other late poems.[17]

His championship of "the American idiom" is less elusive. That American English had diverged importantly from British English was certainly clear by the turn of the century; Whitman's "barbaric yawp" had defied European decorum even before the Civil War. An English novelist like Conan Doyle in the eighties—and Dorothy Sayers in the twenties—could write parodic "American" dialects for occasional characters from the U.S. Yet Williams insisted loudest and almost alone, until after mid-century when he had disciples to join him, that American poetry should sound genuinely American. "I stand squarely on the existence and practicability of an American language—among others *like* English which are not English—and a complete independence from English literature in each case, i.e., that of Joyce and our present-day American writers for example."[18] In his poems, culminating in *Paterson* but beginning as early as the First World War, he collected and juxtaposed and wrought into shape the words of his medical patients, family, and neighbors, "the speech of Polish mothers."

The collage technique of *Paterson* underscores what attracted him in this "idiom"—that it mixes many idioms. English itself is a language compounded long ago of French and Anglo-Saxon, and still resists the homogenization of an Académie Française or the BBC. American English, especially in this century, has had to grow still more supple to absorb grafts from Italian, Yiddish, Spanish, various African languages, Lithuanian, and so on. Within the life of our cities, and within the ear attuned to hear it, modern American is an inherently dialogic language.

As the constant refrain of "authenticity" suggests, our contemporary culture has found the relations between the self and others particularly baffling. In 1956 (a year after "I Know a Man"), Josephine Herbst described "the present phase that tends to the compulsive presentation of people as isolated moral atoms without any sensible relation to society or the ideas of their times"; and this phase has not ended, despite fluctuations during the sixties.[19] But the idea of the dialogic represents a possible liberation from this imprisoning version of individualism. Don Bialostosky, for instance, has made use of Bakhtin to redefine the "authentic voice" in a more productive way:

> "Voice" . . . is not so much a matter of how my language relates to me as it is a matter of how my language relates to your language and to the language of others you and I have heard address our topic. . . . If voice . . . is to be heard in the speaker's responsiveness to the voices of others who have spoken on the topic as well as to the voices of those who now listen but may yet speak, then an authentic voice . . . would be one that vitally and productively engaged those voices. It would be *authentically situated*.[20]

The self or the voice is indefinable in isolation; it is born from a matrix of other voices. Eliot delineated an echo chamber of the past in which each new voice takes its place. But Williams was interested in mining the present speech around him. He sought authenticity for the American poem in the dialogic language of the American people.

This casts new light on his interest in improvisation. For a year (some time before 1920) he wrote a brief piece of prose at the end of every day; later he added short commentary "interpretations" to most of them, and published eighty-one of them as *Kora in Hell*.[21]

These are not exactly improvisations in a jazz player's sense of the word. Their whole history, from conception to publication, was a written one, so that the time-bound nature of the language was much modified as compared with music. "Even if I had nothing in my mind at all," says Williams, "I put something down, and as may be expected, some of the entries were pure nonsense and were rejected when the time for publication came."[22] The jazz player cannot edit. Williams's work only began as improvisation; then he spent time "groping around to find a way to include the improvisations" in a book. This involved rearranging and interpreting as well as selecting. In a later chapter we will see language used as a truly improvisational medium; but by contrast, the only compositional safeguard that Williams refused was the freedom to revise.

Yet this is no trivial refusal,[23] and after more than half a century *Kora in*

Hell (and the prose of *Spring and All* and his other mixed works) retains a wild, puzzling freshness. "It was a kind of automatic writing," says Williams's biographer, Paul Mariani: "Williams' attempt to 'loosen the attention' and descend deeper than ever into his poetic unconsciousness to tap energies so far left dormant" (p. 148). This is a use of improvisation that makes sense only in the context of language—language seen as tending to harden into an "authoritative word" that represses the poet's true voice. Improvisation promises an escape into the internal persuasion of dialogue.

Gerald Bruns, in an essay on *Kora*, treats improvisation as the opposite of a dialogue: "An improvisation is conceived in forgetfulness or in studied ignorance; it is what happens without respect to previous statements, which is why a conversation, although extemporaneous in its development, is not an improvisation."[24] He distinguishes between "rhetorical" and "Romantic" improvisation, essentially as between embellishment and creation: "Romantic improvisation begins with a blank sheet of paper; rhetorical improvisation begins with a sheet of paper on which a poem or score is written but which contains to the knowing or the artful eye large and indeterminate areas of something left unsaid, unsung" (p. 147).

If Konitz's performance of (or "on") "All the Things You Are" is rhetorical, Williams's improvisations would be Romantic, and therefore "hard to distinguish . . . from a spontaneous overflow of powerful feelings" (p. 147). But the page is never blank. Nothing is made of nothing. Bruns's idea of improvisation (though he has much of value to say about its relation to writing) makes sense only if the voice to be released by automatism is a unitary voice. Yet even Bruns's own project of "invention"—a kind of rhetorical soloing on critical topics—is exciting precisely as it eschews authoritative singlemindedness so as to engage in a playful dialogue with various works.

Williams's prose improvisations constitute a special case. And yet the principle of improvisation—not simply earnest spontaneity, but the process of composition displayed on stage in the final poem—is central to his poetry as well. Just as, in the prose parts of *Spring and All*, Williams explicitly stops and restarts whenever the progress of his thought demands it—

> [A work of the imagination shows the individual] that his life is valuable—when completed by the imagination. And then only. Such work elucidates—
>
> Such a realization shows us the falseness of attempting to 'copy' nature.[25]

—so in the verse parts of the same work he sometimes uses the same method:

> The place between the petal's
> edge and the
>
> From the petal's edge a line starts . . .
>
> (p. 108)

In later verse the resemblance is less obvious; but even his most apparently composed poems maintain something of the same insistence on improvisation.

On the page, ''The Yachts'' looks a little surprising for a Williams poem. The lines are long, and of a consistent length. The three-line stanzas might seem familiar, but the general left-justified blockiness of the text contradicts our sense of Williams as a poet who distributes his words through typographical space. The beginning of the poem holds an even greater surprise:

The Yachts

contend in a sea which the land partly encloses
shielding them from the too-heavy blows
of an ungoverned ocean, which, when it chooses

tortures the biggest hulls, the best man knows . . .

This, from the most adamant of nonmetrical poets, is *terza rima*. The lines are not metrical, but they flirt with iambic pentameter; the first and fourth, though quite loose, could be scanned without absurdity.[26] The A rhyme, though not exact, is strengthened by being a two-syllable rhyme; and the B rhyme is entirely conventional. In these opening lines, we may see Williams bearding the expatriate traditionalists in their den: the form is Dante's, and the *Divine Comedy* was an essential talisman for Eliot as well as for Williams's friendlier enemy, Pound.

Yet in the next line Williams ran across an interesting bit of language—

to pit against its beatings,

—and followed where it led:

. . . and sinks them pitilessly.

This line destroys the rhyme and with it the conventional form. It obeys no imposed meter. Its form, instead, is internally generated and controlled: This is a line drawn through two occurrences of the morpheme, *pit*.

The verb *pit* goes back to an Indo-European root meaning ''cut, strike, stamp,'' which would seem appropriate to the context except that the modern verb derives deviously from the Anglo-Saxon noun (meaning a hole cut into the ground) by way of cockfighting. The *pit* in ''pitiless'' is the Latin *pietas*, which may not even be Indo-European. Williams is characteristically uninterested in these histories.[27] Puns of this kind represent the unexpected compounds of meaning formed in the roil and heat of speech as speech, as a stream of sound; their strength depends on the *lack* of historical connection between the words, the serendipity of their coincidence. That is, the virtue of puns is improvisational.

In a way, this brings us back to familiar ground as readers of Williams's work: Though he has begun an experiment with a traditional form, ordained by literary history and imposed on the poem from without, he abandons it in favor of a symmetry organically growing or spontaneously discovered within the line he is constructing. Yet the most startling gesture of the poem's beginning is not this choice, but Williams's decision to leave the traces of his original project. We can easily imagine Eliot, or any poet, beginning with the idea of writing some *terza rima* about yachts, and then getting off onto something more compelling; that is how poets most often work, despite Poe's fantastic claims for rational composition. But it is difficult to imagine Eliot—let alone Poe—leaving such bald clues as to his change of intention.

I am recounting this story backwards from Paul Mariani: "He had begun it with Dante's *terza rima* since he was borrowing the scene from the *Inferno* where Dante and Virgil must cut through the arms and hands of the damned floating beneath them who try to sink their small boat" (p. 370). No early drafts of the poem exist, as far as I can determine, which might settle the question historically. But the point lies elsewhere. The poem's larger method is one of discovery. In the last stanzas, the casual personification of the yachts and the sea suddenly rises (with Dante's help) into political awareness and "the horror of the race dawns staggering the mind." The shock of these stanzas depends on our belief in a casual observer who is similarly shocked into realization. The poet's readiness to change in midstream prepares us for the recognition undergone by the implicit "I" in the poem, who in turn involves us in his discovery.

The speaker's sudden conviction grows out of a conflict among different tendencies in his descriptive language. Through the calm reportage of events, with bits of journalistic color like "broad bellying sails," other tones glimmer at various moments: amused contempt for the "lesser and great craft which, sycophant, lumbering / and flittering follow them"; a kind of fascistic contempt for the crew that "crawls // ant-like, solicitously grooming them"; enthusiasm for "the minute / brilliance of cloudless days"; and a different enthusiasm, tinged with regret, for the yachts that

> . . . appear youthful, rare
>
> as the light of a happy eye, live with the grace
> of all that in the mind is fleckless, free and
> naturally to be desired. . . .

Not only the yachts, but various attitudes toward them, various voices, "contend"—as mildly as in the genteel, "governed" competition of the race, while the uneasiness of the language gradually increases. When the merely decorative, conventional metaphors ("the sea . . . is moody, lapping their glossy sides") are suddenly reversed and thrown into relief ("It is a sea of faces about them in agony, in despair"), the understanding held in suspension by the mixture of voices precipitates. We believe the conversion because of

the unpredictable abruptness with which everything that precedes it is transformed. However the poem was written, if we suspected that it knew too well
where it was going, we would not so wholeheartedly follow.[28] Or to put it
another way, the poem results from a dialogue between a poet whom Dante
has prepared for this race and a speaker who must cover the same ground for
himself for "the horror of the race" to "dawn" and "stagger the mind."

There is a poetry of voice and there is a poetry of image. This dichotomy is so
crude that no poem obeys it. Yet it at least implies distinct ways of reading
poems. "The Yachts" is usually read for image—for the objects and events
Williams describes and the metaphor (yachts:sea::rich:poor) they add up to.
But it can be read with attention to voice, so that the motions and multiplicities
of the telling become the events of the poem, and the adding up to metaphor
is its plot. Many poems or parts of poems lend themselves strongly to one or
the other way of reading. The old name for a poetry of voice is "rhetorical";
it would include most work by Campion and Tennyson and Ashbery. The
modern name for a poetry of image is Imagist.

In the modernism of the first half of our print-committed century, the dominance of the image seemed almost absolute, at least in theory. Certainly many
of Williams's poems, as well as Pound's and Eliot's and Stevens's, demand
that we envision things and scenes. They often carry us through an elaborate
"composition of place" (to use the vocabulary of Ignatian meditation[29]). Language in these poems tends to become transparent, so that we can see the
image through it as if without distraction or distortion.

But poetry, if never wholly musical, is never more than partly visual. Its
chief means of attaining vividness of image is vividness of sound. The great
Imagist lines do not derive their greatness directly from image, any more than
from plot or moral virtue. Pound's "Quick eyes gone under earth's lid" seems
to give us a picture; but if we tried to draw it, we would have to leave out the
influential alternative meanings of "quick" and "lid" (not to mention
"gone"). Even if we filmed it, so as to catch the irreducibly temporal movement of metaphor, what would we film—soldiers, their eyes in metonymic
close-up, falling under fire into trenches which then somehow close like eyes?
The result would be luridly surrealistic if, improbably, it could remain serious.
It would hardly combine the ruthlessness of Pound's beginning and ending
spondees (the double force of "quick" is important) and the incipient grief of
the shift in sound that intervenes ("gone under").

A number of Creeley's most striking poems concentrate our attention on
voice by refusing to satisfy our customary desire for image. "I Know a Man"
lets us envision a situation—two speakers, a car—but with a strict minimum

of dramatic paraphernalia. In other poems, the abstraction from image is even more rigorous.

The Immoral Proposition

If you never do anything for anyone else
you are spared the tragedy of human relation-

ships. If quietly and like another time
there is the passage of an unexpected thing:

to look at it is more
than it was. God knows

nothing is competent nothing is
all there is. The unsure

egoist is not
good for himself.[30]

This certainly defies the Imagist law of concrete language. (''Go in fear of abstractions,'' said Pound.) It strongly tempts us to read it in propositional terms—to ask first and foremost, of a statement like ''If you never do anything for anyone else you are spared the tragedy of human relationships,'' whether it is *true*. The sentence seems a clear declaration, except perhaps in the shading of its tone. (Surely—the title would tell us, even if our expectations about the ethics that poems affirm did not—the poem is warning, not recommending.) The last sentence sounds just as forthright, though when we try to combine it with the first, the question of tone grows even more tangled. (If it implies that the egoist can never be ''sure'' enough to fulfill even his own needs, does the course ironically recommended in the first sentence not become impossible and the warning therefore empty?) Still, these uncertainties lie out at the edge of our understanding of the propositions. The poem seems to take its model from inspirational prose.

But the first sentence of the poem has an effect—a sound—quite different from the trite prose it seems to comprise. The lineation, most obviously at the end of the first stanza, cuts sharply across the incipient fatuousness. This is not semantic lineation, as in the whole range of earlier modernist poets from Williams through Eliot and Auden; in the amputation of a suffix from the tail end of the sentence, no meaning is created through accentual ambiguity. Judged by that archetypal free-verse standard, this lineation is silly. Rather, its point is precisely to undercut the statement the sentence seems to make, not to confirm it. What the poem does is not to make the statement, but to quote it. The poet distances himself from its banality while not disputing its potential truth. In this, we might see Creeley acting toward the statement much as we saw Konitz acting toward Jerome Kern's tune: embracing it as a vehicle for performance, yet at the same time wryly distorting and condensing it. Furthermore, as the poem's line of thought grows to include the idea of "competence" and "all there is" and so on, the hope of clarity seems to require ever more desperately that we ignore the second sentence of the poem. There we confront abstraction of a different order. The syllogistic syntax continues the poem's bent toward logic, but the diction seems oddly concrete, while absolutely refusing specificity. The opening adverbial phrase might fit well into the nostalgic tenderness of certain imaginable love poems; but the subject of the clause (unlike that of the previous sentence) is not "you" or anything like it. "Passage" might go back, picking up "quietly" along the way, to the "ships" cut loose from "relation-"; but an image that depends on so low a grammatical pun hardly accounts for the sudden lyric tone of these lines. In the absence of clear sense, the tone derives from a new delicacy of sound (as in the plays on *l* and long *i*), and above all from rhythm—the intrusion of a full pentameter, "If quietly and like another time."[31] At the climax of the dependent clause, "thing," the ultimate abstraction, finally blocks our groping for sense, and with the sentence's main clause still to come.

What Pound warned against, and what most of Creeley's poem so disarmingly offers, is the abstraction of thought from things and events toward principles or summary generalizations.[32] The language accompanies the mind in its movement away from things. But in this second sentence of the poem, the abstracting movement separates the language from the thought. The immediacy of tone suggests that the speaker is thinking of something perfectly definite—an event, perhaps. But this thinking is not made available in the words of the poem; what is said is fraught with the unsaid. This is language not only *not* transparent to image, but opaque also to rationalization. Yet the result is not meaningless. How can language mean, without recourse either to image or reason?

We can answer either by reference to formal linguistics or by analogy. For analytic principles suitable to this use of language, we would turn to Saussure and those who have developed his idea of language as a "structure of differences" that means by self-reference (*pit* is defined by distinction from *pet* and *bit*, just as a sequence of 0's and 1's in a computer can mean "pangolin" or "add these numbers," according to the encoded context) rather than by reference to things outside itself. For analogy, we would turn to music—which Saussure's version of language closely resembles. Sensory representation or image (birdsong, gunfire, etc.) is peripheral to our understanding of music. And in a different sense, our rational understanding of music—the analysis of harmonic relationships, for instance, that helps to explain and even enrich our sense of order and complexity in listening—is secondary to our fundamental experience of music.[33] Why should poetry require more (or less) than music to attain a condition of meaning?

Yet the music of a poem does not descend anonymously from the spheres.

The speaker in "The Immoral Proposition," though no compulsive talker like the driver in "I Know a Man," is no less compelling a voice. One cumulative effect of the poem's various sorts of abstraction is that we cannot be sure of the speaker's relation to the speech. Is this an address to the self, warning against a foreseen error? Or to us, from the voice of bitter experience? Or a reproach to a more specific "you" from someone who importantly represents "anyone else"?

The poem's haunting effect requires us to be baffled in all these ways. The abbreviated stanzas and the abrupt pause of the word choked off by a hyphen recreate the halting pace that "I Know a Man" gets from its lineation. (In the third stanza of this poem, the lineation returns to that more customary style of Creeley's.) What halts and struggles onward is a voice. Indeed, deprived so completely of any image, we can find hardly anything but voice in the poem. A voice is an intentionality unfolding in time. It may unfold slowly, as here, or fast, as in "I Know a Man," but it must move to exist. For us as listeners, it is "the passage of an unexpected thing"; and "to look at it," to participate by listening, corroborates and validates its speaking. Our participation is "more than it was" as an isolated utterance. The intention can compel our listening repeatedly; it cannot be captured or settled. We are caught by the painful attempt to articulate something that disappears as soon as words seem about to hold it still.

The halting lends conviction. What is "immoral," says the poem, is finally "propositions": smug partitionings of thought and action according to a faculty of judgment that prizes conclusions over mysteries. Creeley's poems refuse certainty with the passion of Socrates disavowing wisdom. They depend on our belief in their spontaneous intensity.

Our experience of even the most spatial of arts involves time: We walk through a building; we scan a painting's parts in some order. On the other hand, our understanding of even the most fleetingly time-bound art ultimately takes a kind of instantaneous shape in our minds. The difference among arts is one of delay, of degree. Yet this difference remains essential. Poetry, straddling the indefinite division, can impress us as striving toward spatial wholeness, as the *Four Quartets* almost explicitly do: "In my end is my beginning," says Eliot. (Yet "Only through time time is conquered.") Or poetry can resist separation from the matrix of time in which it is originally voiced: To forget that "the passage of an unexpected thing" precedes "God knows / nothing is competent" and follows "the tragedy of human relationships" is to have lost "The Immoral Proposition" almost entirely.

Williams insisted over and over that the poem is a made thing, "a machine made of words." "It isn't what [the poet] says that counts as a work of art, it's what he makes, with such intensity of perception that it lives with an intrinsic movement of its own to verify its authenticity."[34] The previous chapter suggested that improvisation does not mean scattered, chaotic eruption; and we see how seriously a poetic composition can pretend to spontaneity. A poet like Creeley or Williams sets himself or herself a problem similar to the actor's (or to that of the poet reading aloud): to make what has the authority of print sound or act like internal persuasion. The poem is a text and a speech, rather as light is a particle and a wave.

Consequently, these poems risk two opposite kinds of misreading. On the one hand, if we accept their claim as improvisations too naively, they dissolve into triviality or mechanical reportage or mere idiosyncrasy. (This is the danger they present as objects of imitation for young poets.)[35] We begin taking them simply as talk, all talk as equally illuminating, and the poems as undistinguished snippets. If we then discover evidences of skill, of making, we are likely to feel practiced upon; we hate poetry, said Keats, that has "a palpable design upon us."

On the other hand, if we take these poems too simply as compositions, we are apt to worry them into rigid, overfamiliar shapes. Saying that in "I Know a Man" clues like "goddamn" and "for christ's sake" constitute a pattern of imagery that also attracts "John" into sacramental significance, we would betray both the poem and ourselves.

To believe simultaneously in the dance and its choreography may seem to require doublethink. More properly, though, it invites us to a richer understanding in which acts of speech neither spring from nowhere, nor transmit a foregone conclusion, but embody a feeling out.

On Silence

Kind of Blue—many people's favorite great jazz record—has liner notes by Bill Evans, the pianist on the date, entitled "Improvisation in Jazz":

"There is a Japanese visual art in which the artist is forced to be spontaneous. He must paint on a thin stretched parchment with a special brush and black water paint in such a way that an unnatural or interrupted stroke will destroy the line or break through the parchment. Erasures or changes are impossible. These artists must practice a particular discipline, that of allowing the idea to express itself in communication with their hands in such a direct way that deliberation cannot interfere.

"The resulting pictures lack the complex composition and textures of ordinary painting, but it is said that those who see well find something captured that escapes explanation.

"This conviction that direct deed is the most meaningful reflection, I believe, has prompted the evolution of the extremely severe and unique disciplines of the jazz or improvising musician."

(In such paintings the influence of Zen Buddhism, with its emphasis on the Void, on *clearing*, is visible in the predominance of empty space. Cf. Evans's piano, Davis's trumpet, Creeley's emulation of Davis.)

Three

Ornette Coleman: The Shapes of Jazz

ONCE between sets, Ornette Coleman was beaten up and his saxophone was smashed. Criticism by his fellow musicians was less physical than that, but no less violent. When Coleman arrived in New York in the fifties, "his unique playing, already formed, alienated club owners and other musicians, and he found little work. He even had trouble sitting in. The tenor saxophonist Dexter Gordon ordered him off the bandstand, and when he attempted to play with the Clifford Brown–Max Roach band the rhythm section packed up."[1]

Many forces converged against Coleman. The jazz tradition, to begin with, had its fiercely competitive side. "Cutting sessions" weeded out the incompetent and valorized the most fluent, prolific, indefatigable improvisers. The young Charlie Parker himself was scorned off a stage by Jo Jones, the Swing drummer.[2] Miles Davis (later among those who condemned Coleman as a charlatan) during one famous recording session refused to let Thelonious Monk accompany his solos.[3] Then too, throughout the late fifties jazz fans and critics and players were conducting an obsessive search for "Bird's heir," the alto saxophonist who would extend Parker's revolution—extend it, of course, in the direction he had made familiar. Nor was Coleman helped by the portentous album titles foisted on him by producers: *The Shape of Jazz to Come*, *The Change of the Century*. His own opacity of speech recalls Williams's frustrating attempts to articulate his aesthetic. Finally, the contemporary style stressed "cool" for a variety of reasons, including complicated responses to the continued oppression of African-Americans after the Second World War; but Coleman's heated music refuses restraint.

These considerations lie well outside the music itself, in the realm of personality, historical accident, and group demonology. Yet no art, certainly no evaluation of artistic work, is wholly separable from its social context.[4] Jazz derives its special power (and its resonance for those who contemplate relations among the arts) partly from the way it expresses and transmutes tensions within that social context—as a black music in a white society, an American music in a culture derived from Europe. We should not expect simple judgments of new voices.

Fury took root in a ready soil of bewilderment. Whitney Balliett notes the real basis of Coleman's rejection: "At first hearing, Coleman's music sounds obscure and perverse, as if he were deliberately playing flat, in the wrong key, and out of time. But after a while the listener enters his world and dons his

logic. . . . [His solos] move melodically with such freedom and originality
and surprise that they form an independent music'' (pp. 65–66). To treat this
music on its own terms, we must begin by noting that it diverges from everyone else's. Coleman's recording of his tune ''Lonely Woman,''[5] for instance,
now strikes anyone on first hearing as not merely idiosyncratic, but genuinely
original. Strangeness does not guarantee authenticity, but authentic work may
well seem alien to the authority of stylistic fashion. The same otherness that
now—after twenty-five years—allies itself with the stunning lyric beauty we
have become free to hear in the piece, at the time struck many knowledgeable
listeners as an ugly assault. Exploring the relations between strangeness and
beauty, authenticity and conviction, we might learn more about the issues we
have seen surrounding the idea of voice.

To treat the work itself on its own terms—this is the critic's accepted job,
or a basic part of it, in the world of poetry. We write and read criticism because
we want to understand more fully how certain poems work, so as to bring them
more completely into the sphere of our enjoyment. The situation in music
differs somewhat—in jazz, almost completely. For many jazz fans, jazz musicians, and even jazz critics, analysis is sacrilege: It breaks into holy places
and writes on the walls. Consequently, there is very little of it, as compared
with the self-sustaining industry of literary analysis.[6]

In 1958, Gunther Schuller—composer, conductor, French horn player, mu-
sicologist, later the author of *Early Jazz* and *The Swing Era*—collaborated
with Martin Williams and others in founding the *Jazz Review*, one of the few
American journals devoted to jazz criticism in the common literary sense of
the word. Schuller's first contribution was an article that became famous or
notorious; it remains one of the most elaborate examinations of a single jazz
performance, Sonny Rollins's ''Blue Seven.'' A note of defensiveness inter-
rupts his discussion:

> I realize fully that music is meant to be listened to, and that words are not adequate
> in describing a piece of music. However, since laymen, and even many musicians,
> are perhaps more interested in knowing exactly how such structural solos [as Rol-
> lins's] are achieved than in blindly accepting at face value remarks such as those
> above, I shall try to go into some detail and with the help of short musical examples
> give an account of the ideational thread running through Rollins' improvisation that
> makes this particular recording so distinguished and satisfying.[7]

What literary critic would feel called upon for such an apology? Yet the sort
of response Schuller anticipates apparently came often enough for Martin Williams to mention, in introducing a collection of articles from the *Jazz Review*,
''letters from readers which said, in effect, you can't talk about jazz that way''
(*Jazz Panorama*, p. 7). Rollins himself reacted to Schuller's essay by declaring that he would never read his notices again. (Of course it was not Rollins,
but his listeners, that Schuller was addressing.) A year and a half later, in a

detailed review of several records by Thelonious Monk, Schuller's tone takes on more exasperation. He begins a paragraph about Monk's change of an A♭ to a B♭, but breaks off: "I gather that for many jazz enthusiasts, any remotely analytical thinking about notes, pitches and chords is simply odious. Nonetheless, musicians deal with sounds, chords and notes; and it is precisely what they do with these basic ingredients, how they 'select' them, that we are able to differentiate one from another" (pp. 236–37).

People did not object to analysis as boring, we should notice, but as offensive. The complaint focuses on spontaneity as the most essential characteristic of jazz. At an extreme, this principle raises the occasional claim that recorded jazz is not jazz at all, lacking the true Paterian transitoriness. More subtly, it leads to the doctrine that only improvisation can be jazz—a position hotly contested by such orchestral jazz composers as William Russo.[8] The prizing of spontaneity both derives from and reinforces the idea, easily oversimplified, that the most original player is by definition the best. When Schuller speaks of the selection of notes differentiating "one from another," he is referring to players, not directly to pieces of music.

What is at stake is again authenticity: but not really of the work, nor even of the artist; rather of the audience's reception of the work. Analysis is looking a gift horse in the mouth. Though in some cases the objection originates in a simple distrust of thought, or a misplaced concern about murdering to dissect (misplaced in that the life of a written or recorded work of art is peculiarly renewable), resistance often reflects a more profound concern with the community that unites player and listener. If the relationship among player, music, and listener is to resemble a dialogue, we must yearn toward simultaneous conversation. The long time it takes to analyze, so much at odds with the fleeting time of playing or listening, threatens to alienate the devotee. Only the small fraction of jazz that is recorded even offers itself for analysis. Finally, as Walter Ong points out in his highly illuminating work on *Orality and Literacy*, analysis is a literate activity: "Human beings in primary oral cultures, those untouched by writing in any form, learn a great deal and possess and practice great wisdom, but they do not 'study.' . . . Study in the strict sense of extended sequential analysis becomes possible with the interiorization of writing."[9] Ours is no primary oral culture. Yet our secondary orality has interested many writers. Jazz seems to exemplify it; as everyone knows, for instance, many early jazz players could not read music. To analyze jazz, then, might be to threaten it with reabsorption into the literate and potentially repressive mainstream of the culture.

An analogy invites us: Improvisation is to orality as composition is to literacy. Jazz obviously belongs on the left side of this equation. But before the impulse to elaborate such a system carries us too far, we might return to the actual piece, "Lonely Woman."

In his recording, Coleman alters the proportions of the standard structure of

jazz performances: melody, string of solos, melody. Konitz's "All the Things
You Are" partly suppresses the melody choruses in favor of free improvisation (taking "free" with the necessary qualifications); Coleman goes just the
other way. Whereas in most jazz, particularly by small groups and particularly
since the early forties, the point is the solos, "Lonely Woman" concentrates
heavily on its melody. Only Coleman takes a solo, and it is only one shortened
chorus. Two-thirds of the piece is occupied by composed material; the normal
modern-jazz proportion would be nearer a quarter or a tenth.[10] Such an emphasis on compositional structure suppresses our association of this jazz with
orality.[11]

This revised emphasis bends our attention toward the stunning tune itself,
which has helpfully been published in *A Collection of Twenty-six Ornette
Coleman Compositions*[12] (as reproduced below). Examining the written melody, we can begin to pick out features that contribute to the effect of originality.

"Lonely Woman": published transcription of melody

D.C. al Fine (2nd End.)

| Em | Fm | F#m | F#m | A | A |

"Lonely Woman" by Ornette Coleman. Copyright 1960, 1968 by
MJQ Music, Inc. All rights reserved. Used by permission.

The harmonic character of "Lonely Woman," established by the "D pedal
point in bass" indicated at the beginning, holds a first surprise. Though the
key signature says D minor, this pedal point, maintained throughout most of
the chorus, implies a tonal center rather than a conventional key. (The absence
of a chordal instrument such as guitar or piano increases harmonic ambiguity.)
Serialism and true atonality were almost unknown in jazz at this date;[13] the
likely alternative to tonal harmony was modal harmony. My earlier historical
sketch noted that the first modal jazz (Davis's *Milestones* and *Kind of Blue*)
was recorded more than a year before Coleman's album, and by 1960 this
method belonged among the available resources of the avant-garde.

Yet the tonal center in "Lonely Woman" is not a modal center. Which
mode would it be? A mode is defined as much by exclusions as by the notes it
includes, like a club or a constellation. The ambiguous sixth degree of the
scale used in "Lonely Woman"—the successive B natural and Bb in measures
8 and 11—seriously undermines the Dorian, which is the most common modal
choice in jazz.[14] The resolution on F# in the twelfth measure at least temporarily suspends both the Dorian and the Aeolian as possibilities. If we see these
incidents as extensions of modality, then the closest parallel would be John
Coltrane's work a year or two later. But the effect is very different: This
sparse, highly singable melody has little to do with Coltrane's "sheets of
sound" that dissolve modality in profuse chromaticism. Nor do the extra-
modal notes function as passing tones or occasional ornaments. Rather, "Lonely
Woman" seems to move from one selection of the chromatic scale to another
by its own internal logic, with hardly a glance at (European) historical categories and associations; and calling various fragments Dorian or harmonic minor or Mixolydian will not capture their unity of sound. For this it is harder to
find a precedent; and the true successor is Coleman's own *Free Jazz* album a
few years later.

Furthermore, the melodic phrases are asymmetrical in length.[15] They add
up to a fifteen-measure main strain. Since most of the rhythmic units in Western music are powers of two, this is very unusual—though actually it *sounds*
quite natural. The first six bars can be divided into two phrases, each of three
measures containing two sub-phrases:

Ex. 3.1. Phrases in beginning of melody

The first phrase moves away from the tonal center on D, the second returns
to it. But the next two measures, rather than beginning a contrasting or answering section as we might expect, seem to extend this otherwise neat construction, while filling it out to a deceptively neat eight bars. So the nascent
symmetries of the beginning, the divisions and allegiances of the various melodic fragments, are obscured; the phrases never quite grant completion of a
closed unit. The "tonic" in the eighth measure, undermined by the harmoniz-
ing B natural, does not feel like an end to the main strain.

The next brief phrase

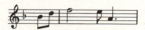

Ex. 3.2. Melody, measures 8–9

—set apart by the isolation of the saxophone, by the saxophone's sudden intrusion up into the trumpet's register, by the B♭ that contrasts with the preceding B natural, and by the first shift of the bass pedal point from D to A—
somehow counterbalances the whole preceding complex of phrases. This solo
phrase follows the first note on which the two horns play in harmony rather
than in unison or octaves, and is followed in turn by the only extended passage
of harmony (measures 10–12). This penultimate phrase, also distinguished by
its sudden slowness and metric regularity, occupies three measures, which
begins to seem the normal unit for this tune. Finally, the strain ends with
another three-bar tag that is again most peculiar for sounding neither short-
changed nor long-winded.

Even the division into three-measure phrases is deceptive. The structural
accents—the ones that, in the absence of a written score, might suggest the
beginnings of measures—arrive at quite irregular times:

Ex. 3.3. Time values and accents in melody line

This shifting around of the implied measure may remind us of Konitz's accentual play—or of Creeley's. It also recalls Charlie Christian and the Bebop style
he helped to found twenty years before this recording. But the effect here is

not nervous, tricky, brilliant.[16] To find any similar naturalness, we would have to go back to Louis Armstrong's duet recordings with Earl Hines; but they pay much more allegiance to the four-beat measure and four-measure phrase. Coleman's tune instead moves as if it hardly lived within measures at all.

Yet none of this asymmetry and tonal ambiguity seems to account for what we began by being interested in—the lyric power of "Lonely Woman." In noting the irregularities of scale and phrase length, I have had to add repeatedly that the effect of each oddity is not odd at all. Moments like the G in the third measure—not the obvious A, which would act like a dominant and go far to establish functional harmony; not separated by an obvious interval from the preceding C♯; not sustained for an obvious length (three and a third beats); and followed by so sharp a rise to high A—such moments certainly contribute their share to the force of the tune, bringing us to our toes. But though we begin to see elements of the relation between beauty and strangeness, something is escaping, some sense of why we would be willing to hear the piece repeatedly. Inspecting the written melody, we are losing the point the melody has in the ear. We can abandon analysis, as some enthusiasts would recommend; or we can look a little harder for what is evading our attention.

If we have been looking in the wrong place for "the work itself," this reflects a fundamental puzzle about *text* in jazz. A case like Konitz's "All the Things You Are" presents this conundrum in its most usual form. Jerome Kern wrote a tune; Konitz played a series of variations on it. The tune served as Konitz's text, in something like the way a biblical verse supplies the text for a sermon. But already there are complications. The preacher, like the jazz soloist, is not immune to the attractions of virtuosity, which shifts or blurs the focus of attention. And though the soloist's purpose, like the preacher's, may be primarily to interpret the precedent work (Kern's or God's), the interpreter's attitude and authority necessarily differ between the two cases. To give the metaphor more play, Konitz does not much resemble the monk who reads scripture in the refectory. He might more trenchantly remind us of practitioners of the Higher Criticism, using metaphorical interpretation to dissolve recalcitrant literalities; or of more recent deconstructionists, recontextualizing Kern's tune to expose its allegiances and assumptions. Like the preacher, he is conscious of previous interpretations; but for him they are more likely to represent predecessors to be bested than authorities to be obeyed. He brings to his "text" kinds and degrees of irony that would get a minister defrocked.

The complications of the tune's status as text can grow Byzantine. Consider the recording, by the nine-piece band called Supersax, of a harmonized transcription of Charlie Parker's improvised solo on the tune called "Ko Ko," the melody of which Parker wrote by more or less transcribing a chorus he improvised on Ray Noble's "Cherokee." Where is whose text? From Parker's almost disdainful mastery of a tune that had long served as a test piece, to the reverent archaeology implicit in a group like Supersax (which records almost nothing but harmonized Parker solos), to Noble's idea of what Red Indian music ought to sound like, we move through a hall of mirrors.

The case of "Lonely Woman" seems simpler. I have already produced a copy of the text; Coleman recorded a performance of it. Yet one fallacy inherent in this view emerges as soon as we turn a page in the collection of Coleman's compositions, and find a vocal version of "Lonely Woman." I spare my reader the lyrics (not by Coleman); but the melody begins like this:

Ex. 3.4. Beginning of melody, vocal version

The pitches are the same, but the time has changed drastically. The whole first strain has been shortened to twelve bars—it has become a blues line—which necessitates many changes in the relative values of the longer notes.

In fact, there is some question about the authority of both these written versions. We usually feel sure that a poem in a contemporary book was not only written down but seen through the press by its author. (Indeed, it is a customary and convenient shorthand to think of the words written and printed and proofread on the page as being the poem itself.) But the title of the book from which this printed music comes, *A Collection of Twenty-six Ornette Coleman Compositions*, presents the pieces as if they were collected by someone else. So does the title of *The Collected Poems of W. B. Yeats*, in a sense, and there the implication is quite spurious. But it remains hard to imagine Ornette Coleman reviewing proofs. The practice would be unusual in the world of jazz; and would Coleman have been content with two such different notations of his own piece?

We must even doubt the provenance of the original notation. Did Coleman himself write down his tune this way? Many jazz melodies are notated only by scholars or publishers. If he did, when—before or after recording it? If not, who did? Another collection is advertised on the back cover of this one as having been "edited and transcribed by Gunther Schuller." According to Martin Williams's liner notes on *The Shape of Jazz to Come*, the tapes for the album were also edited with Gunther Schuller's assistance. Williams says that this conjunction between Schuller and Coleman took place at a summer session of the School of Jazz at Music Inn, in Lenox, Massachusetts. The School of Jazz was a project in which Martin Williams also had a hand, and its most significant exponent was John Lewis, the pianist and musical director of the Modern Jazz Quartet, or MJQ.

Since this *Collection of Twenty-six Compositions* was published by MJQ Music, which also holds copyright on the individual tunes (the copyright for "Lonely Woman" is dated 1960, like the recording; for the book, 1968), it seems reasonable to suppose that John Lewis and the quartet began from something like this transcription when they set out to record Coleman's tune in 1962 (*The Art of the Modern Jazz Quartet* [Atlantic SD 2–301]).

Perhaps comparison with this second version will clarify our understanding of Coleman's composition. But although it is conventional—almost unavoidable—to say that the MJQ recorded "the same tune," the impression given by their piece of music contrasts absolutely with Coleman's. In part this can be traced to different instrumentation. Coleman's quartet is fronted by two wind instruments, the MJQ by piano and vibraphone. Piano and vibes are percussion instruments, whose notes can barely be manipulated after they are struck; and their pitches are much more rigidly confined to the tempered chromatic scale than are saxophone and trumpet. The disparity between the two versions, however, involves far more than the expressiveness of the instruments employed. In fact, the MJQ has radically reconceived "Lonely Woman."

Several points of comparison stand out. First, the MJQ version is much more elaborately arranged. It does, like Coleman's, begin and end with the melody (though the ending is truncated), bracketing a single solo chorus. But the MJQ subdivides each of the three AABA choruses very sharply into its separate strains. The chorus of solos provides a good example. It is introduced by several repetitions of a two-bar riff derived from the ending of the melody, which establishes for the first time in the piece a steady tempo, approximately $\quarternote$ = 132. Over this riff, the piano then plays a spare, blues-oriented solo for the duration of two strains, the AA part of the chorus. (Since the solo is about twenty-four measures long, it seems that the MJQ, as in the vocal version, assumes a twelve-bar blues underlying the tune.) An out-of-tempo bass solo follows, unaccompanied except for occasional atmospheric rolls on tom-tom. Though this passage clearly corresponds to the bridge or B-strain (the only section of the tune that has no composed melody[17]), this bass solo is built on thematic variations on the main-strain melody—the only solo so constructed. Finally, Milt Jackson's muscular and elegant last-strain improvisation (on vibes) again strongly recalls the blues. The sketchy accompaniment to this solo, by bass and drums, reinstates the steady tempo, but remains full of confident empty space. The arrangement of the whole chorus insures a steady build-up toward the repeated melody chorus. It entreats our attention to intricate structural contrasts and linkages; set beside Coleman's version, it feels self-conscious.

Furthermore, the melody chorus itself (both at the beginning and at the end) contradicts the feeling of Coleman's original recording. The first strain completely avoids any beat; vibes, bass, and drums provide various kinds of sostenuto behind the piano's statement of the melody. And in this sostenuto background, in contrast to Coleman's ambiguous tonal center, we hear solid functional harmony: It moves from i to V and back again to establish the key, and then progresses by way of modulating dominants through full, half, and deceptive cadences (V-of-V to V, V-of-iv to VI, and so on).

The second A strain (which, in the final iteration of the melody chorus, ends the performance) is notably regularized not in harmony, but in rhythm:

Ex. 3.5. Second A strain, Modern Jazz Quartet version

Nothing could be farther from Coleman's fluid rhythm, so essentially impossible to notate. The precise beat throughout the arrangement insures good coordination among all the members of the quartet; but it stands an immense distance from the character of Coleman's version. The MJQ seems to have found more or less conventional rhythmic patterns implicit in the tune, which they render distinct and show off in turn like facets; whereas for Coleman, exactly the point of the tune's rhythmic structure is its continuous, simultaneous ambiguity.

In short, the MJQ's performance of "Lonely Woman" much more closely resembles its performance of Lewis's "Django"—another dirge with a singable melody, strong clear harmonies, and sections of contrasting rhythmic character—than it does Coleman's performance of his own tune. In 1957—perhaps a year before editing the tapes of *The Shape of Jazz to Come* at Lewis's School of Jazz—Gunther Schuller had coined the term *Third Stream music* to describe a series of attempts to combine jazz and "classical" music.[18] Schuller and Lewis were the leaders of this movement, which came to include dozens of players, composers and improvisers. From a certain academic critical point of view, this movement represented a coming of age for jazz:

> It is likely that the artistic objectives of third stream music were logical outgrowths of the "advancement" of the jazz of the fifties. Whereas in previous times, jazz and European fine-art music had been distant in technical regards, actual musical language, and emotional content, the gap between the two musics had been considerably diminished. . . . It was the appearance of musicians who could bring together improvisational skills and the sense of timing found in jazz performance and the

disciplined requirements of fine-art music that differentiated the third-stream move-ment from earlier attempts to fuse the two idioms. (Budds, *Jazz in the Sixties*, pp. 72–73)

The MJQ's complex and explicit arrangement, with its studious attention to overall form and the interrelation of sections; the alternation of composed (ar-ranged) and improvised segments; the domestication of blues material (blue notes and syncopations) within a foreign context; the readiness to shift tempo and meter, but in ways that recall Beethoven rather than the singers of field hollers: such features help to identify this "Lonely Woman" as a Third Stream composition.[19]

Leaving aside the question of whether the Third Stream movement was suc-cessful in maintaining a "jazz feel" in compositions shaped by European aes-thetic principles, we can still feel some vertigo in thinking of Ornette Coleman as a Third Stream composer. He did improvise a solo over the twelve-tone background of "Abstraction," written by Schuller for the second important Third Stream record.[20] In Schuller's liner notes for the album, he tries to link Coleman's playing with his own serial composition by pointing to the atonality or freedom from conventional tonality characteristic of both. But despite the intriguing comparison, the contrast between jazz solo and "classical" back-ground in "Abstraction" remains sharp; Coleman enlivens the piece by evad-ing its capture. For the same reasons, the MJQ's reconception of "Lonely Woman" seems a *mis*conception born of John Lewis's preoccupations. Most of the tune's wonder has been supplanted by pretentious and misplaced refine-ments, the tune's own subtleties dispersed into melodrama.

This disappointment has nothing to do with competence—the Modern Jazz Quartet was a constellation of skill. Rather, it carries us back to our riddle of text and tune. A partial solution to the puzzle might lie in extending our idea of "composition." In preparing the MJQ's version, John Lewis assumed—as did my analysis earlier in this chapter—that "Lonely Woman" can be identi-fied with its melody. If instead we restore to the piece certain elements that Coleman certainly "composed," such as the more nearly vocal instrumenta-tion of his quartet, the austerity of harmonization, and the metrical relation between the lead and rhythm instruments, we return quite some distance to-ward the original satisfactions of the piece. The question, though, is how far we need to go in this direction.

When Whitney Balliett says that "Coleman's music involves the melodies he writes, the instrumentation he sets them in, and his own playing" (p. 65), he offers not a tautology but a definition, one that reminds us of fundamental differences between the jazz composer and the composer in the European tradition.[21] Like any composer, and unlike a painter, Coleman does not have complete control over the production of his music; he has to trust the performers. But this includes himself. He preordains a smaller percentage of the music than most European composers (smaller even than modern aleatorists, who leave various aspects of structure and detail to the musicians themselves, or the Baroque composers who expected extemporized ornamentation); yet Coleman, as a member of his own quartet, is directly responsible for a larger percentage at the time of the music's realization.

Balliett's reminder encourages us to keep extending the idea of "composition" to include acts like bringing together the remarkable playing group, counting off the tempo, and so on—whatever our listening demands that we identify as "Lonely Woman." As we do so, the line between composition and performance grows fuzzier. By the same token, the distinction between composition and improvisation loses importance. It arises in the first place, as I noted in the previous chapter, from the time-orientation of musical art, which allows us to distinguish what was made up beforehand from what is extemporaneous. But the dichotomy also implies the existence of notation, of a printed text that the performer may adhere to or depart from. In this sense the distinction belongs to a print culture, in which literacy is assumed and orality, or its musical equivalent, is a phenomenon.

"Music" can mean the art of arranging sounds into coherence; or the pattern of coherence; or the sounds themselves, so arranged. Or it can mean the paper notation of the sounds. Consider these possible ways to write down the opening of the melody of "Lonely Woman":

Ex. 3.6. Alternative notations of melody

These all have some plausibility. Musical notation of our familiar kind has arrived fairly recently. In the past three centuries or so—a period coinciding with the European hegemony of composed tonal music—it has developed into a highly elaborate system, so that a page of music contains many times as much *information*, in a technical sense, as a page of prose.[22] This complexity grew for the sake of exactitude. Yet there is no way to decide among the four notations shown here. When the notational system is applied retrospectively to an existing performance, the exactitude is deceptive, because it is inadequate.[23] Earlier forms of musical notation, such as that used by the Greeks, were naturally even sketchier.

Notation is unessential to music. It aids memory, and probably began with that purpose. But this mnemonic function requires little elaboration; a modern singer may tape to a guitar the first phrases of a song's verses so as to recall their order, but require no prompting at all to remember the notes. Modern notation expanded to serve a different convenience, that of the composer. The problem was the same one that gave rise to the writing of language: to communicate with people distant in space or time. The notation, then, carries with it implications of the social system we glanced at in chapter 1, in which the composer produces works in studious isolation, and then passes them in written form to players who realize them in performance. The performance is what music essentially requires in order to exist—as jazz, especially in its uneasy relationship with notation, insists even more than European music.

The emphasis on performance that helps to define jazz, combined with Coleman's particular emphasis on reiterative presentation of the melody rather than on improvisation, gives special weight to the ensemble in "Lonely Woman," rather than to solo instruments. This is one place to look for the aspects of the music missing from my first analysis.

The first thing we hear in "Lonely Woman" is the bass and drums, playing together quite fast. When the saxophone and trumpet enter together a few moments later, they are playing much more slowly. If we decide on the first notation of the four I have presented—it corresponds to the published instrumental version given in full at the beginning of this chapter—then we have something deceptively like hard fact to work with. The main strain of the melody occupies fifteen measures, each of four beats; it takes (on a close average) twenty-four seconds; its tempo is therefore $\quarternote = 150$. The bass and drums can be timed at about $\halfnote = 176$, or about two and a third times faster than the lead instruments.

Of course these facts are spurious in an important sense, being deduced absurdly by means of a stopwatch and some arithmetic. Anyone who can reliably play along with the melody instruments on the record (as they do with each other) does so by "feel," not by statistics. What we actually hear is a two-layered rhythmic construction. In itself, this is not unusual. Most jazz ensembles adopt, as a primary structural principle, a hierarchical separation of instruments according to their rhythmic function.[24] But usually the lead instruments—the ones that are higher in pitch, more flexible technically, and more often foregrounded as carriers of melody—keep the fastest time, dividing the quarter notes of the bass, for instance, into eighths and sixteenths. "Lonely Woman" turns the hierarchy upside down: The bass and drums keep fast time behind the slow melody. This exaggerates the effect of both tempi. The background seems desperately urgent, and the melody becomes still more eloquently mournful.

More astonishing than this inversion is the quartet's maintenance of two incommensurable meters. Keeping regular time presents enough difficulties without someone else keeping radically different time at the same volume. In a sense, the players as well as we must perceive the melody tempo not as some obscure fractional multiple of the background tempo, but as "free" rhythm.

No word in the rhetoric of the arts delivers a lower ratio of information to argument than "free." Balliett is right to say that "when he improvises, [Coleman] dances around outside the harmonic and rhythmic cage that Parker eventually locked himself into. He has cast aside chords and keys and harmony and conventional tonality" (p. 65). And Coleman himself uses metaphors that suggest the same sense of liberation:

> My music doesn't have any real time, no metric time. It has time, but not in the sense that you can time it. It's more like breathing, a natural, freer time. . . . I like spread rhythm, rhythm that has a lot of freedom in it, rather than the more conventional, *netted* rhythm. With spread rhythm, you might tap your feet awhile, then stop, then later start tapping again. That's what I like. Otherwise, you tap your feet so much, you forget what you hear. You just hear the rhythm.[25]

Yet Cecil Taylor, an avant-garde pianist sometimes associated with Coleman, is also quite right to remark that it "is not a question of 'freedom' as opposed to 'nonfreedom,' but rather a question of recognizing different ideas and expressions of order."[26] "Freedom" suggests the restraint overcome, but tells us little about the order that replaces it. Coleman comes closer when he says that one can "play flat in tune or sharp in tune. If I play an F in a tune called 'Peace,' I don't think it should sound the same as an F that is supposed to express sadness."[27] The issue centers not on escape, but on the liberation of certain aspects of the music from rule-governed regularity, so as to make them variable, and so potentially expressive. What can be significantly varied can make meaning.

The metrical relation between the two pairs of instruments in "Lonely Woman" serves as a vehicle for musical meaning in two ways. First, it directly increases the complexity of our awareness of passing time, a primary resource of meaning for all music. Second, rather than simply establishing and maintaining the two tempi, Coleman plays with the relation between them. During his solo, he approaches and then briefly joins the beat set by the bass and drums. (When he reaches it, about half way through his solo, someone in the group gives a little cry of delight.) Yet when he and Cherry restate the melody, their timing is exact enough to keep the total duration of a fifteen-measure strain from increasing by much more than a second. The tempi, we learn as we move through the performance, are not truly independent, but interdependent. Haden on bass not only matches the tempo of Higgins's drums, but also shifts his pedal point note at moments dictated by the horns playing the melody. Rhythmically, the piece represents a remarkable feat of inclusive and mutual consciousness by four people, an awareness made manifest by unexpected alterations in an apparently strict metrical structure.

The emphasis Coleman's arrangement places on melody, as opposed to improvisation, also tends to emphasize sound, rather than invention. This is the other major aspect of the performance omitted by any consideration simply of the written tune. Coleman's distrust of the tempered scale, his belief in expressive intonation, leads him sometimes into explicit vocal effects—horse laughs, wails, and so on. More continuously, it makes him adjust his pitch according to context, sliding up to one note, allowing another to sag halfway through, pushing at all the boundaries of what formally defines a "note." In this he differs from other jazz musicians only in degree. The difficulty of notating jazz pitches is proverbial.

This inaccessibility of jazz to notation brings us back to the comparison with European music, and we begin to glimpse the real meaning of that difference. Consider what Michael Budds has to say about thirties Swing music: "In contrast then to the individualism and the self-realization of talented folk musicians which had characterized the dixieland styles, the subsequent period of large ensemble jazz exhibited the prominence of European aesthetic criteria. 'Clean' rhythmic precision, 'correct' intonation, symphonic tone quality, and a higher level of instrumental virtuosity became conspicuous artistic goals" (p. 7). Despite these careful quotation marks, the potential condescension remains embedded in the standard critical language. Budds is not alone. At least until recent years, when rising interest in ethnomusicology has accompanied changes in middle-class America's own cultural values, few scholars of Western music, drawn to jazz for whatever reasons, have been able to transcend the feeling that "fine-art" players with their "legitimate" tone—the word has long been used by jazz players themselves—constitute a norm from which "primitive" musicians depart only to their disadvantage.

The misunderstanding revolves around a different relation between the music and the musician. In the system of aesthetic thought that has developed with European music, one can insist without oversimplifying too drastically that the musical composition is more important than the musician.[28] The symphonies of Brahms—it is too deep an assumption even to be an article of faith—will survive all the best and worst performers of them. The best performers are *legitimate* because they honor the *lex* which is the score, or rather the spirit that moves in the letter of the score. This is the real force behind Wanda Landowska's remark to an upstart: "You go on playing Bach your way, and I'll go on playing Bach his way." The performer works with details of timing, touch, and so on, infinitely subtle, variable within a range far smaller than in jazz. The virtuoso performer is one whose treatment of these permitted variables most accurately brings to life the written work. Of course styles change; Landowska's behemoth Pleyel harpsichord now strikes us as a sad hobble for a great player. But what the sophisticated listener might now prefer is not something *newer*, more original on the part of the musician (Bach on the synthesizer remains more synthesizer than Bach), but something more "authentic"—Bach "on original instruments."

In jazz, the authenticity of the performance derives from that of the performer. The player more nearly *is* the point. This helps to explain why the greatest jazz can sometimes be made out of the worst composed material; Billie Holiday's recordings provide the most obvious examples.[29] When jazz moves too far from concentration on the players—whether as a cooperative group or as a sequence of soloists—murmurs arise that it is no longer jazz. Thirties big band music is one example; Third Stream music is another.

So if Coleman insists with unusual force on the sound of the horn, he only moves a little farther in the direction natural to jazz. Budds once more traces this characteristic of jazz to an African origin: "Another Africanism in jazz is the presence of a heterogeneous sound ideal. . . . The development of an individual 'voice' has always been a major concern of jazz musicians" (p. 3). Again we see why the MJQ's well-tempered piano and vibraphone would be out of place in Coleman's quartet. The sound of the horn is the jazz performance's most literal "voice"—that term by which we assimilate music to musician, speech to speaker. The metaphor comes easily, as when jazz players talk about "telling a story through their horns," or a scholar points out the melodic influence of tone-oriented African languages.[30] The word's transference from the human voice to the instrument is metaphorical, but barely.

The literal and metaphorical applications of "voice" to a jazz performance threaten some confusion. One voice, for example, can alter another. One singer can pronounce the terminal sibilants for a whole chorus—as is often done to keep down the unmusical hiss; one wind player's vibrato can sound as though it belongs to a whole horn section. Another example: After playing an octave apart for most of each melody chorus, Coleman and Cherry reach up to a high, close dissonance; whose "voice" do we hear wailing, when only the two horns together wail?

We transcend (if not solve) this riddle by recalling what we have learned about the metaphor of voice in relation to poetry. The previous chapter suggested that "voice," or at least "authentic voice," is never simply single, but arises out of dialogic relations among voices.

"Lonely Woman" offers us, first, the dialogics of the jazz quartet. Coleman's quartet is in a sense his voice, like Ellington's or Akiyoshi's bands. Coleman's and Cherry's horns converse with Haden's bass and Higgins's drums; the fact that the two groups seem at first to talk at cross-purposes, and only later discover their tentative shared ground, strengthens the impression of dialogue. The horns themselves, abiding largely by the difference-in-sameness of octaves, separate at moments into harmony.

It is tempting to revise the analogy that suggested itself earlier, by contrasting Coleman's highly oral composition with Konitz's highly literate improvisation. Konitz's solo is a complex piece of work, but not difficult to transcribe into standard musical notation; while Coleman's composed and reiterated bridge defies at least my pen. Certainly the existence of the MJQ's arrangement of "Lonely Woman" presumes writing, while Coleman could certainly have taught his group the tune by ear and described the treatment he wanted to give it. Coleman's attitudes toward intonation, rhythmic intricacy, melodic repetition, group participation, and so on, show him to be engaged in a dialogue with oral African music—which also means that his orality is of a secondary kind. Coleman is no African musician, but an American one as ready to transform into his own material the music of Africa as the music of Europe (which supplies his instruments, his compositional structure, and most of the harmony he does use). In this respect he carries forward the principles of vocal and instrumental blues, with which his music is so obviously allied that we have seen two versions of "Lonely Woman" that truncate it by three measures to fit the traditional twelve.

Coleman's music also constitutes a dialogic sally toward the jazz contemporary with it—a forceful mixture of rejection and adaptation. Unique as he seemed and still seems, his style certainly includes echoes of Parker's kind of virtuosity. The makeup of the quartet, too, follows the Bebop standard, except for the absence of a chordal instrument—which rather recalls the very different quartet of Gerry Mulligan a few years before. And the basic structure of "Lonely Woman" (like the majority of Coleman's tunes) abides by the conventions, though Coleman distorts the normal proportions.

Finally, it seems important to consider the musicians' dialogic relation to listeners. The great preponderance of jazz being made every day goes unrecorded—meaning that it is' lost, phrase by phrase, the instant it gets made. It may remain in memory, but memory is far from exact or complete. "Sound exists," as Ong points out, "only when it is going out of existence. It is not simply perishable but essentially evanescent, and it is sensed as evanescent" (p. 32). Why do people devote their lives to such an art? And how can we sit and listen to such an art being made and disappearing, without succumbing to overwhelming sadness? The answer, of course, is that the music appears as continuously as it disappears. The constant loss is only the inverse, logically entailed, of constant plenitude.

This sense of what jazz performance means to us can lead in two directions. On the one hand, it may make us marvel at the copious genius of the musician—perhaps generally at the amazing resourcefulness of human mental fertility, but more particularly at the inventive prowess of this soloist in front of us at this moment. Our admiration is appropriate; but in that direction also lies the whole folklore of jazz, its hagiolatry, its apotheosis in the cutting session. On the other hand, jazz arose out of highly participatory music in which the audience were also performers. While we attend to the players before us, the sense remains that we are being allowed to participate in something irreplace-able. Perhaps any music could give us that sense, heard in the way that jazz— through the intimacy among player and instrumental voice and the sound it-self—*demands* to be heard. In any case, unless we play it ourselves, listening to such music is the very closest we ever get to a perfectly sharp and consistent consciousness of our continuing being in time, ''so that,'' as Eliot says, ''you are the music while the music lasts.'' That is what the tragedy of music essen-tially celebrates, and live jazz never lets us forget it.

The fundamental point, then, is not improvisation but presence. Spontane-ity and authenticity must finally be referred to the dialogic engagement of the musical performance. This is the legitimate root of the worry about analytic criticism of jazz, and the emphasis on recordings that follows from analysis. How much does the recording of jazz subvert presence? Both much and little. We belong ineluctably to a literate culture; and the literate imagination has necessarily developed a talent for reconstruction. Certainly the presence es-sential to jazz is affected far less by recordings than by notation.

To value recordings for the wrong reasons—because what is repeatable is safely predictable and at our command—is indeed to lose the plenitude of jazz by fleeing its loss. But there is something to be said for what we can learn from records. Certainly young jazz musicians do; they carry cassettes around in their instrument cases, and listening (even in the emerging college jazz programs) is the substance of their education.[31] Recordings not only make the analysis of jazz possible, but give analysis most of its point as well. Without them, if we could somehow analyze some aspect of one performance we might hope to increase our appreciation of the next one to come along; as it is, we can also expect this one to gain depth when we return to it, therefore to inform our listening to other music in more comprehensive ways.

We know that hearing again is not the same as hearing for the first time— except in imagination. But we also find that many experiences can be repeated without diminution, and that we can do without the sentimental existentialism of believing unrepeatable ones to be generically purer. Listening to jazz on record, we relearn our complicated relation to time, over and over.

On Choreography _____

Paintings and sculptures are their own notations—though there are also repro-ductions.

The advent of movies (later videotape, now computer graphics) at last gave dance a notation. Earlier systems of written notation—literally choreo-gra-phies—were terribly inadequate. Dance was the last of the oral arts; Petipa's *Swan Lake* is known because one set of dancers showed it to another by danc-ing it. Movies are two things to dance, a means and an end. They preserve a choreographer's work from generation to generation; and dance movies (which are also song movies and are called musicals) become themselves the medium of distribution.

Music has a traditional notation worked out between the seventh and sev-enteenth centuries. Then beginning with piano rolls and seizing quickly on wire, acetate, tape, vinyl, laser, and computer information-storage media, mu-sic has found a different kind of repository. Recordings do not replace scores in European concert music because they are more accurate as to sound, but less perspicuous as to structure; and scores will never replace jazz recordings.

Not many people are musically literate enough to make the analogy between a poem's relation to its printed text, and a piece of music's embodiment in a score, exact.

Four

David Antin: Culturology

Some years ago the poet David Antin stopped
writing poems and began talking. He would go
into a public space, turn on his tape recorder and
to all appearances talk off the top of his
head. . . . When Mr. Antin had given a number
of these talks, he made transcriptions of the tapes,
revised the transcriptions to accord more naturally
with his normal patterns of phrasing, and
published them in 1976 under the title, "Talking
at the Boundaries."[1]

ANTIN'S procedure draws together ideas we have been exploring. We could
begin by asking about *genre*, about the kind of thing Antin is making—or
rather, doing; the questions start even in this choice of verbs. He recalls a
lecturer, a storyteller, a stand-up comic; we think also of a sermon (whose
"text" is often the title of the piece, such as "real estate"), a one-man play
(Hal Holbrook doing Mark Twain, David Antin doing . . .)—and finally, of
course, a poetry reading. Antin's activity resembles all these kinds of speaking, and none of them.

Though Antin can be very funny, comedy is not his end. Most comics'
"material," prepared by themselves or their "writers," can be "delivered"
in many performances; the occasion and the speech are mostly separable, and
our sense of being immediately addressed is the skillful illusion an actor creates. Spalding Gray's monologues (such as *Swimming to Cambodia*), though
comparable to Antin's improvisations in their narrative bent and casual tone,
closely follow scripts Gray has worked out beforehand, and are repeatable.
They do not depart far from the traditional poetry reading, which, as perfected
by Dylan Thomas in the fifties, remains "a cross between a lecture and a
dramatic reading. Proscenium or podium oriented," such recitals emphasize
"the distance between the poet and audience,"[2] much as concert music divides musicians from listeners. They also separate the poet-reading-now from
the poet-writing-then (the composer versus the performer), and so reinforce
the hieratic image of the poet as hermit alchemist—Yeats in his tower, Moses
on the mountain. Antin, instead, is finding his words right before our eyes.

Even the most impromptu lecturer—no matter how famous—at least ostensibly draws our attendance by means of his topic. But Antin's topics are not meaningfully announced beforehand (the title is often given him by someone else), and are too fluid to be easily named in retrospect. Even during the talk we might be said not to know what he is talking about, because he can radically shift our sense of his focus several times in an hour. Emphasis on the talker rather than the topic might ally him with the Roman oratorical tradition of epideictic rhetoric, the virtuoso treatment of a commonplace theme—except that Antin is so clearly interested in getting something *said*.[3] In discourse that is neither the philosopher's, which aims at rigorous originality, nor the scholar's, which acknowledges its sources in detail, Antin draws from an exhilarating range of the linguistic, scientific, sociological, and aesthetic thought available to a cultured contemporary mind.

It is a kind of jazz talk. As in Coleman's "Lonely Woman" (but not the MJQ's), it is impossible to value either the composer or the performer at the other's expense; as in Konitz's "All the Things You Are," we attend to Antin because of what he can do with (possibly) familiar tunes. Poetry, unlike concert music, interposes no interpreter between us and the work; Antin brings poetry to the same point as jazz by also eliminating any gap of time. His art— more than a concert musician's, and more also than other poets'—requires him to be an interesting person. He *needs* to have been a linguist, an art critic, an engineer, a poet, a technical translator, a curator, a teacher, a member of a big complicated family, and a perpetual talker and listener.

Can these talks truly be improvisations? Hugh Kenner calls them "quasi-improvisations," quoting Antin's description of "improvised pieces that I have considered before doing, but which I have gone to a particular place to realize."[4] He not only "considers" general ideas beforehand, but reuses bits of talk. For example, in a 1975 interview with Barry Alpert, Antin distinguishes the person who merely feels bad, merely has a *complaint*, from the person who has gone to the doctor and now (having a name for it) has a *disease*; and he draws the obvious inference that doctors give people diseases (*Vort #7*, pp. 28–29). This is typical Antin: simultaneously a witty linguistic play and a shrewd observation about the linguistic social web that enmeshes and defines "doctors" and "patients." The idea is too good to drop; he rephrased it in "The Principle of Fit, II," released on cassette by Watershed Tapes in 1980, and again in a talk given at Brown University in 1987.

Furthermore, though Antin's publication of transcribed talks certainly reverses the conventional poetic relation in time between text and speech, the reversal allows him to revise the transcriptions (as Michael Davidson says) "to accord more naturally with his normal patterns of phrasing." This is an oxymoron; we must take the word *naturally* in the same fictive sense in which Creeley's poems can be said to be *speech*. Marjorie Perloff reports that Antin makes "some changes when he transcribes a talk poem on the typewriter. The

basic structure and movement remain the same, but he may add a related nar-
rational unit or clarify a point."[5]

Still, this is no more "quasi" than jazz improvisation. Probably the most
prolific and inventive improviser in jazz was Charlie Parker, whose impromptu chorus on a familiar tune could become a jazz standard in its own
right; whose four-bar solo break on "Night in Tunisia" stopped one recording
session dead in its astonished tracks. Yet a voluminous dissertation by Thomas
Owens shows how Parker's improvisations are built out of a little store of
about a hundred "motives," which Owens catalogues in all their variations.[6]
Parker's method bears a similarity to Homer's use of verbal formulas, as described originally by Milman Parry and at length by Albert Lord in *A Singer
of Tales*. Homer's phrases and Parker's motives are not simply fillers for moments when invention flags; they are responses to local contingencies of meter
or harmonic progression within a broader sweep of narrative or musical statement. Stephen Fredman calls Antin's talk poems "epic narrations—where the
elements (stories, ideas) are *arranged* musically like a succession of riffs,
rather than being spontaneously invented."[7] Antin himself talks intriguingly
about Homer as a talker in a talking situation, rather than a writer, and bluntly
sums up improvisation's limits:

to improvise at all   you need some kind of cliches

(boundaries, *p. 191*)

The fact that Charlie Parker in any particular solo played mostly fragments of
phrases he had played before, like the fact that he might be playing a known
tune, will not prevent us from calling the solo "improvised" if the word is to
have any use whatever.

The question of revision is more vexed; but we might note that the jazz
improviser is prevented from revising only in one sense, which is peculiar to
a print culture. Like the playing, our listening is borne along and away by the
moments; so another turn in the solo can retrospectively revise what we feel
we have heard. Konitz's last chorus on "All the Things You Are" revises his
first much as his first revises the original tune. Any simpler view of "revision" depends on our having access to two differing texts. Our ideas about
revision involve assumptions about time, labor, and the order of composition.
Mozart is said to have conceived whole symphonies as if instantaneously;
when "composition" takes just the time required to write down the notes, it
becomes difficult to distinguish from the act of notating a preexisting mental
construct. Jazz too, as we saw in the previous chapter, complicates the relation
between composition and improvisation, and Antin amplifies the same complications.

Standing up in front of a lot of people and talking for an hour entails a kind
of boastfulness. The occasional grumble that this is too easy to be art (Antin
just talks, Coleman just makes noise) stems from worry that we might befool

ourselves in conferring the mantle of Art, with its call on our reverence. But
"It is not like just anybody talking, who talks like David Antin?"[8] The bravado recalls again one idea of the jazz improviser: the man of prowess, the
cutting session's hero. As Antin establishes his personality on the stage or the
page, though, he emerges not as agonically inclined but as hedonic, aiming
not to overpower or convince but to fascinate us.[9] Like the jazz player seen
less trivially, he is driven to improvise by an urge to maintain what he calls
"my sense of the present" ("how long is the present," *tuning*, p. 84).

>   i try not to be too prepared   i mean im aiming not
> to be prepared   so that i can do what i dont expect to do   in
> terms of something i want to say   and which is what one means
> by improvisation   to do something you want to do in a way you
>   didnt know you were going to do it   which is to do something
> new
>
>   (boundaries, *p. 240*)

>   whatever im doing   i want to be doing it now
>   at whatever cost   and there is always a cost   for wanting
> anything and insisting on it   which is here the cost of not
> coming with a fully prepared well designed script . . .
>   but if i had it all worked out before i got here   the
>   whole design   i couldnt take you into account or even myself
>   at the time i got here
>
>   (tuning, *p. 150*)

The desire to surpass one's own expectations and act beyond one's own knowing, to take the whole present fully into account, recalls John Cage (whose
lectures have clearly influenced Antin) and the Zen inspiration behind his introduction of chance into musical and verbal compositions. Perloff quotes
Cage as praising Americans for "our air way of knowing nowness." If that is
what our poetry and music are to enact, then improvisation becomes an inevitable method.

The other side of "aiming not to be prepared," of course, is being very
ready. As Antin describes what turned out to be the first talk poem,[10] "I decided I wouldn't prepare anything to talk about before I got there. . . . I fig-
ured I was as prepared as I was ever going to be. Most of my life had prepared
me for this, as well or ill as I was ever going to be" (*Vort* #7, p. 27). Charles
Altieri, seeking exact grounds for admiration, refuses to "praise the immedi-
acies of speech per se—to me that route seems only to repeat the naturalizing
gestures of an outmoded romanticism."[11] Skepticism justifiably dogs any ex-
cessive delectation of inspiration over homework; but Antin himself (as Altieri
demonstrates) is not interested in "naturalizing gestures" of any simple kind.
By endless practice, at first unconscious, later perhaps conscious, he has made

the scales and arpeggios of American speech his own; now he is a smart man
standing up and talking, about as prepared and unprepared as any of us at a
party or a panel discussion or a first deposition in a lawsuit.

Say then that Antin's talks are improvised. But are they *poetry*? "You have
no idea," Perloff wrote to Sherman Paul, "what hostility he arouses. . . .
When I gave a talk . . . at the Folger Symposium on Contemporary Poetry last
year, Harold Bloom, Richard Howard, John Hollander, and Donald Davie
were dismayed at my even having the nerve to talk about someone as awful as
Antin. The conference organizer . . . phoned me a few weeks later and said,
'Well, after all, Marjorie, that stuff just isn't poetry!' "[12] Antin himself aggressively questions his relation to "poetry":

if robert lowell is a

poet i dont want to be a poet   if robert frost was a

poet i dont want to be a poet   if socrates was a poet

ill consider it[13]

Just as he aims beyond what he can expect of himself, he sidesteps what we
expect a poet or lecturer or performance artist to do. "A morsel of mashed
potato on the tablecloth can be horrible if you pick it up thinking it's a bread-
crumb,"[14] but it does make vivid the textures of both.

Revising the expectations defined by genres is recurrent literary business.
If the purpose of the arts is to shake thought's cages, an art should question its
own borders either intermittently or constantly. If we suddenly notice that a
supposedly poetic event we are attending feels as much like a night club act or
a charismatic church service as a lecture or recital, it may enliven us to the
event and help us to fulfill it. On the other hand, arguing over the generic
definition of Antin's work—if the terms of debate presume that a fixed cate-
gorical definition of "poetry" is possible or desirable—merely entangles us
in fretful ambiguation and unresolvable muddle.

Yet "Is it poetry?" and "Is it improvised?" meet in a real question about
what *improvised poetry* might mean. Poetry is made of language, but music is
made of music. (Or music is made of sound, or noise; either way, it is not
words.) We all use language all the time in the indifferent conduct of our daily
lives; while even the least music—blowing on a jug or whistling past a grave-
yard or just beating time while someone else makes complicated sounds—has
some aura of the artistic, the special, the privileged. However much we assimilate music into our lives, it is *not* our lives as language is. Actors can pretend
they are talking; but playing music makes us musicians.

Since there is no presumption that an act of language has to be composed
(we all do it as easily as Mozart), "improvisation" is an idea with less to brace
itself against in poetry than in music. From a certain critical perspective, the
more convinced we are of Antin's improvisation, the more problematic it becomes as poetry. If the separation of poet and speaker is a sacrosanct defining

condition of poetry, these talks cannot be poems. The Romantics and their offspring bequeathed us an obsession with drama, which eventually, despite the ostensibly expressivist nature of Romantic poetry, made any speaking person in a poem a persona, at most a mask of the playwright-poet. Hence the New Critical conviction that the relation of poetry to speech *must* be a fictive one (as it is in Creeley's and Williams's poems). As for the modernists Antin singles out, Lowell's "confessional" claim to speak *in propria persona* leaves the persona quite intact; and Frost, whose resonance depends on his cagey refusal to affirm statement as knowledge, never toys with the confessional stance at all. With other powerful exemplars in Yeats, Eliot, and some versions of Auden and Stevens, these are the modes that poetry has made conventionally available in postwar America.

Antin and other "postmodernists" imply a change. Marjorie Perloff describes the historical shift in terms of a new balance among Aristotle's six aspects of poetry—

> *mythos* (plot), *ethos* (character), *dianoia* (thought), *lexis* (diction), *melopoeia* (rhythm and song), and *opsis* (spectacle). Romantic and Modernist theory elevated the second, fourth, and fifth of these elements: poetry, it was and still is assumed, involves the presentation of a self (the "ethical argument") in terms of appropriate *lexis* and *melopoeia*. In practice, lexis means connotative, multi-layered language and symbolic imagery, whereas ethos has generally been construed as some form of psychological depth. (*Pp. 288–89*)

Now, she continues, poetry has begun to emphasize performance (and therefore *opsis*), to "reintroduce narrative [*mythos*] into the lyric structure," and in the case of Antin and a few other representatives of "the new didacticism" to make *dianoia* the central feature of poetic discourse.

Thought? Ezra Pound did insist that poetry be "at least as well written as prose," and Altieri notes that Antin treats "the work as if it had the same obligation to discursive clarity as any other mode of discourse" (p. 13). The continuous precision of Antin's thinking—

> i should have absolutely believed it
> regardless of whatever bullshit it was intended to seem like
>
> (boundaries, *p. 223*)

—might vaguely recall Pound's commendation of *logopoeia* and the modernist nostalgia for Metaphysical wit. Yet Antin's interest in thought is not tropical and poetic, but structural and philosophical. He sees the Western philosophical tradition (he names Bacon, Descartes, and Kant) as having walled poetry off from thought, reality, truth, or any profound responsibility for or to the human situation. What is left may be called Beauty, but from Antin's perspective it looks inane. Just as Williams worried that without poetry we would be left with newspapers for the truth, Antin struggles against the cultural separation of imagination from reason. Once that division has been instituted, the province of imagination shrinks to recreational fantasy: "Disneyland is the construction of the culture, which has committed itself, so far as it cares, to the belief that the imagination is everything excluded by reason and has a rather impoverished view of both."[15]

So the countermove is to stand before us, thinking, inventing, offering anecdote in place of both abstract argument (though highly abstract arguments punctuate some of the talks) and the immediate sensory details that have been the realm and material of lyric poetry since early in the last century. "Invention," Altieri says, "is the lyricism of the mind."[16]

Antin's cultural and philosophical concerns dictate both his method and the domain in which his thought—though he ranges and leaps with verve—is concentrated: a kind of anthropological perspective on the interactions among language, art, and culture. Defying the schism he blames on Kant, he claims the territory of philosophy (linguistic and social categories, problems of knowledge, truth) for an activity characterized by spontaneous inventive storytelling—which he reasonably calls poetry. He needs to "slow down the fantasy and illusion of understanding."[17] Finally it is *because* the talks are improvised that they are poems.

An oddly common complaint about Antin is that his work is cold, without emotion, as if he exemplified Eliot's "perfect" poet in whom are perfectly separated "the man who suffers and the mind which creates." Antin's is no such dissociated sensibility. He rejects a conventional "emotional vocabulary" of interior "depths" because it "takes you on bridges past the cracks in the real";[18] it sustains the schism between reason and imagination. From inside that schism, Antin looks "cold," just as musical criticism looks antithetical to jazz. But as soon as all the faculties of mind are united in its present working, these anxieties collapse.

———————

Inevitably, the most influential criticism of Antin is that his work is formless. The same was said of free verse at the beginning of the modernist era. Marjorie Perloff's answer—the issue has been the central topic of her defense of Antin—employs Northrop Frye's distinction among verse, prose, and an "associative rhythm" of speech, prior to prose and verse which are "conventionalizations" of it.[19] The "associative rhythm" (William Spanos calls it "the rhythm of exploration" [*Boundary2*, p. 602]) is of course less finished than the form we expect in verse or in prose, more "intensely continuous," more "process-oriented." There is a link here between Antin's interests in improvisation and in *dianoia*: The metonymies of the "associative rhythm" tend to run along the level where we do most of our thinking, somewhere between the particles of sound or object and the abstractions of structure or idea, in a middle realm where concepts are embodied in instances and anecdotes. As Perloff shows, it is possible to analyze a talk poem by Antin in terms of a series of moves, an unfolding rhythm of discovery heightened from or simply made more conscious than in ordinary speech.

Take the title piece from *talking at the boundaries*: To begin, Antin places his talk by telling how he received its title on the voucher for his honorarium (under the joint sponsorship of "a department of english a department of art and a library"). This leads naturally to discussion of his improvisation, its roots in a need to address a knowable audience, the problem of the book as a "totally dislocated occasion," professed mystification about the system of book distribution, the midwest as an arbitrary place books go, Fort Wayne, Indiana, which he once drove through—and then *here*:

```
                          but its ok
        were in bloomington       not in fort wayne      and its because
    of this        and because this talk was sponsored by a library an art
    department and an english department were on a boundary       or at
    the intersection of three boundaries       so there is no opportunity
       for shop talk
```

(boundaries, pp. 56–57)

The "its" in "its because of this" is never resolved syntactically; and the following "and," together with the repeated list of his varied sponsors, conceals a leap from what threatens to descend into stock comedy about the Midwest (not very promising in Indiana) to the idea of boundaries—familiar ground on which he knows he can profitably deliberate. The sudden intrusion of the phrase *shop talk* announces the arrival at a topic, and blurs in our recollection the wandering that brought us here.

For twenty lines (a couple of minutes) he meditates on the implications of "shop talk" (professional groups maintaining the boundaries of their disciplines to reinforce their status as experts), matching and rematching the phrase with the word *boundary*, which gets transmuted into *border*, which suggests a metaphor of nations: "the state called art," and a poetry-state. In contemplating these borders along with Antin, we stand at them; and now they become concretely imaged ("and you look over the boundary and you see him sitting there"). This is an instance of what Keats called "stationing"; it makes our imaginative position definite in what feels like a sensory way, and so heightens our sense of arrival, of significance.

Antin goes on to describe people in these "states" doing things we know are usual enough in the contemporary world of the arts: painting from a photograph, reading poems to an audience. But these activities, instead of being named—the word *poetry* does not occur, for instance—are described as if by an uncomprehending foreigner. This defamiliarization is a constant tool for

Antin. "He regularly presents himself," says Perloff, "as a kind of passive register, although his knowledge of art or language or science is a persistent element, hovering at the edges of his discourse. The 'I' of the talk poetry is consistently 'confused' or 'puzzled' or 'surprised.' He sees the things around him as if for the first time" (p. 333).

This technique has literary predecessors (it resembles the Lilliputians' descriptions of Gulliver's pocket watch and gun, and Elizabeth Bishop's "Seven O'clock News," and more subtly the catalogues in Flaubert's *Bouvard et Pecuchet* and in the Ithaca section of *Ulysses*). Beyond that, Antin uses it to underscore the presentness of his talked thinking, as if it were too immediate to be filtered through the generalizations of common knowledge. Then too, it lets him describe conventional poetry readings in such a way as to naturalize the alternative he is presenting to us. (*His* delivery of poetry is more like traditional painting, it says.) Finally, the comparison between painting from photographs and reading written poems emphasizes how current art activity depends on previous activity; and this in turn helps make our idea of verbal improvisation more precise.

The metaphor of nations leads on to the idea of translation, which recurs throughout the rest of the talk and might, in one abstraction of the whole, be called its topic. Under pressure of scrutiny, "translation" comes to include not only the idea of boundaries that led to it, but the whole concept of interpretation, whether in language or in action. Yet the amount of conceptual territory that "translation" can be made to cover, for this nonce, is clearly not the *point* of the talk. The point lies embedded in the course of the piece, which comprises a series of gestures: sequential instantiations of an abstract principle; sudden literalizations of metaphors; diagrammatic forays like geometric demonstrations; and above all, stories.

Some of Antin's stories come from anthropology texts, some involve members of his family, some are first-hand anecdotes. Most center on conversations. These stories often unfold under a double allegiance: to their own force and closure, and to the talk that contains them. For instance, the four-page account of Antin's political discussion with a cab driver is rich in color and character and also in structure—a story containing an elaborate theory and another story. But the point of it, for the poem as a whole, is one small instance of misleading translation between Yiddish and English. What makes the anecdote belong in the talk is peripheral to the anecdote itself. Like Homeric similes—and perhaps for some of the same improvisational reasons— the stories offset the momentum of the whole as much as they further it. As enjambed lines do on a smaller scale in verse, they double our sense of the talk's motion, of its procedure through time, like a doubled rhythmic layering.

Similarly, the final move of the piece is a recounted dialogue in which Antin Socratically questions a young Marine about what he would do in various violent situations. On its face, the story says that one needs to take responsibility for one's own life. But the context of the talk poem shifts and refines our understanding: The boy is attempting to substitute preparation—a single absolute decision, joining the Marines—for continuous present thought, which in the last line Antin equates with translation (in the broadened sense of "interpretation"). The story is chilling and exemplary, though what it signifies seems different for the Marine, for Antin as the conversation happened, and for him and us now as he retells it. All the first-hand anecdotes show us Antin himself thinking all the time; and this both authorizes his talk (he has worked on this matter before; it is not just off the top of his head) and authenticates it (right now in front of us he is thinking, as he always does). Even more visibly than the rest of his talk, the stories are simultaneously something Antin says and something he does.

This is finally what makes Antin's performances poetry—that at his best he attends so exactly to the what and the how of his speech at once. He neither gets so carried away by ideas that the language goes pale and abstract, nor falls so in love with the sound of his words as to weave beautiful rhythms that affirm nothing.[20] These qualities make him a great talker, and they make him a poet, discovering form in content. This is what Perloff means to point out by using Frye's idea of "associative rhythm" to legitimize talk as poetry.

Yet Perloff's answer to the charge of formlessness is only partly adequate. I do not mean to return to the old worry that we might not know poetry from the mere talk that surrounds us. Antin is too good a talker for that concern to be relevant; more to the point, he is not just a talker. In attending to the striking origin of Antin's poems, most of his critics largely ignore the fact that what we are talking about is a text.[21] Antin speaks before audiences, and then in his transcriptions he strives to duplicate that presentness; but the means of duplication are textual, typographical means. He expresses distrust of literature and the commerce of its distribution; but he does write books, and it is in the books that most people usually "hear" him. In order to substantiate the "associative rhythm" of the beginning of "talking at the boundaries," I had to study the poem with some care, reading and rereading to find the points at which one path turns into another. The turns—the open-parenthesis shifts—are easy to locate, but one cannot tell without very attentive judgment where (if at all) the close-parenthesis moment occurs, or readily distinguish an important pivot from a digression. That is the essence of the "associative rhythm"; but such study requires print.

This suggests a simpler approach to the question of form. In poetry, "form" has traditionally referred to such features as rhyme, lineation, meter, stanzas, and so on. It may extend to assonance and even to patterns of imagery or of ambiguity; it may be distinguished as more "external" than something called "structure"; in any case, the term's application in literary criticism has always been regulated by the possibility of pointing to something on a page. The sonnet form, having found its niche in a literary ecology, is about as definite as a zoological species.

In this sense, Antin's form has the following characteristics:

1. no capitalization;
2. no punctuation (except for quotation marks);
3. unjustified left and right margins;
4. pauses made visible as gaps about seven ems wide;
5. line breaks arbitrary;
6. (added in *tuning*:) something like paragraph breaks; a part-line is dropped straight down or (if the previous partial line is too long) three-quarters of a line of whitespace is added.

This form is meant to *recreate* in our reading some aspects of how we hear talking—not to *preserve* the fact of talk in some simple, impossible way. The transcription is not neutral; the form is chosen, not automatic or conventional, but invented.

Indeed, one can trace its invention in Antin's history. There are two possible ways toward Antin's current activity: A talker searching for a wider audience might be led to transcribe his talk, like a minister who publishes a series of sermons or a comic who releases a book of routines; but Antin's history shows him instead to be a writer, whose foray into the medium of talk never led him far from the page. He reportedly wrote much of a novel, which he abandoned in a revulsion against prose (''all that syntax had come to look to me like padding'' [*Vort* #7, p. 7]). He published four books of relatively normal-looking poetry during the late sixties and early seventies.[22] Some of them—especially *Definitions*, a powerful and eccentric book that should not be out of print—indicate various ingenious kinds of dissatisfaction with conventional forms. Perloff remarks that ''conceptually, 'definitions for mendy' [in *Definitions*] looks ahead to the talk poems, but Antin has still to master . . . the 'associative rhythm,' the forward movement of speech when it is allowed to evolve according to its own laws'' (p. 303). It is not clear how Antin, who had been speaking since he was two, could have failed to ''master'' an ''associative rhythm'' that belongs naturally to speech; more accurately, I think, he had not yet found a form that would adequately convey that rhythm to the reader from within the confines of the page. ''definitions for mendy'' remains an uncannily moving poem in its own right.

Though in retrospect we can locate in the early books important aspects of the Antin to be, there was little at the time to make him seem much different from other poets—more different than serious poets always are from each other. The 1972 collection, *talking*, begins with a poem (''The November Exercises'') whose time-stamped, prose-like chunks resemble *Meditations* and parts of the other early books. But the next two pieces, partly improvised but with much preparation, restarting, and editing, are for two or more voices. This change of speakers is indicated by typographical variations that begin to resemble the later work, but seem more simply motivated. Finally, in "talking at pomona," Antin locates both the improvised talk poem and the typographical form to embody it in print.

The disavowal of punctuation and capitalization were retained from the bulk of his previous work; the visual pause had also appeared before. Combining these elements, he achieved what seems by definition impossible—a form neither verse nor prose. Yet it combines the attentive responses elicited by both. Antin does not write lines, as he says; but the chief virtue of verse (defined as language in lines) is that it stands against the conventional absence-of-discontinuity that eases the reader's way through prose—eases it too much for the attention Antin wants to sustain. Like verse, Antin's form claims the control over silence and pace that prose gives over to syntax. Like prose, his form blurs the small-scale edges by which verse defines its intention, the tendency of lines to depart from the poem at a right angle, into eternity.

When speaking of his form, Antin prefers the term *notation*, or sometimes *score*. The parallel with music is intriguing. He recognizes that any notation has limits of accuracy:

> I want it understood that my page is just that—a notation of some performance—which is the real work or some relation between *performance and intention*. I am not fussy about my notation—the way a Black Mountain poet might be—or maybe I'm just fussy in a different way. I don't give a damn about 'lines,' I want the flow of talk—Yet I won't bother to use two different kinds of pausal notation (e.g., two different space breaks), because I assume that an intelligent reader/speaker can get enough information about that from the sense of the language and I refuse to insult his or her intelligence by offering redundant clues. Once you begin with this kind of worry there's no end to it—You make the passage *con brio* (define 'brio' metabolically—basal metabolism—give metronome markers, leave an exemplary metronome made of platinum/iridium in a vacuum at 5° Centigrade with the Bureau of Standards, etc.)—This is the way of the fussy line break—The composers of the figured bass tradition knew better. Any harpsichordist of intelligence knows what the usual civilized ornaments should be—no? (Vort #7, p. 80)

This problem of accuracy varies from one kind of transcription to another. Lectures are easier to transcribe with sufficient accuracy using conventional prose than are dramatic performances. In the previous chapter we noticed that jazz, in contrast to European concert music, offers special challenges to any standard system of notation; Antin's talks make enough demands on printed language to render the visual blocks and regulated syntax of prose—which Antin is fond of calling "concrete poetry with justified margins," pointing out

its artificiality as a container for talk—inadequate to the task.[23] This is the
necessity of his invention.

If Antin's "notation" is also a "form" in the conventional sense, it should be
possible to put other "matter" into it. Antin himself does this in the italicized
transitions, a page or a few pages each, that he inserts between the poems in
talking at the boundaries and *tuning*. These passages fill in the narrative of his
travels between talks, and give a sense of the context of talk among friends
and colleagues into which the poems are directed. They help sustain in the
printed book the sense of "address" that is so important to Antin, and they
subtly underwrite the continuity of the poems with the life of the mind that
makes them. But what are they transcriptions or notations of? Possibly Antin
composed them by speaking into a tape recorder—but surely not before an
audience. In these transitional passages, at least, the form is a fiction of talk,
just as a sonnet is.

Perhaps, then, like the sonnet, this form ("the Antinine talk poem") could
surpass its originator. Could other poets use it? Surely not: If they did not first
talk before an audience, the fiction would be transparently bogus; and if they
capably did, they would be poets with sufficient interest in the individuality of
"voice," both literally and metaphorically, to need to invent their own systems of transcription. But could the form be used, after the fact, for other
material originally talked?

Here is a piece by Lord Buckley on Jonah and the whale, transcribed as best
I can in Antin's form:[24]

```
        my lords and my ladies        of the royal court        the
religious fantasy        of jonah        and the whale        now the great
     lord was sitting in his rosy rocking chair one        hallelujah
     morning        when he looked down and observed by a great body of
water        a little mortal about five foot two        and the lord
dug the mortal        and he called for gabe and gabe put down his
horn and swung with the book        and the lord flipped the pages
   a b c d e f g h i j        and it was jonah getting his kicks on the
beach he say "man        sure is crazy out here on this here beach
   mans got a lot of room to groove in the suns shining down and
   everythings a melody in fine"        now when the great lord has
something he must have        done upon the earth        he calls upon his
   favorite children to do it        so the great lord put the sound on
jonah he says        "i dig you jonah        i dig you jonah        i dig
   you jonah cause jonah is the lords        sweet        boy"
   jonah said "man where is all that jazz music coming from anyway
```

sound like seventy two jazz bands is jumping off here man it makes me
want to jiggle and wriggle" he say "whew   mm   say i know them
     seagulls aint wailing up no breeze like that"   he said "the
whopperwills and the canary birds dont care"   say "heh heh
he he   i got the craziest feeling all over my body   oohoo
feel like i want to stretch my wings and   ooooooooowee   good
morning lord" and the lord said "good morning jonah"   he said
     "jonah   i got a little favor id like to" jonah say "aint that
crazy   ninety six million cats for the lord to put his finger on
an he select jonah aint that groovy"   and the great lord said
"jonah   i want you to cross the red sea   and put the message
on the israelites   theyre squaring up over there"   and jonah
said   "man you dont mean this here   big pool do you lord"
hmm boom   "say man look at them waves"   hmm boom   he say
"you must mean some   little old jonah size pool dont you lord"
the great lord said "jonah   put your nose into the wind   and
the message will come to you"   and jonah put his great nose
into the north wind   wh whew   it was not there   he put it
in the east wind   wh whew   it was not there   he put it in
the west wind   wh whew   it was not there   but   when
he put it in the hallelujah south wind   whoo wheew   it was
     there   so he traveled for twenty two days   and fifteen
minutes and came to a   great cathedral like group of trees
lifting their glorious arms up to heaven   in supplication of the
master   and down at the bottom of these giant   sequoias
     jonah saw growing a   strange green vine   and he said "just
like brigham young"   bam   "this is it"   and he sat down
beside it   and he observed of it   and he admired of it
and he plucked from it   and he rolled of it   and he selected
of it   and he swung of it   and he said "where is that fool
pool the lord want me to dig   look out here comes jonah   and
he ready as the day is long"   mmmmm boom cutting a gigantic v
right through the breast of the waves   and suddenly fatigue
hit jonah   in the back of his soul   and he lay his great body
back in the water   and he lulling and the waves of morpheus
hhhaa   was goofing on his eyebrows   and sleep   came to
jonah   and he slept for twelve hours and fifteen seconds
when he woke   what did he see   ill tell you what he saw
he saw the whale   and what did he say when he saw the whale he
said "get me from this scene   immediately"   and the whale say
"heh heh   man   heh heh   every time i stick my nose out of
this pool   i sure see some crazy jazz but heh heh   this is
the bending end"   he say "what you mean the bending end mister

whale''   say ''look at that he talk too what do you know about
that''   he said ''course i talk mr whale'' he say   ''dont you dig
the marine news   aint you hip to whats going down round these
here waters''   say ''wait a minute here take it easy now''   he
said ''aint no taking it easy mister whale'' he say   ''its a big
pool   you groove your way   ill groove mine   ill swoop the
scene   and dig you later''   whale say ''look a here heres a
little old bit of nothing a million miles from no place he going to
hip me the king of the deep what the lick is''   he says ''i got a
good mind to gobble you up''   jonah said ''dont you do that mister
whale   cause if you do   im going to knock you in your most
delicate   gear''   the whale say   ''that blew it''
harrumm   and he swallowed jonah   and here was jonah
slipping and sliding from one side of this great sea mammal to the
other   fear and terror in his heart   he couldnt go out the
front end and hes afraid to go out the back end   and all of a
sudden he fell down on these great thick blubbery rugs   and a
piteous sound came from jonah   he said ''loorrrd   looorrrrd
can you dig me in this here fish''   and the lord said   ''i got
you covered jonah''   jonah said ''man the lord sure got a crazy
sense of humor'' he say   ''maybe thats the reason i dig the cat so
much   tell me hes got me covered the cat got me surrounded''
and the great lord said ''jonah   reach in your watertight pocket
and take from there   some of the   cigarettes you got from the
great   tree   and   courage will return to you''   and
jonah did   and we see jonah inside this   giant whale
smoking this   strange cigarette   watching the pistons
pound   driving and   poom   pushing and the great valves
aww ooh   spanding and   eee aah   expanding   and
finally the whale say   ''uh   jonah''   and jonah say
sssp   ''what is it fish''   the whale say '' 'what is it fish' ''
say ''you got a new captain on this mass mess now mister fish''   he
say ''i aint on the outside no more   im inside now''   whale say
''jonah what in the world is you smoking in there   i thought i was
off the phlibidee islands here i is two minutes for the panama canal
this jazz has got to go''   jonah say ''what do you care what im
smoking in here im the captain of this mass mess as i done explained
to you before''   said ''jonah what are you doing stomping all over
the engine room like that for boy   why dont you sit down
someplace and cool yourself   you getting the ride for nothing''
jonah say ''ill stomp all over this here engine room as long as i want
say what is this wheel''   said ''look out there boy you messing
with me down the wheel   jonah look out man no way   messing

with that equipment like that here"   jonah say "what is this here
     lever here"   he say "look out im at you jonah   jonah
jonah   boy   boy   look out what you doing you got my full
speed ahead lever   jonah   jonah look out for the rock on the
     right   the rock on the right jonah"   "cool"   he say "it
aint cool at all   we in the shallow water"   jonah say "thats
     all i want to know"   and favamm he hit the whales big sneez o
meter and   wh whheeww   blew him out on the cool   groovy
          sands of   serenity
                                        which only goes to
prove   as confuci said many many years ago   "lan gai sao ton
go lo tao i sai si sao"   which translated   briefly means
if you get to it   and you can not do it   there   you
     jolly well are   whew   arent you

Interesting as the experiment is—at least for the transcriber playing out the
formal decisions—its failure will be clear to anyone who has *heard* Buckley.
The transcription may suggest some of his manic humor, or remind one of it,
but can't effectively include it. Like a song reduced to printed lyrics, the story
seems both flat and overblown; the jokes range from the obvious to the em-
barrassing; the timing is merely puzzling (the notation of rhythm not being
sufficiently exact); the repetitions tend to annoy and the ellipses to confuse.
The music is missing.

What the experiment reveals, then, is that Antin's transcriptive form and
his oral style are uniquely suited to each other. His speaking style is not especially dramatic—"spectacle" hardly seems an appropriate term. His appearance is striking but unchanging; he makes little use of expression or gesture. His stage business is limited to a slow, almost subliminal dance:
beginning behind a podium, eventually picking up a glass of water, moving
very gradually out into the open, finally taking a sip, returning (over fifteen or
twenty more minutes) to reach his starting point together with his peroration.[25]
The talk itself, not the spectacle, holds us. This is a style that goes relatively
easily into print. He uses none of Lord Buckley's nonverbal sounds and dialects and snatches of song and abrupt changes of voice and pace, except what
remains visible in the words themselves.

Far from making the transcription obvious and "natural," this match between talk and form indicates a successfully deliberate translation across the
boundary from one medium into another. Though he gives talks that he never
publishes, these seem to represent partial failures—the kind inevitable for any
improvising artist, who may be off, or covering too-familiar ground, or wandering too long too far from what turns out to be the point. The best of his
talks, we assume, wind up as texts. So a view of Antin's art that excludes this
act of translation seems incomplete, and unable to account for either its new-

ness or its value. For Antin, performance is the first stage of composition. To simplify him into either a writer or a performer is like criticizing *The Band Wagon* as artificial or praising Creeley's poems as real speech.

The translation from spoken word to print engenders paradox, which runs deeper not only into Antin's work but into everyone's. *Distribution* and *presentness* are opposed. Any mode of working that tries to combine them—and what artist in our culture would not want to combine them?—is bound to employ paradoxical means. Print is an old solution to the problem, but it troubles Antin: "because once ive established my love for the present through my talking i dont give it up when im writing" (*tuning*, p. 94); and yet, "in looking at my own book and feeling   that as i look i lose my sense of the present   my sense of the present disintegrates for me as i read" (*tuning*, p. 84).

Antin's choice of the book as a means of distribution is no longer technologically inevitable. Yet he has remarked that tape recording—though an integral part of his own artistic process—turns out to be a deceptive medium for the publication of his work.[26] It changes what we do and do not hear. It emphasizes distance, not presence. (He also agrees that "live" recordings of jazz are similarly deceptive, while "studio" recordings—including those we have examined in earlier chapters—are not.) Text is not so false, perhaps, because it does not pretend to be true.[27] Barry Alpert notes that though Antin has worked with videotape and his wife is a video artist, he has apparently decided that that obvious medium too is unsuitably removed.

The paradox intensifies when we consider Antin's insistence on "address." It is not immediately clear how to reconcile this idea of "address," which suggests that some kind of dialogue with the audience is a necessary condition of his work, with his self-described "uninterruptible discourse."[28] Books are uninterruptible (you can abandon a book, but not interrupt it); address characterizes talk among present persons. Antin's admiration for "Socrates' great interruptible inventions" is tempered by distance; his own art is not so directly interactive.[29] Some critics have seen this as duplicity—he pays lip-service to dialogue while egotistically hogging the stage.

We could ease the paradox by arguing that what he addresses is a topic (as he suggests at one point in the Alpert interview). Or we could follow Perloff in assimilating "uninterruptible discourse" to the "intensely continuous" nature of the "associative rhythm" (pp. 304, 318), as if the discourse were merely prevented from interrupting *itself*, a pencil never lifted from the paper. But finally the puzzle arises, again, from a misperception of the genre of Antin's work. When Paul Gonsalves played twenty-seven consecutive blues choruses at the 1956 Newport Jazz Festival, no one complained that he was being egotistical.[30] Several thousand people did cheer and whistle, which would not have happened during an equivalent duration of Haydn, but which did not constitute an interruption. In Europe, sound during a performance is catcalls;

in Africa, it is encouragement; as in some places it is impolite not to belch after a meal. Though he composes words not notes, Antin is not engaged in conversation.

His choice of "talk" rather than "speak" is a careful one. (Compare the plausible "speak the sentence written on this card" and the nonsensical "talk the sentence written on this card.") *Talk* being both verb and noun helps unite his activity with its product, and so make the whole process seem more straightforward than perhaps it is. But though improvisation makes the pieces poetry (in the sense of authentic response to both what the mind discovers in the moment and the language in which the discovery is embodied), turning them into *poems* requires that the discourse be uninterruptible. His talks are neither speeches, nor simply speech.

But if he is not conversing, he is engaged in dialogue. He and his audience are present in the same time with the same occupations, at "a private occasion in a public place." The traffic from him to them is obvious; the return traffic is mysterious only if we take the boast of his talk at its own individualistic word. It is only our attention that warrants his continuing.[31] Explicitly in his stories and analyses, Antin calls attention to the cultural community that makes language possible, difficult, and necessary; and the occasion of his talking repeats the lesson implicitly. Within the talks themselves we can see at play such habitually separate categories as poetry and criticism, poetry-as-music (-as-structure) and poetry-as-content, imagination (stories) and reason (examples). It is the immediate presence of the audience, however, that grounds his entertainment of these possibilities. Again as with the jazz soloist, we contribute a kind of witness to the occasion, without which it would be meaningless, an "unnatural language act," a "radically displaced occasion."

The potential textuality of his talk yields a more complex dialogic interplay, even in the minds of immediate listeners. As we listen he defines for us a situation with at least four poles:

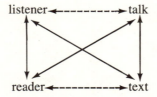

Some of these dialogues are familiar, such as the direct horizontal relationships of listening and reading. Yet even these are transformed by others that are special to Antin's work: his potential or actual translation from talk to text, and the influence the anticipated text has on how he talks; our ability (if we know his books) to imagine as we listen how the text will look; our ability as we read to reconstruct the living voice. These latter intricate skills are adapted, by the instigation of Antin's art, from our training as literate people (we can visualize a spoken sentence well enough to write it down) and as readers of poetry (we can resurrect a speaker from the tomb of print). The boundary Antin crosses in his act of transcription parallels the boundary condition of our own dual relation to language, reader-listeners and listener-readers.

The most tempting partial view of Antin is as an "oral poet." It seems legitimate to speak of "the New Orality," or (as in the issue of *Boundary2*) "the oral impulse in contemporary American poetry"; but this new orality is not the old, Homeric orality, intriguing as the parallels may be.[32] Neither Antin's memory nor ours has been shaped by lifetimes of nonliterate experience. His talk would probably not be very exciting to someone raised in an oral culture. Above all, he and we are aware of the potential book. Antin's work is literate because the culture it belongs and attends to is literate; if it gives a taste of the "postliterate," that is not the same as preliterate. Like modern jazz, his work complicates the relation between text and performance, but does not eliminate it. As I noted in the previous chapter, our very idea of improvisation depends on the existence of a potential notation. In this sense preliterate jazz players were not engaged in any distinctive activity of "improvising." It is not the dream of a return to an archaic cultural state that makes Antin's work exciting, but the adventures of talk within a culture partly alien to it.

I have suggested that instead of the unmixed traditional categories of work that is oral-improvised (the *Iliad*) or literate-composed (literature), we can understand jazz better in terms of mixtures: the oral-composed work of Ornette Coleman, the literate-improvised work of Lee Konitz. Antin clearly belongs with Konitz. It is hard to think of any real predecessors in the verbal arts (perhaps Blake's marginalia on the lectures of Reynolds?). The biographer and the cultural historian might ask whether Antin's poems could have existed without the preceding few decades of jazz.

On Signatures

In *The Pirates of Penzance*, three different declarations of identity—

for I am a Pirate King
for I am a Major General
for I am an orphan boy

—are sung to the same tune. Three selves (distributed between two people; part of the joke is that a major general can also be an orphan boy and therefore safe among the soft-hearted pirates) use, or accommodate themselves to, or take on the coloration of, a single melody. It is hard not to hear this as a parody of the contemporaneous Wagnerian idea of the *leitmotif*—a musical theme that announces a character and distinguishes him or her from all others.

It is tempting to trace this difference beyond parody to the fact that Gilbert and Sullivan wrote comedy, while Wagner's operas are tragic. Tragedy—it is a commonplace—individualizes, while comedy leads us back into the fold.

_____

Five

Joni Mitchell: To Whom It May Concern

WHEN Joni Mitchell's first album was released in the late sixties, the songs on it would still have been called folk music. Nothing could be less apt. Mitchell's artful attention to poetic technique (the album bears a dedication ''to Mr. Kratzman, who taught me to love words'') makes these songs the opposite of anonymous.

Michael from Mountains

Michael wakes you up with sweets
He takes you up streets and the rain comes down
Sidewalk markets locked up tight
And umbrellas bright on a gray background
There's oil on the puddles in taffeta patterns
That run down the drain
In colored arrangements
That Michael will change with a stick that he found
(REFRAIN:)
Michael from mountains
Go where you will go to
Know that I will know you
Someday I may know you very well

Michael brings you to a park
He sings and it's dark when the clouds come by
Yellow slickers up on swings
Like puppets on strings hanging in the sky
They'll splash home to suppers in wallpapered kitchens
Their mothers will scold
But Michael will hold you
To keep away cold till the sidewalks are dry
(REFRAIN)

Michael leads you up the stairs
He needs you to care and you know you do
Cats come crying to the key
And dry you will be in a towel or two
There's rain in the window

There's sun in the painting that smiles on the wall
You want to know all
But his mountains have called so you never do
(REFRAIN)

Someday I will know you very well[1]

Twenty years later, no one expects such care in a popular song. Some detailed analysis might be salutary.

The eight-line verses and four-line refrains suggest a structure of quatrains, and the light end-rhyme

x a x *a* / x x x *a* // x b b x

confirms it. Within that fairly conventional scheme flourishes an unconventional richness of sound. It could be sketched as internal rhyme:

```
   a                 b              (wakes               sweets)
   a        b        c              (takes     streets   down)
                     d                                   (tight)
            d        c              (bright   background)
========
                     x
                     e                                   (drain)
                     e      x                       (arrangements)
            e        c              (change            found)
========
                     x
      f        f     g              (go          go    to)
      f        f     g              (know     know you)
               f     g      x                 (know you)
```

This is a complex pattern, comparable to the intricate ballades and virelais of Old French poetry, or to Welsh forms with their frequent internal rhyme and strict syllabic meter. Even this enlarged diagram of the rhyme scheme does not include all the recurrences that the alerted ear picks up. In the first pair of lines, the rhyme is not simply between "wakes" and "takes," but between "wakes you up" and "takes you up"; two different uses of "up" sharpen the juxtaposition. Each verse rings with supplementary rhymes as well. In the first, "rain" (line 2) chimes distantly with "drain" (line 6) and its attached sequence ("arrangements," "change," lines 7–8). In the second verse, three consecutive lines constellate "up," "puppets," and "suppers," outside the main scheme; and the third verse introduces another internal rhyme ("crying" and "dry" in lines 3 and 4) that clinches the first quatrain into even tighter parallel unity.

Furthermore, this network of rhyme serves as scaffolding for irregular, abundant, local auditory effects. "Sidewalk markets locked up tight / And umbrellas bright on a gray background" is perhaps the clearest example. The staccato repetition of *k* sounds integrates the first line, as the modulation from *-br-* and *br-* through *gr-* to *b-gr-* does the second. A more delicate web of *l* and *m* sounds links the two lines. Sound thickens to support sense when the tight consonantal clumps of the first line vivify the "locking up" the words image. More generally, this shower of visual and verbal color deepens the contrast with a rainy "background." ("That again for six stanzas," says Pound of Arnaut Daniel, "WITH the words making sense.")[2]

Analyzing the "music of poetry" this way is not an unusual exercise. But here something is radically wrong with it. "Michael from Mountains" is not a poem but a song; and the demands made on words by the situation of song differ from the demands made by poetry.[3] Though it may be useful to separate a song's lyrics and its music temporarily and analyze them in isolation, we risk a falsification like forgetting that *Macbeth* is a play, or that *Die Zauberflöte* is not. For example, successful songs are likely to be insistent about the marking of prosodic structures, because song is confined to temporal perception by the ear. Poems—in their usual situation as texts on a page—have the help of the eye with its spatial and structural aptitudes; the eye can brachiate contentedly among subtleties of sight-rhyme and lineation that fall dumb on the ear. But the ear's work is facilitated by rhyme and strongly defined stanzas, and almost all songwriters gratify these demands. As a result, the reader of contemporary poetry may find printed song lyrics formally ponderous or naive.

The inside cover of Mitchell's album displays the lyrics of the songs, presumably under her direction, with her lineation, and so on. The genesis of this printed, lineated version may resemble the genesis of Antin's printed talk poems, or it may not.[4] But in any case, the notation of the song's words as verse is exterior to the song, a mere listening aid adorning the wrapper of the phonograph record that gives us the real thing: the song itself. Unlike Antin's pieces, of which the notation is an integral part, songs are complete in their auditory form. From that perspective, lineation looks like a mere substitute. Some of the turn-of-the-century resistance to free verse might have arisen out of nostalgia for song's happiness with "form" in the traditional sense—with rhyme and meter.

In the case of "Michael from Mountains," the confrontation between printed words and sung song alerts us to a paradox. These lyrics of Mitchell's go well beyond the requirement that a song's words be ordered clearly enough for us to hear their orderliness. John Hollander has analyzed the common metaphor of "the music of poetry," reminding us that it *is* a metaphor, "yoking

by violence together what have become dissimilar activities.''[5] In a famous
essay ''On Musicality in Verse,''[6] Kenneth Burke analyzed the richness of
sound patterning that lyric poems impose on language. In one critical vocabulary, this imposition is known as ''overdetermination'': While the language
system semantically dictates a speaker's choice of words, the extra, deliberate
patterning of sound adds further constraints to the choice. Thus ''cats come
crying to the key'' not only because ''crying'' is a plausible name for a sound
cats make (though the sense of the word jars a bit), but because it begins with
a *k* sound and its first syllable rhymes with ''dry.'' Such poetic ''music'' developed as a substitute for actual musical settings, from which Hollander
traces lyric poetry's history of ''divorce.'' This development paralleled the
invention of properly poetic meter to replace the quite different meter of music.[7] In short, there is no obvious role for this kind of ''musicality'' in songs.
Taking on the obligations of both poetry and song, the lyrics of ''Michael from
Mountains'' seem super-overdetermined.

　　Before delving farther into this mystery, however, we should look more
closely at the apparently familiar territory surrounding it. The peculiar essence
of song, to put it as baldly as possible, lies in the relation between the lyrics
and the music. The details of this relation are rarely discussed—at least by
critics coming from the literary side of the river—and are far less automatic
than the naturalness of a good song makes them seem.

Ex. 5.1. ''Michael from Mountains''; first verse and refrain

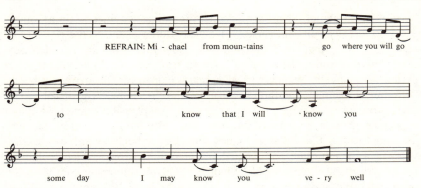

REFRAIN: Mi - chael   from moun-tains   go   where you will go

to   know   that I will   · know   you

some   day   I   may   know   you   ve - ry   well

When we shift from talking about poems to talking about songs, even the terminology can hold some surprises, as in the ambiguity of words like *phrase* and *meter*. For instance, we can make a sort of scansion of Mitchell's first line:

    /   /   /   /
Michael wakes you up with sweets.

But to construct metrical feet around these accents would be inappropriate. The song's meter can be described not in terms of iambs or trochees, but in terms of either the time signature or the musical rhythm

Ex. 5.2. Meter of "Michael from Mountains"

which consistently overlies that basic pulse and is reiterated by the accompanying guitar.[8]

In this first line the four verbal accents are aligned with the music in two ways, rhythmically and melodically. The song's basic rhythm emphasizes the first beat of each measure, as is usual; the third beat, normally just weaker than the first, is displaced forward by half a beat and thus strengthened, which also crowds any emphasis away from the second beat. Again as usual, the fourth beat of each measure is somewhat lighter than the first and the displaced third. In the first line of the lyrics, three of the accents fall on the first beat of a measure, the anticipated third beat, and the first beat of the next measure, respectively. These syllables demand this stress: The first one begins the beloved's name as well as the song; and the other two turn out to be rhyming points. The remaining, lighter accent ("up") coincides with the secondary musical accent, the fourth beat of the measure.

Ex. 5.3. First verse, measures 1–2

The melodic correspondence is similar. The points of maximum melodic emphasis in a musical phrase are usually the highest note or notes, then the lowest, while those in between carry the least weight. (In descending phrases, the emphasis of high and low is usually reversed.) Here the three main stressed syllables are all set to the same pitch, which is the highest in the phrase; while ''up'' falls on the lowest. In all these ways, Mitchell closely aligns the pitches and the rhythms—the melodic and rhythmic shapes of the musical phrase, and the rhythm of the words as governed by contextual emphasis as well as by the patterns of pitch inherent in English speech.[9]

One difficulty in describing correspondences between lyrics and music is that so many of them seem too obvious to be clearly noticeable or demonstrable. It is too unnatural for us to imagine alternatives, against which these correspondences could emerge as choices. *Naturally* musical phrases coincide in length with verbal phrases. Thus a rest naturally follows ''sweets,'' where a line break in the printed lyrics also points out a syntactical juncture; and the next rest (after ''streets'') matches the ending of the next verbal phrase (though no printed line break underscores the audible syntax). But this kind of correlation is not simply a matter of course. In this case it is reinforced by the rhyme on ''streets,'' which also

1. is the only strong accent in this (half-)line of lyrics,
2. falls (uniquely in this phrase) on a strong musical beat,
3. is the highest note of the phrase, and
4. is the first point at which the underlying harmony shifts away from a tonic chord.

Matching lyrics and notes is a process of choices, often intricate ones, juggling the mutually independent logics of music and words.

Mitchell's third phrase offers a different kind of correspondence, one that comes more easily into our awareness. While the melody, beginning with a quick patter of sixteenth-notes, falls steadily in pitch, the words tell us: ''and the rain comes down.''

Ex. 5.4. First verse, measures 3–4

(Here the lowest note is the point of maximum emphasis, and accompanies the primary verbal stress on "down"; the stressed "rain" falls on a strong third beat.) Hearing this, we remember what we may have missed before: that the second phrase—"He takes you up streets"—was set to a consistently rising melody.

Ex. 5.5. First verse, measures 2–3

This kind of onomatopoeic setting would become cloying if it were maintained at this level. Throughout the song, though, there are hints of a consistent attention to such effects: the upward melodic leap on "sky," for instance, or the pendulous rise and fall of

Ex. 5.6. Second verse, measures 5–6

Almost a corollary of the congruence of musical and verbal phrases is the relation between larger musical and verbal units, both of which tend to be built on powers of two. Quatrains are by far the commonest song stanzas, and four-, eight-, or sixteen-measure sections (frequently in 4/4 time) are the musical units most comfortable for Western audiences. Thus in "Michael from Mountains," each quatrain occupies eight measures. But again the relation is complicated by additional determinations. The unity of the first quatrain is emphasized by a variety of formal closures in both melody and lyrics. The end rhyme "down / background" verbally marks a completion. The second four measures are melodically identical to the first, except for the final note of each. At both those points (halfway through the quatrain, and at its end) the harmonic structure returns to the tonic after a brief excursion, while the pitch first descends to the dominant below and then ascends to the dominant above the melodic center of gravity. In each case, despite the stable tonic harmony, the melody's emphasis on the dominant gives the phrase ending some flavor of a half-cadence. This feeling is stronger the second time ("on a gray background"), where the sudden upward leap simultaneously rounds off the previous unit (eight measures, the first quatrain) and prepares us for the next.

The quite different melodic shape of the next eight bars reinforces the separate integrity of the two quatrains. The second quatrain of each verse seems

less crammed with verbal pattern, but this quatrain gets extra cohesion from
its melody. ''That run down the drain'' and ''In colored arrangements''—
which do rhyme, since word-boundary is no more audible in song than in
speech—are set to nearly identical sequences of notes, transposed downward
half a tone.

Ex. 5.7. First verse, measures 11–13

Nor is the final line of this quatrain (and of the verse) allowed to secede from
the tightly interlocked couplet preceding it. It rhymes internally with the previous lines' terminal rhymes; and a nearly identical *verbal* rhythm runs
through all three:

(x / x   x /)
That run down the drain
(x / x   x /)   x
In colored arrangements
 (x   / x   x   /)   x (x /   x x /)
That Michael will change with a stick that he found

Verbal and musical kinds of verve and momentum support each other. And
the result of all this engineering feels as simple as any cri de coeur.

Though the alignment of notes and syllables seems nearly automatic to the
ear, it is far from inevitable. And it follows, from the skill required, that errors
are possible, with at least awkward results. Consider ''The Star-Spangled
Banner.'' The initial dotted-rhythm descending triad accommodates the first
verse easily enough:

Ex. 5.8. ''Star-Spangled Banner'': beginning of first verse

When in the second verse we try to cram ''Whose broad stripes'' into the same
musical phrase

whose broad stripes

Ex. 5.9. "Star-Spangled Banner": beginning of second verse

the result is a stadiumful of Americans mumbling.

Like any aesthetic resource that can be used or misused, the matching of words to notes can also be subverted expressively. The purpose is usually humorous. The first album by that remarkable trio of sisters, the Roches, opens with an introduction ("We") whose sardonic amiability depends on rhythmic deformations in word-setting. The background is a quick strum on one guitar, executed with crisp mock efficiency and a jaunty back beat. The lyrics begin in camp plainness:

> We are Maggie and Terre and Suzzy,
> Maggie and Terre and Suzzy Roche;
> We don't give out our ages,
> And we don't give out our phone numbers
> (Give out our phone numbers).
> Sometimes our voices give out,
> But not our ages and our phone numbers.[10]

This looks like free verse—in the simplest sense, meaning only that, unlike many song lyrics, it has no obvious allegiance to poetic meter.[11] Instead, on the page the words cohere by means of repetitions like those that have shaped much free verse since Whitman, here deflated by a nervous pun. If these lines do not sound much like the Psalms, it is not for prosodic reasons. In the ear, the rhythms gain complications that are much funnier:

Ex. 5.10. "We": first verse

The first hint of trouble is the "and" that, twice in the first phrase, gets unwonted emphasis from a rising melody. (The quirk would be lessened by the word's relegation to a note off the beat, if it were not the same off-beat that the guitar is emphasizing.) In the last phrase, completing the offense, "But" takes not only the highest note in the phrase but also the position of maximum metrical emphasis, dead on the first beat of the measure. Between these one-word pratfalls we hear a bit of rhythmic play:[12] In the repeated run of syllables, "we don't give out our," the accent falls first on "don't" and then on "give" as the words shift from one part of the measure to another. Finally, "phone" is twice robbed of its accent by the adjacent "numbers" (as "broad" is robbed by "stripes"); at the end, "phone" triumphs on the downbeat of the measure, which then tumbles into the disaster of "num*bers*."

This may be low comedy, but it is certainly not accident. A later song on the same album reminds us how subtle the semantic service of the music to the words can be. The refrain repeated after the first two verses of "Runs in the Family" contains the list, "my uncle did it, my daddy did it." In speech, contrastive stress would fall on the first syllable of "daddy" (and "uncle" if the contrast were premeditated). So the harmonized melody, basically a repeated downward scale, lifts just once, on that syllable:

Ex. 5.11. "Runs in the Family": refrain

In the last verse, the contrast changes: "just like my mama did, just like her mama did." The switch suggests that "mama" should be stressed the first time; but now the contrast calls for stress on "her"; and finally, the progression of the verses demands that the contrast be stronger this last time around. So now "mama" (unlike "uncle" and "daddy") falls on the beat, and the voices move up not once but twice in the second phrase. This also creates a sharp drop of a fourth on the repetition of "mama"—a kind of anti-stress that underscores the inevitability of the recurrence:

Ex. 5.12. "Runs in the Family": final refrain

This shrewdness about formal possibilities peculiar to song leads the Roches to treat syntax in unusual ways. In most songs, musical phrases are associated with syntactical units that are not only discrete but more or less complete, usually clauses or detachable imagistic phrases. The auditory equivalent of enjambement is rare. But ''The Hammond Song'' extends one sentence over three musical phrases separated by longish pauses, by major junctures in the harmonic structure, and by changes from one solo voice to another to the full trio:

Ex. 5.13. ''The Hammond Song'': second verse

There may be some intention to make ''That would be just'' stand on its own, a kind of punning lineation used often enough in poems. But the more general result is to make the listener suspend conclusions about what is being said until the saying is finished. That attitude militates against continuous instant involvement (of singers or listeners) with the words and notes. In a sense, it militates against lyricism.

The resulting irony combines naturally with the Roches' project of importing flat, clichéd speech into the traditionally more rarefied atmosphere of song. They do for popular song something of what John Ashbery has done for poetry. This colloquializing project, in turn, is associated with a radical shift in subject matter and therefore in style, forced on American song in the sixties by Bob Dylan and others.[13]

Joni Mitchell, too, has written ironic songs ("The Gallery," "The Last Time I Saw Richard"); but few appear on her first album. In "Michael from Mountains," the force of setting presses all in the opposite direction, toward imagistic immediacy and emotional engagement. In the songs of all these writers, however, ironic or lyrical, and in any song that uses the relation between words and notes to control the semantic and tonal development of meaning, the musical setting has an obviously dramatic function. It is an agent of voice: It characterizes the singer.

This is the life of opera. In that medium, the "songwriter" (usually two people, one responsible for words and the other for music, as is true also of many popular songs) creates individualized characters largely by distinguishing the musical materials to which their lines are set. The corporate author bears the same relation to the singers as a playwright does to the actors. For an artist in such a position, the appropriate ethic is the one Keats called Negative Capability, speaking of Shakespeare's ability to distribute himself imaginatively into a dramatis personae. Being absent from the stage may make this easier to achieve for the composer than for the lyric poet. (Having to collaborate with a librettist may help too.) But the situation of a songwriter who also sings her own material is more complex and, evidently, risky. What makes the more narcissistic popular singer/songwriters (Neil Diamond and John Denver come to mind) so painful to listen to is the failure of that imaginative ethos—the failure to separate, as Eliot said, "the man who suffers from the mind which creates," in the absence of a mind that brings any original attention to the self's internal weather.

By means of irony the Roches create a doubleness of voice that saves poignancy from sentimentality (a good example is "Mr. Sellack") and lifts cliché into a convincing rhetoric. Looking for a parallel tension in Mitchell's song, we find ourselves returning to an earlier unanswered question. What I called the super-overdetermination of prosodic elements—the flourishing assonances and consonances, the onomatopoeia, the overabundant internal rhymes— keeps us continually aware that a *writer* is present, standing somewhere behind the singer. And now a peculiarity in the song's use of pronouns begins to make sense.

"Michael from Mountains" is a song about how love transforms the world in the lover's eyes. Michael's presence draws the motor oil on street puddles into "colored arrangements"; it makes the "umbrellas bright on a gray background.'' Of course, Joni Mitchell effects this transformation by talking about what the two people say and do, not by eulogizing Michael directly. It is usual to say of good modern literature that it does not describe but enact, that it shows not tells, but there is nothing especially modern about this. Homer knew that the way to impress us with Helen's beauty was to describe not her but the reaction of the old men who see her from the city's battlements when she first comes on stage in the poem. What Mitchell shows us is how the woman in the song sees.

Negative Capability is more than a playwright's problem. The ability to ''identify'' with someone different from ourselves is the fundamental responsibility of the imagination, as Shelley insisted. True, the desire to identify may be—or may be subverted into—a mere wish to escape from ourselves into fantasy, to cast aside the drab particulars of our one life while the ego revels in a new disguise. That, paradoxically, is what makes the narcissistic artist popular; narcissism is commercially successful because people are often glad to share it by proxy or take it as a licensing example. But it is possible to argue that what we get from most enduring literature is the chance to practice in relative safety the harder task of feeling someone else's feelings.

Perhaps, then, Michael's lover's love is enough to keep us involved in the song. But I do not think so. Her experience is, from our inevitable distance, too banal, too familiar from other literary encounters. To identify with the woman in love with Michael is not impossible, but not very interesting. Mitchell, however, provides us with a more immediate engagement: the sound of her words. The singer's delight in ''Michael from Mountains'' is of two kinds, erotic and aesthetic; one in the company or memory of Michael, one in the elaborate and sensuous arrangement of words. We feel this second delight every time she finds a new rhyme for her preposterously, playfully complex scheme. It is one we can share directly; she teaches us to love words.

These are the pleasures, as it were, of two different people (perhaps sharing the same name—the question of autobiography is no more pertinent than in Shakespeare's sonnets), a writer and a lover. Yet in the singer, can we distinguish writer from lover? The pleasures are similar, as any eroticist of textuality will attest. Each becomes a metaphor for the other so easily in the song that we hardly notice. Our taste for the one pleasure leads us to appreciate the other, and Mitchell exploits this progression to make an ordinary love story ''bright.''

The verses are not in first person, as one might expect, but in second person. ''You'' surely does not refer to the listener, about whom all the song's statements are untrue. The ''you'' whom the singer addresses is that other self, the lover of Michael. It resembles the ''you'' we use colloquially for the (ostensibly) impersonal ''one,'' a ''you'' that does and does not mean ''I.'' These two selves in the song share the same faculty of memory; this doubleness, playing itself out, is what draws us along from one to the other kind of pleasure and of experience.

The refrain reverts to first person. This does not represent a shift by the singer from talking about someone else to talking about herself; the "you" in focus in the verses is herself, while the "you" addressed here is Michael. Yet the refrain does bring us a sudden sense of intruding on privacy. This paradox is one whose twists we negotiate often in speaking to each other. Though the singer apparently sings the verses to her (other) self—"Michael wakes you up with sweets," she remembers—it is easy enough to imagine these recollections being addressed to Michael or to the audience instead. The resulting tone would be only slightly coy. The refrain, on the other hand, though ostensibly addressed to Michael, seems rather to be internal meditation, thought rather than speech—an incantation on behalf of unspoken desire. On the whole, the verses' apparent self-communion feels more public than the deceptively straightforward declarations of the refrain.

The balance between these two modes of address, each richly ambiguous, is vital to the tone of the song. If we were given only the refrain, we would be shut away from the experience of which it generalizes one element; the song would be merely oracular. On the other hand, if the refrain were missing, the distinction between the song's two selves would be too absolute, the singer's aesthetic distance making her sound a little smug. Though we might share the purely aesthetic pleasure of verbal manipulation, our indirect communication with the lover's pleasure would again be interrupted.

The refrain is, as always in songs, more intricately integrated than the verses can be, with their different words set to the same music; and Mitchell uses this extra measure of control to underscore the rhetorical shifts in person and in tense. While the verses are recollections clothed in a historical present, the refrain presses into an indefinite but passionately imagined future. The binding together of the words becomes still tighter—the connection between the lines "Go where you will go to / Know that I will know you" exceeds internal rhyme. These lines are set to a melodic sequence like the one in the second quatrain of the verse. But now the downward transposition is diatonic (remaining within the key), which replaces uncertainty with confidence; and the melodic intervals are much larger, more ardent than before:

go where you will go   to   know that I will   know you

Ex. 5.14. "Michael from Mountains": refrain, measures 3–6

The last line of the refrain is set apart from the rest rhythmically, with a strong rhetorical effect of contrast.

some day   I   may   know   you   ve - ry   well

Ex. 5.15. "Michael from Mountains": refrain, measures 7–10

Isolating "Someday" between rests, setting it to an ascending pair of notes, and making those notes fall (for once) directly on the second and third beats of a measure, all help to give the words that intensity of longing and determination which the context demands for them.

The separation of the last two words from the rest of the line is especially striking at the end of the song, where Mitchell repeats the final line with one change: "Someday I *will* know you very well." Previously, "very well" has simply intensified "I may know you." But at the end those two words follow the rest of the line after a pause sufficient to make us hear them alone, denoting temporary and reluctant acceptance. The fact that songs have no punctuation sometimes liberates their words from the chore of meaning singly. (Lineation can play the same liberating role in verse.) In the last lines of the last verse, the singer has told herself, "You want to know all / But his mountains have called so you never do." Now the lover acknowledges the setback, but refuses to equate "never do" with "never will."

Mitchell's deftness with the literary strategies of voice and address may tempt us into the banal error of calling her (honorifically) a poet. But she is in fact a songwriter, and in songs "voice" is always also literal. In "Michael from Mountains" and the rest of *Song to a Seagull*, Mitchell's pure delivery keeps this fact discreetly at the margin of our attention. To hear how powerfully the physical presence of the voice can interact with its metaphorical extensions, we must turn to a different sort of song. We can begin by thinking briefly about the relation between voice and Voice, between the sound and the things the sound can be made to mean.

———————

Bobby McFerrin's best album to date is called *The Voice*.[14] The title risks preposterous pretension, which perhaps no other contemporary singer could justify in such multiple and subtle ways.

First and most obviously (and perhaps least helpfully in redeeming pretentiousness), McFerrin is a stunning vocal technician. As compared with most modern musical instruments, the human voice takes more easily to sustained, fairly slow melodies rising and falling within a relatively narrow range. (Even "The Star-Spangled Banner"—an octave and a half from top to bottom—strains most throats.) McFerrin, in contrast, has recorded a version of Bud

Powell's "Hallucinations." Powell was the first great Bebop pianist—meaning, among other things, that his solos, and the tunes he wrote to solo on, move fast enough to have daunted other pianists. Technically, the piano is one of the fastest instruments. Not only does McFerrin sing Powell's melodically and rhythmically tricky melody, and improvise a still more intricate solo of two choruses; in the recording studio he also overdubs himself singing an accompanying line whose timbre is that of a string bass and whose range is a high string-bass range, more than an octave below the lead.

This multitracked recording, however, though by far the most exciting piece on his earlier album *Bobby McFerrin*, does not speak to the real miracle of McFerrin's singing, which is how much he does with how little. *The Voice* was recorded entirely in concert, the singing entirely unaccompanied. Sometimes he sings tunes, sometimes songs; but his voice is never simply (as ours can seem to us in the daily business of speech, and as the discretion of a performer like the early Mitchell can make hers seem) a vehicle for words. Sheer virtuosity calls attention to McFerrin's voice in itself. His charm as a performer is to seem merely the voice's custodian; so virtuosity becomes a form of modesty. McFerrin's first aesthetic gesture is to separate his singing voice from his individual self, to treat it as an instrument. (Classical singers do this, too, speaking never of "my voice" but "the voice," as dancers speak of "the body").

The next step becomes clear as soon as we recall how the term *voice* is most frequently used in music. A "voice" in this sense is one of several separate musical lines, as in a fugue in four voices. The history of the metaphor is obvious: Contrapuntal music began as vocal music, one singer (or more) per separate melodic strand. Once the contrapuntal style matured as an instrumental medium, keyboards became its natural home, as Bach's work abundantly shows; in that case, "voices" are distinguished by notation, and by very careful playing and listening. Sometimes counterpoint could be adapted to less obviously suitable instruments, to solo lutes and cellos and violins (Bach being again the master in each of these cases), even to solo flute (as in Telemann's flute sonatas). The main trick of adaptation is called *style brisé*, the broken style. If a single melodic line is made of phrases separated by large jumps in pitch, the ear interprets the phrases as belonging to different melodic lines, different voices. The literal human voice, however, seems ill suited to this ruse, because abrupt large shifts from one range to another are so hard to make accurately; some passages from Baroque choral works defy the compositional difficulty, but only by passing it along to the performer.

McFerrin's solo performance on public radio of Bach's Air ("on the G string") from the third orchestral Suite has become famous by word of mouth. On the record album, he uses *style brisé* on Paul McCartney's "Blackbird," singing both the voice part and the guitar part:

black-bird sing-ing in the dead of night

take these bro-ken wings and learn to fly

all your life

you were on - ly wait-ing for this mo-ment to ar - rive

Ex. 5.16. McFerrin's "Blackbird": first verse

In the course of this performance he whistles, imitates the rustle of a bird's wings, duplicates the sound of a studio echo-delay unit, and creates out of thin air an astonishingly complete tone poem.

In fact, McFerrin has an irrepressible tendency to turn himself into a stage full of people (and animals and things and instruments). The result is most spectacular when the juxtapositions are most quick and immediate. But listening repeatedly to the record, one is struck instead by the sheer multiplicity of voices he has at his command:

West African singing: "The Jump," "T.J."
String bass: "Blackbird"
Children's singing: "The Jump"
Yodeling: "Music Box"
Courting conversation (both sides): "I'm Alone"
African drumming: "T.J."
Jazz drumming: "Big Top"
Soul singing (in "I Feel Good" he imitates James Brown's voice, as well as bass, drums, and guitars)
Parodic minstrel-show singing: "Big Top"
Street talk (the rhythm, not the words): "El Brujo," "I'm My Own Walkman"
Baroque or Renaissance (portative) organ: "Music Box"
Miles Davis's trumpet with Harmon mute: "I'm Alone"
Someone else's Harmon-muted trumpet: "We're in the Money"
Guitars of all sorts
Jazz scat singing: "Donna Lee"

Scat singing—the nonverbal vocal imitation of jazz horn playing—is only one of McFerrin's voices; it is not the genre of his performance. In "A-Train" he does both scat singing and a marvelous parody of scat singing. The catalogue given here is far from complete, in either items or instances. Indeed, it is so short only because I have limited it to the most definite, more or less unmistakable items. Deliberately and with great precision, McFerrin takes on a repertoire of different voices. This is apart from his mining of various musical "languages" (Baroque, African, soul, Rococo, jazz).

Clearly we have arrived at yet another meaning of the term *voice*. We have returned somewhat closer to definitions I suggested in earlier chapters, a voice as a sentience or an intentionality unfolding in time. We are closer also to the conventional literary-critical use of the term; but as long as a performer like McFerrin is our object of scrutiny, the metaphor cannot sever its tie with the physical or recorded presence of the singing voice.[15]

McFerrin shows us two sides at once: A Bakhtinian dialogism of voices, like that of a novel or a city; and the bundling of them all into one Antin-like package standing alone on stage, seeming for all the world like an unequivocal lecturer. In his performances the contrast is sharp and stunning. Yet the same tensions are implicit in any vocal performance, however restrained by some performing styles. Especially in jazz singing, the physical sound of the voice has as much to do with meaning as do the words and the composed coordination of words and notes.

Joni Mitchell has a beautiful voice, which entails risks as well as benefits. Too easy a beauty entraps. A certain song demands certain tones and inflections from the voice; but on the other hand the singer-songwriter is inclined to shape songs to her own resources. The Roches' scrappy, flattened, precariously athletic voices perfectly command the range of tones their songs require: not just sardonic, but capable of pathos enriched by wry self-awareness. At the time of Mitchell's first album, it seemed that she would find a narrower and more conventional home among love songs and quiet character portraits. Only the intelligent exuberance of some of her lyrics saves most of those early songs from charming but unambitious prettiness.

Yet succeeding years produced records that explored a wider range. She found subjects for songs in parking lots and radios as well as flowers and seashells. Her musical backup expanded from her own acoustic guitar—always harmonically interesting, though it has never gotten much attention—to a full band of top-quality Los Angeles studio musicians, the instrumentation pushing out from folk styles toward the zone where rock and jazz overlap, the players beginning to take on roles beyond mere accompaniment.

Still, not much in this progress would have led most listeners to predict Mitchell's 1979 album *Mingus*. What was this blonde Canadian folksinger

ensconced in Laurel Canyon doing with an album about one of the most ag-
gressive black musicians in modern jazz? Apparently it was Charles Mingus,
the great bass player and composer, who initiated the contact with Mitchell;
he proposed a joint project (which did not work out), and asked her to write
lyrics for several of his tunes.[16] Though he died before Mitchell's album was
released, he followed its progress through all its early stages, and to some
extent collaborated with her. The record includes taped snippets of his conversation, a birthday party, and so on, as well as songs about Mingus and
songs that attempt to recreate something of his view of the world around him.

Fittingly, the last song on the album is one of Mingus's own compositions,
"Goodbye Pork Pie Hat," with lyrics by Mitchell.[17] The rhetoric of the choice
is complex. The "pork pie hat" is the one habitually worn by Lester Young,
the tenor saxophonist of jazz's middle years whose oblique phrasing and sound
paved the way for much of the postwar style that has become the mainstream.
Mitchell completes her tribute to Mingus by reworking his tribute to Young.
Not that she seems to be claiming a mantle. Though the words begin "When
Charlie speaks of Lester, you know someone great has gone," the song is not
chiefly concerned with a musical greatness passed from one jazz generation to
the next (and perhaps therefore by implication to Mitchell herself). Instead,
she focuses on the racial persecution by the American musical world of the
very people who created the only indigenous classical American music.[18]

Ex. 5.17. "Goodbye Pork Pie Hat": melody and solo choruses

Les - ter took him a wife arm in arm went black and white and

some saw red and drove them from their ho - tel bed

love is ne - ver ea - sy it's short of the hope we have for

hap - pi - ness bright and sweet love is ne - ver ea - sy street

now we are black and white em-brac-ing out in the lun-a-tic New York night it's ve-ry un-like-ly we'll be driv-en

out of town or be hung in a tree that's un-like-ly

to - night these crowds are hap - py and

loud chil-dren are up danc-ing in the streets in the stick - y mid -dle of the

night sum-mer se-re-nade of tax-i horns and fun ar-cades when right or wrong un-der ne-on

ev-ry feel - ing goes on for you and me the side-walk is a his-to-ry book

and a cir-cus dan-ger-ous clowns bal - anc - ing dread-ful and won-der-ful

per-cep-tions they have been hand-ed day by day gen-er-a - tions on down

After this point, Mitchell enters into a wordless exchange of phrases with Jaco Pastorius's electric bass and Wayne Shorter's soprano saxophone. Then she returns to the beginning melody, with this final new set of words:

We came up from the subway
On the music midnight makes
To Charlie's bass and Lester's saxophone
In taxi horns and brakes
Now Charlie's down in Mexico
With the healers
So the sidewalk leads us with music
To two little dancers
Dancing outside a black bar
There's a sign up on the awning
It says ''Pork Pie Hat Bar''
And there's black babies dancing
Tonight

In this song Mitchell shows that she can sing in a style that diverges sharply from her earlier work—though the inner core of the voice, its physical basis as it were, remains recognizable. (In the next chapter I will have more to say about vocal recognitions.) Innumerable popular singers have recorded songs that are jazz pieces in other mouths, or that have also been recorded in jazz versions, without sounding in the least like jazz musicians. Two factors identify Mitchell's ''Goodbye Pork Pie Hat'' with a jazz performance: the structure of the piece, and the ''instrumental'' use of the vocal line.

First, the structure of Mitchell's song is that of a jazz solo. Mingus's tune is basically a blues: a twelve-bar chorus, the harmony moving to the subdominant in the fifth bar. (This reference to the long development of pre-jazz adds another strand to Mingus's tribute, and Mitchell's.) The traditional blues harmonies are very much elaborated, though, and the tempo is very slow, so that the circuit of one chorus feels like an especially extravagant adventure. But Mitchell does not simply put words to the written melody, like a normal lyricist. Her song begins there, but then proceeds through two further choruses whose melodies differ entirely from the official tune but fit its distinctive harmonies—two solo choruses.

Second, Mitchell makes her voice sound as much as possible like a jazz horn. She emphasizes changes in timbre; for example, she treats changes between chest and head voice as a saxophonist might use shifts between registers, expressively, rather than trying to smooth out the transitions.[19] Unlike a European concert singer obeying a score, she bends notes and blurs their pitches. In this dialogue of voice and horn within a vocal jazz performance, there is some difficulty deciding which is a metaphor for which, because we have come full circle. Jazz horn players differ from ''classical'' players in their emphasis on individual sound, ultimately imitating the human voice; "telling a story through the horn" is the partly fanciful traditional phrase. But as the music came of age, jazz singing began to follow, not lead, jazz playing. Listening to Mitchell sing—though less obviously than when listening to McFerrin—we are bound to think of her voice not as a vehicle for words, but as a musical instrument, and one played in a jazz manner.

This jazz use of the voice makes its movements difficult to notate. One example among many: In the eighth measure, should the word "admission" be set to eighth notes (as I have shown it) or sixteenths? The actual stopwatch time probably falls somewhere in between, and the phrase's precise relation to the beat is especially difficult to determine in so slow a performance. The point is simply that notation, as always in jazz, works within very obvious limits of accuracy. It can certainly never substitute for a live or recorded performance, even with the same degree of satisfaction as in European concert music, or in "Michael from Mountains." Indeed, musical notation is never exact. My transcription of "Michael from Mountains," too, contains simplifications that in one sense falsify the music. When Mitchell sings "and the rain comes down," which I showed as ending in straight quarter notes, the voice's delays accumulate to make the last note nearly a beat late. Our notation developed as a way of publicizing the intentions of a composer. When it follows a performance instead, its responsibilities, like its uses, change.

Yet notation after a performance does have uses in clarifying what we hear in a performance. At the end of Mitchell's first chorus, I show the phrase "cellars and chitlins" set to five equal notes within a beat. Of course the equality is a mere artifact of notation. But the confinement of the whole phrase within one beat demonstrates graphically how Mitchell achieves a tonal finesse, making the phrase a wry, parenthetical comment rather than an angrily earnest one.

The solo is composed of tensions between low and high pitch ranges, between crowded phrases and sustained notes, and between a slow meter, loosely treated, and more swinging rhythms at twice the speed. Several of these contrasts come together in the three phrases that end the melody chorus ("black musician / in those days they put him in an underdog position / cellars and chitlins"). The first is stretched out so that it both begins before and ends after the official melody's phrase. At this point in the lyrics, standard syntax is breaking down—the chorus began with a full sentence, then a complex but dangling dependent clause, and here a single noun phrase, which the vocal phrasing lets linger in the air for comment or development. What follows "black musician" could logically be straightforward and bitter; but Mitchell instead gives us a sentence, light and brittle in tone, whose crux is a reference to Mingus's autobiography *Beneath the Underdog*. Much of the ironic lightness that makes the phrase effective comes from the sudden shift to double-time rhythms: the words "put him in" fall squarely on straight eighth notes, and the rest of the phrase syncopates the same doubled beat. Then comes a relatively long pause, and then the quick, dismissive "cellars and chitlins," sung as if it were quoted.

Shifts in timbre keep the vocal line continuously alive to its own meaning. In the second chorus Mitchell declaims "love is never easy" in a full-throated, tumbling phrase that revalidates the platitude; a measure later, she gives "bright and sweet" the breathy delicacy that once seemed her whole vocal style, but that acts here as one appropriate color from a much broader palette.

The contrasts deepen as we move from the first to the second solo chorus. The second begins with very slow, isolated pairs of notes. These are followed abruptly by a phrase that can cram "children are up dancing in the streets" into half a measure. The next phrase, again fast, climbs through an octave and a half, from the lowest to the highest note in the solo. The rest of the chorus concentrates on rhythmic variety, beginning with phrases (measures 6 through 8) that toy with the same few notes placed asymmetrically around the bar, and ending with one more long phrase ("perceptions they have been handed day by day, generations on down") that summarizes most of the solo's range of pitch and its vocabulary of double-timed rhythms.

Mitchell's vocal suppleness has a different purpose from McFerrin's virtuosity. McFerrin's voice is an actor taking on roles; his sincerity is an actor's. In a sense any singer, anyone singing a composed song, is taking on the role of that song. But this need not be the center of attention in the performance, as it usually is for McFerrin. Mitchell ventures on a more intricate and problematic authenticity. To begin with, she is taking on a role that she has not earned in the ways that it is often thought to require earning: She is not (that is: was never before seen as, and does not have the accepted background of) a jazz singer.

A more interesting problem—of which we have seen other facets before—arises when improvisation comes into question. This "Goodbye Pork Pie Hat" *sounds* like that ultimate feat, maybe impossible to sustain more than momentarily: improvised singing with words. But in fact, Mitchell's melody throughout the solo choruses is closely modeled on John Handy's tenor saxophone solo from Mingus's original recording of the tune.[20]

The precedents for this procedure—not like a standard lyricist putting words simply to a tune, but verbalizing an existing, previously improvised jazz solo on a tune—begin with Eddie Jefferson, sometime during the thirties or forties. He vocalized James Moody's recorded saxophone solo on "I'm in the Mood for Love";[21] King Pleasure heard Jefferson perform it, and himself recorded it with great popular success in 1952. Within a year several other singers were producing other works in the genre. One of the first was Annie Ross, whose clever "Twisted" was built on a tenor solo by Wardell Gray, and who then became one third of the most popular group in the field, with Dave Lambert and Jon Hendricks. More recent groups (Manhattan Transfer, the Ritz, Rio Nido) have extended the genre with the technical verve of a second generation.

Matching words and notes, in this style of lyric writing, differs somewhat from the usual mutual jiggery-pokery, the shaping of musical and verbal phrases to each other that we examined earlier in this chapter. Instead, the process requires the verbal artist to hear, in the musical phrases, some kind of meaning that can articulate a verbal equivalent. The equivalence must include compatibility of rhythm—the common ground of music and speech—but it may also grow out of the interplay of melody and harmony, and it must result in a suitable, coherent statement. This procedure turns the idea of "telling a story through the instrument" on its head, at the same time making it less fanciful.

Usually we think of meaning as governing tone. (He means that I should not go, so he uses a sarcastic tone in saying, "Oh sure, go right ahead.") Voice, tone of voice, is the vehicle of meaning; what is being *said* controls those secondary aspects of speech—pace, pitch, timbre—that can be imitated fairly directly by, say, a saxophone. But in the vocalized jazz solo, the songwriter turns this sequence around; it is the "voice" of the solo that shapes the other, now secondary aspect of actual vocal performance—the words.

Works in this genre can be seen as the singer's back door into jazz, after the technique of horn players has grown too formidable to be emulated and can only be copied. More constructively, however, the point of the genre is usually a tribute to the improviser whose solo constitutes the singer's material. (The Supersax harmonizations of Charlie Parker solos manifest the same tributary impulse in a more slavish medium.) Perhaps we can see Mitchell as letting this generic history add John Handy to Mingus and Lester Young as objects of her tribute.

But the point of her tribute to Handy is not very precisely to an improviser (though in later works such as his amazing performance recorded at the 1967 Monterey Jazz Festival, Handy certainly proved himself a fine improviser). His solo on "Goodbye Pork Pie Hat" shows at least one sign of having been worked out in advance: He opens his second chorus with long notes flutter-tongued, while Mingus plays matching tremolos on the bass. The coincidence—both of technique (Mingus rarely uses tremolos) and of timing (they begin exactly together)—is too close not to have been planned. Mingus often dictated solos to his sidemen; Handy's later records make his flutter-tonguing a kind of trademark. What these bits of evidence add up to is not perfectly clear.

Furthermore, Mitchell does not simply sing Handy's solo, as Jefferson and others sing the solos that are their material. She is not interested in the kind of accurate fidelity to the original that constitutes the standard in this genre. In several ways she reworks Handy's solo, adapting it for voice (raising a too-low phrase by an octave, simplifying his too-fast phrases at the end of the first chorus), clearing out some repetitious sections (near the end of the second chorus), adding phrases (the whole of "dangerous clowns / balancing dreadful and wonderful," as well as stretches of the melody chorus), and rephrasing rhythms in many places. She preserves the basic lines of Handy's solo, while freely altering the details.

We have reached a point where it truly seems not to matter whether the music is improvised or not. The heroism of improvisation is beside the point. Responsibility for the music is ineluctably multiple, and Mitchell never pretends otherwise. Quite the opposite. She does everything possible to enhance the dialogism latent in this artistic situation. Into the dialogue enter Mingus the composer, Young the inspiration, Handy the soloist, Jefferson and Ross and others the generic innovators, as well as Pastorius the bass player (electric, but impossible without Mingus's example of horn-like bass playing) and Shorter the saxophonist (soprano, but like any contemporary player well aware of Lester Young)—the ensemble not so much directed by as centered on Mitchell the lyricist, and Mitchell the performer.

On Equivocation

From time to time a poem or song makes the multiplicity of voice explicit. John Ashbery's "Litany" (printed in two columns "meant to be read as simultaneous but independent monologues") is a recent example. Thirty years ago W. D. Snodgrass's " 'After Experience Taught Me . . .' " enacted a fiercer confrontation.

Among songs, an obscure example is Mason Williams's "Three Song" (once recorded by the Smothers Brothers). In each of the three stanzas, a voice sings an apparently self-contained set of lines; a second voice sings a second set; then the two combine their verses into longer melodic and verbal lines. The gain in completeness is satisfying; even more, the tricky skill is impressive.

A more famous example is Simon and Garfunkel's "Scarborough Fair/Canticle," in which a new song of anger against war is entwined with an old song of bitterness in love.

Why is it so exciting to hear two songs (or read two poems) at once? How many voices do we hear? Ashbery says two; Snodgrass's speakers are mortal enemies. But Mason Williams puts together by surprise a single song; and by overdubbing, *both* Simon and Garfunkel, with their closely matched voices, sing *both* parts of their double song.

Six

Jazz, Song, Poetry: Toward Speaking For

In 1985 Larry Coryell and Emily Remler released an album of guitar duets.[1] Coryell helped pioneer the fusion of jazz and rock styles in the mid-sixties, and has developed that border area ever since. Remler, a more recently risen star, has more closely followed a jazz line of development. The two performed together at various concerts before going into the studio. Their common ground included a shared respect for past guitar masters and a repertoire ranging from jazz standards through Latin and flamenco-influenced originals. On the record, they both play jazz electric guitars (arch-topped, hollow-bodied) except on the two tunes written by Coryell, on which they play identical acoustic guitars (steel-stringed, graphite-topped Adamas models manufactured by Ovation, a company whose instruments Coryell has long endorsed).

It is usual in duet recordings to segregate the two players on the two stereo channels, adding a footnote on the album cover to identify who is heard on the left channel and who on the right, as if the musicians were sitting in separate booths—as, in the studio, they may well be. But as if to underscore the sense of confluence in this musical occasion, Remler's and Coryell's album, called *Together*, is mixed so that both instruments sound near the center, the reverberations of both guitars spreading out to the sides as the sound does for the audience in a live performance. The resulting ambience is in auditory terms more realistic. But a live audience can usually *see* who is playing what, who is soloing and who is accompanying. Listening to the album, we can identify which notes belong to whom only *by* listening—and listening not for the mere uninformative location of the sound but for its personality.

Neil Tesser, who wrote the liner notes for *Together* and praises not only the music and the musicians but also the engineering decision to mix the stereo this way, remarks that "it's not hard to tell these two guitarists apart." Nevertheless, he offers a crib for the hard of hearing by stating that Emily Remler "solos first on the opener, 'Arubian Nights,' " and referring to Larry Coryell's "break (the second solo) on 'Joy Spring'." But Tesser is wrong. On "Joy Spring," Remler does solo first and Coryell second; but Coryell solos before Remler on his composition "Arubian Nights."

How did I know who was who, more or less without thinking about it, the first time I heard the album? Only when I reread the liner notes and realized the discrepancy between them and my hearing did I begin to doubt my own recognition. After that, of course, I needed repeated listenings before I could feel absolutely sure.[2] Before thought tangled the millipede's feet, recognition was as immediate as my recognition of any familiar voice on the telephone or radio or tape recording, or floating in from the next room. With doubt, though, came analysis.[3]

In the intimate and immediate process of recognition, whether of human or of instrumental voices, we combine facts from both ends of the scale of auditory experience, from the millisecond to the minute—from the finest discriminations between atoms of sound that the ear can make, to the broadest patterns of repetition and variation that the memory can retain. When instead we seek to establish an identity for a problematic voice, or to confirm and explain an identification, we turn to some sort of conscious analysis; and since analysis gains depth and precision by sacrificing breadth, we are likely to focus on one end of the scale or the other. At one end, the details of sound can be subjected to experimental exegesis in the psychologist's laboratory. The critic, on the other hand, wants to address more macroscopic issues of style than duplicable experiments could comprehend. Someone who finds a unique oscilloscopic measure for the quality of Emily Remler's picking attack discovers a fact that will *only* identify her playing, not indicate its character or its coherence. So the critic naturally aims high. We try to name the aesthetic premises and decisions that define the player's style, and gather them into systematic characterizations and discriminations. More specifically, we select phrases that seem characteristic, and try to pinpoint the character they express. I began by transcribing all four solos, to set before myself exactly what the phrases were.

There are countless famous earmarks in jazz playing: Johnny Hodges's scooped long notes, Thelonious Monk's whole-tone runs, the public library of phrases to be mined from Charlie Parker, and so on. The student player learns these licks, and may come to distinguish the exact quality of a rising minor-ninth arpeggio played by Jim Hall from one played by Joe Pass. In one sense, then, a sufficiently extensive collection of techniques invented by or habitual to a certain player might be thought to define that player's style. By the same token, though, anyone equipped to make such a collection is probably equipped to duplicate it. Many jazz disciples learn their mentors' styles thoroughly enough to fool a listener. Duncan James's imitations of George Barnes are sometimes that flawless; Jon Faddis, who has since "found his own voice," began by digesting much of the sound and awesome technical flexibility of Dizzy Gillespie. Identifications based on "signature" phrases can be precise; but they can also be false.

Only Emily Remler, on this record, plays variations on this figure, derived from a technical exercise in slurring:

Ex. 6.1. Remler's phrase

Near the end of her second solo chorus on "Arubian Nights," she uses the
figure twice in different positions to underscore how the harmonies shift at this
point in the tune:

Ex. 6.2. "Arubian Nights": chorus 5, measures 30–31

A few measures later she uses just the first half of the figure, though for much
the same purposes:

Ex. 6.3. "Arubian Nights": chorus 6, measures 3–4

In "Joy Spring," on the other hand, halfway through her third chorus she
repeats the first half of the figure in such a way as to build up to the whole
again:

Ex. 6.4. "Joy Spring": chorus 4, measures 13–15

These examples share (aside from the left-hand technique itself) the common
function of outlining a harmonic progression. But they show very different
structural impulses: toward continuity, syncopation, and progression, respectively. It would be hard to say whether Remler's style is better defined by the
sameness or the difference, by consistency or variation.

Another kind of technique—based more in the right hand than in the left—
marks Coryell's solos. Once or twice in each solo, he releases nervous energy
in a way that at these tempos (♩ = 196 in "Arubian Nights," ♩ = 212 in
"Joy Spring") transcription can only approximate. In "Arubian Nights,"
near the end of his second and final chorus, he plays something like this:

Ex. 6.5. "Arubian Nights": chorus 3, measures 17–26

Similarly, he punctuates his second chorus in "Joy Spring" with this sudden shower:

Ex. 6.6. "Joy Spring": chorus 6, measures 18–19

And the first half of his next chorus is dominated by almost equally fast triplet runs.

Both of these stylistic signatures—extended slurs, prestissimo scale runs— have an exercise-based quality. They "lie under the fingers" for a guitarist after hours and years of practice. Yet they differ greatly in character: the precision and strength of the left hand required by the hammer-fingered slurs, versus the overwhelming blur of the speeding pick. One could begin to base a description of Remler's and Coryell's musical personalities on such differences.

But the picture is complicated by other, equally distinctive playing patterns. As far as I can determine, it was Larry Coryell who invented this flashing, incantatory riff, which he uses in both "June the 15, 1967" and "Good Citizen Swallow" on the Gary Burton Quartet's *Lofty Fake Anagram* album from 1968 (the third of Burton's albums on which Coryell played, and the second which led the jazz-rock fusion movement):

Ex. 6.7. "June the 15, 1967": chorus 6–7 break

Close similarity, both in sound and in finger movement, suggests that the player of these exuberant notes near the end of "Arubian Nights" is Coryell:

Ex. 6.8. "Arubian Nights": chorus 6, measures 9–16

—as Tesser assures us; but he also assures us that in "Joy Spring" the solo that includes this passage

Ex. 6.9. "Joy Spring": chorus 3, measures 16–24

is played by Emily Remler. In fact, Remler plays both of the solos that include the phrase that was "patented," as musicians sometimes say, by Coryell. Whether she is consciously quoting and extending those old, widely known Coryell recordings, or is instead developing what has become a standard guitar lick, even she could probably not be sure.

The undisputed guitar patent on octave double-stops is held by the late Wes Montgomery. So clear an influence is Montgomery on Emily Remler (through George Benson, through Pat Martino), and so far has Coryell's work over the last twenty years taken him from that jazz mainstream, that we might expect passages in octaves to mark Remler's solos. She does indeed use them frequently on this album as on others. But at many points Coryell seizes on the technique, a good odd instance being this striking passage from "Arubian Nights":

Ex. 6.10. "Arubian Nights": choruses 2 and 3

It is possible that performing with Remler reminded Coryell of stylistic materials he had not used for some time, to which he returned with new enthusiasm; but the strands of influence are too braided for this to be more than speculation.

The predictions about identity generated by these signature phrases turn out to be incorrect half the time—a result no better than random guessing. Adding to the inventory of both players' resources does improve the score. (Remler plays more extended, syncopated sequences; Coryell plays more repeated notes; and so on.) Yet these inventories are not only unreliable as stylistic touchstones, but also insufficient for stylistic definition. Large parts of each solo—including not only filling or bridging passages and half-idle pauses for thought, but also some of the most distinctive moments—cannot be assigned to either player on the basis of proprietary materials. Some are apparently brand new, thought up by Remler or Coryell on the spur of the moment. Others belong to a vocabulary either traceable to specific forerunners—Django Reinhardt, Pat Martino, Charlie Christian—or general to all players. When accompanying rather than soloing, both guitarists use a rich technique that combines punctuating chords and an almost independent bass line—a method that seems to have been invented in the fifties by Jim Hall when his guitar was the only harmonic instrument in the Jimmy Giuffre Three. Coryell plays the melody of "How My Heart Sings" in fingered harmonics, which Tal Farlow developed in the late forties. Into their solos on "Joy Spring," each guitarist inserts one quotation, a device as old as jazz, developed into different forms of wit by various players; Remler and Coryell declare their allegiance to Bebop by quoting, as Charlie Parker so often did, not show tunes or the jazz repertoire itself, but that common fund of music we all know well enough to make it nearly anonymous: Remler, a few bars of "The Irish Washer Woman," and Coryell, an answering phrase from the English round "Christmas Is Coming."

As I marshal my reasoning, then, my argument that Tesser must be mistaken in his identification of the soloists on "Arubian Nights," I find that however long I pore over my transcriptions my real evidence belongs to the original experience of hearing, and resides in details that remain unexplainably minute. An exasperated voice saying, "Just listen!" keeps interrupting what strives to be generalized stylistic analysis.

Not that this recognition is a purely sensory act, distinguished from intellectual activity by its perfect immediacy. Some of the preconditions include my having listened to both players almost since Coryell began to record, and my having transcribed solos by other players with different styles. Most relevant of all may be the fact that I play jazz guitar. I have a sense, not only of how the left hand feels while fingering a certain series of notes, but of how the right hand plucks a string or moves a plectrum—the infinitesimally graded differences in pressure and timing and position, in both hands, that bring the guitar as close as it can come (without electronic manipulation) to the varying resonance of vowels in a human mouth. It is more difficult for me to identify pianists; it requires more conscious thought, more deliberate attention. Even identifying trumpeters or saxophonists is a less immediate act for me, though those instruments bear a warmer relation to the voice than does the guitar. It is possible that if I were mute I would find recognizing my wife's voice a more intellectual exercise than I do—that some ground of possible imitation underlies our finest, most unconscious knacks of knowing. We know the feel of our voices in our mouths, and can therefore imagine ourselves possessing the mouth that produces a different voice.

If "voice" is an idea about style as personal (identifiable, individual, authentic), it has two inseparable but logically distinct aspects; for the jazz player we can think of them as *sound* and *invention*. To identify a player, we consider how harmonically adventurous and melodically cogent and rhythmically alert the improvisation is; and we listen to him or her making the notes. (The balance between sound and invention is altered, not very subtly, by the fact of recording, which on the one hand alters and distances the sound, and on the other hand emphasizes invention by making it possible to study the solo.) Tesser's descriptions of the two players quite properly combine these aspects. He calls attention to Remler's "fuller, rounded tone," and he also observes that "she rarely plays a note that's rhythmically out of place. Coryell, on the other hand, has always maintained a noticeable twang to his guitar sound, in deference to his rock 'n' blues roots; what's more, his solos are rhythmically quirkier, wilder." Remler's rhythmic precision feels willed, a result not of abandoning herself to the music but of riding it with superlative control; every conclusion she reaches is airtight, every challenge definitively met, every flight of fancy solidly rooted. Coryell, on the other hand, ranges dissatisfied through his choruses, all bravado and trial; sometimes he leaves a gesture sketched, unfinished, as if its conclusion were too obvious.

The danger is that such summaries may come no closer to defining individual style than describing Robert Frost as a poet of cagey wit who writes moralized rural landscapes—a description that fits Andrew Marvell about equally well. In further refining my descriptions, I would be abstracting more and more distantly from the music. Nor do the generalities prevent Tesser from making (unless it is a slip of the pen) his outright mistake in identification. The descriptions come after the fact of recognition. They would not be likely to help another listener very much in learning to tell the two players apart. The audience that can be informed and pleased by Whitney Balliett's impressionistic descriptions of jazz players' characteristic solos is not an audience that does not know the players' styles, but one that has not made the reasons for the recognition conscious. Stylistic analyses can substantiate and help explain recognition, but not initiate it or prove its correctness. Listening, analyzing, and recognizing reinforce each other: We hear the details of touch, abstract from them an image of personality, listen through that filtering image to further details, refine the image, and so on. Analysis traces or imitates the path of the listening mind as it sorts the auditory world into identifiable persons.

When we return from instrumental music to song, we find that recognition partakes still more of our daily skill in knowing each other. This is the fun of

"Dida," a pleasant, wordless interlude in Joan Baez's album *Diamonds and Rust*, on which she is joined by Joni Mitchell. Baez's voice is unmistakable in its strength and characteristic vibrato; Mitchell's has a distinctive throatiness and vertiginous sense of range; both voices are as familiar to a generation or more of listeners as those of presidents and TV anchor men. In "Dida," they exchange statements of the brisk, sentimental melody, and then entwine comments on each other's brief improvisatory phrases. The fun, that is, consists in our having to pay attention so as to know who is singing, but not to endure great difficulty at it.[4] The reason for this relative ease is not so much that Baez and Mitchell are better known to most of us than Remler and Coryell, but that these are literal voices, not translations of the immediate human reality of voice into an instrumental extension.

Another tune from Baez's album reinforces the point, yet complicates it. In one stanza of Dylan's "A Simple Twist of Fate," Baez—whose relation to Dylan is old, famous, and subject to glancing and direct comments throughout this album—mimics Dylan's singing. The mimicry is obvious; yet Baez cannot possibly make her voice sound very much like Dylan's. Instead, she employs the usual tools of parody, imitating the most distinctive elements of Dylan's vocal style: the speech rhythm breaking across the musical meter; the free treatment of pitch halfway between the nonce tunes that help encode the meanings of speech and the sustained curves of chant or song; a hint of Dylan's nasal tone. When a singer's voice masquerades, it does not fool or confuse us, but it renders our act of recognition double: We hear Baez *doing* Dylan.

Tom Waits's song "A Sight for Sore Eyes" realizes some of the serious dramatic potential implicit in this method of vocal impersonation. The song is included in Waits's album *Foreign Affairs*,[5] which offers a number of striking experiments in diction and form. There is "Potter's Field," an extended, imagistic narrative chanted in a dreamlike gigantization of crooks' slang, with no definable melody and—very unusually in popular song—no regular rhyme. There is the almost-title song, "Foreign Affair," which uses an inflated polysyllabic diction to both mock pretension and insist on an absurd but irreducible dignity. There is a bar scene with Bette Midler; an impassioned love song addressed to the eponymous logo on Muriel cigars; and a Rabelaisian Beat road adventure culminating in a double-entendre version of "California Here I Come." All this zest is heightened by Waits's voice—a gravelly, half-lisping, surprisingly supple vehicle for tones ranging all the way from gross through sardonic to poignant.

Halfway through the album, after this voice is well established in our ears, Waits opens "A Sight for Sore Eyes" with a piano introduction that is a tinkling eight-bar quotation of "Auld Lang Syne"; then his playing shifts to the childish tidiness of the song's accompaniment, at once a waltz and a lullaby. (His own piano will remain the song's only accompaniment—as on the other most remarkable song on the album, "Burma Shave"—except for a discreet bass.) Singing across the tardy beat of the waltz, as if he could barely keep up with it, he begins the string of clichés that are the foundation of the lyrics: ''hey sight for sore eyes it's a long time no see / workin hard hardly workin hey man you know me . . .''[6] Waits is a master at the technique (familiar throughout twentieth-century poetry, rarer in song) of recontextualizing platitudes for ironic or revelatory effect. It goes along with his ear, which Williams might have appreciated, for a kind of debased patois that has been utilized only marginally by literature.

What is striking about this opening verse is that the voice in which Waits sings it is not his own. To explain how the physical sound of a voice can be recognizable (we never doubt that it is Waits singing), and yet different from itself (the personality is not the one we hear consistently in the rest of the album), might be a task for the scientist of vocal production. Listening, we simply hear the difference. The voice masquerades, not in its essential qualities (just as Baez cannot really sound very much like Dylan), but in its gestures of personality. The physical voice remains the same; but Waits uses it to *do* a character.

If the voice is not Tom Waits's, whose is it? Supposing that a voice projects, among other aspects of personality, a somatic type, we can hear this one as belonging to a man of a certain age and girth, settled into a certain degree of dissipation and failure. Waits revives the word *palooka* to describe him (though in his mouth it describes the others in the bar where we find him). He is, as he says, ''half drunk all the time and i'm all drunk the rest,'' maudlin, vain, pathetic; he thinks almost exclusively in clichés. He is a type.

That we assign the clichés to him rather than to Waits is the result, as well as one of the causes, of our distinguishing the character's voice from the songwriter's. This is the elementary function of what in poetry since Browning has been called ''dramatic monologue.'' Waits thinks in dramatic terms (especially in terms of the movies: the record sleeve speaks of ''I Never Talk to Strangers'' as ''co-starring'' Bette Midler). The monologue is a natural form for him.[7] In ''A Sight for Sore Eyes,'' the separation from the character in whose mouth the words are put is no subtle distinction like the one in ''Michael from Mountains.'' The writer stands as distant as the painter of portraits, not of self-portraits; and this distance is announced first by the very quality of Waits's voice, which he constrains to a mellow obesity belied alike by his other songs and his photographs. As for stylistic qualities more readily available to literary or musical analysis, they do not much help us in the fundamental act of distinguishing this voice from Waits's ''own''; instead they proceed, *after* we make the distinction, to inform us about the person being spoken for.

Elsewhere Waits has carried on formal experiments begun by Dylan: jamming long verbal lines into short musical phrases, opening out the almost universal foursquare quatrains of popular song, delaying or crowding rhymes to make their recurrence less automatic and more expressive. But the form of ''A

Sight for Sore Eyes'' is as conventional as the lilt of the tune and its harmonization in thirds by the piano, or as the blandness of the clichés. All these aspects of dullness work to characterize the man we hear speaking. On the record sleeve the lyrics are printed as couplets, many of them with internal rhyme (''guess you heard about nash, he was killed in a crash''), emphasizing even more than the usual typography of quatrains the straightforward rigor of the form.

In fact, the rigor is even greater than convention would lead us to expect. Alliteration and assonance abound (''hey sight for sore eyes it's a long time no see''), along with more complex morphemic repetitions (''and hey barkeep what's keepin you keep pouring drinks''). While most songwriters allow themselves great liberty in rhyming (as Waits does elsewhere, sometimes suggesting Wilfred Owen's slant rhymes), the refrain of this song emphasizes a strict rhyme: ''keep pourin drinks / for all these palookas hey you know what I thinks.'' In this rhyme, where a formal nicety enlists a grammatical solecism, the songwriter and his invented character meet head on.

Again, more strikingly than in ''Michael from Mountains,'' where the separations are more tentative, our consciousness of Tom Waits as a performing artist—the singer as well as the writer of his song—adds a kind of shadowy third level to the complex of identities confronting us. Not only does he sing, and in the manner of his singing present the dynamic relation between the song he has written and the character he has created, but he plays the piano. (Here is the commonplace miracle that in music one may *accompany oneself.*) The gentle, inexorable sound of that accompaniment becomes the most constantly eloquent commentary on the whole monologue.

Contempt is not what we finally feel; the character is *not* a type, though his ability to express an individual self is severely limited—so limited that it becomes the job of the song to do it for him. Our recognition of that personal uniqueness, despite the limitation, is partly the result of eloquent simplicities scattered here and there among the verbal detritus. The penultimate stanza, about Nash's death, is the most oddly powerful, at least as sung (like most good lyrics, it looks irredeemably flat and awkward on the page):

> guess you heard about nash he was killed in a crash
> hell that must of been two or three years ago now
> yea he spun out and he rolled he hit a telephone pole
>   and he died with the radio on

The farce of the opening internal rhyme is minutely undercut by the hint of automotive nostalgia in Nash's very name—even the most blatant of lines has its quirk. The next line reminds us how intermittent is the speaker's contact with such old friends as he is addressing. The diction of the third line (''spun out'' and ''rolled,'' and especially the grammatical identification of the car with the driver) evokes the macho romance of cars even while the context freezes the bravado. The chill settles most in the rhymes, whose closure is satisfying, reductive, funny, and horrifying. And the last line, whose disavowal of rhyme helps give it the isolated timelessness of an epitaph, achieves the song's height of improbable, unsentimental poignancy. By this point in the song we have advanced at least from contempt to compassion.

Marvelously, we do not remain even at that half-comfortable distance. The breaking point in our detachment comes in the last repetition of the refrain. Any singer is likely to vary his or her delivery of a refrain, often altering the last occurrence, especially, in the direction of speech rhythms (as Mitchell does in "Michael from Mountains"). So does Waits here. But much more strikingly, his vocal mask slips for just a moment; on the word *palookas* his own voice, the one we know from the rest of the album, breaks through the donned voice of his character. Suddenly, momentarily, the distance among character and writer and listener that makes dramatic monologue possible, and is made possible by it, collapses, as if an actor caught sight of himself in a mirror. Here is the moment—perhaps unexpected in a song like this—where Aristotelian pity for undeserved suffering (who deserves to be as pointless as this speaker?) is joined by the consequent Aristotelian terror for ourselves. The voice becomes the vehicle of imaginative identification.

That we use the metaphor of voice in talking about poems suggests a powerful belief in language, a belief that we *are*—even more than we are what we say— how we sound in saying it. Hence the injunction to young poets to "find their own voice," a formula that also acknowledges the difficulty of transferring vocal identity to the foreign medium of print. Yet the dramatic monologue, more than any other poetic mode, confounds this simplistic faith in the individual lyric voice.

With regard to monologue, the whole situation of poetry differs markedly from song. Written poetry has no physical voice to act directly on our hearing, and no immediate sensory recognition takes place. All our discriminations among characters, narrator, author, and whatever other entities we need to posit in reading, derive from the mute, unifying facade of print. Voice, in poems, has to be constructed or reconstructed by a reader's imagination. The relation between the reading imagination and the printed material on which it dwells is dynamic and ambiguous; and so is the result. Because of this fluidity, a written monologue can exfoliate in more directions than a song.

Dramatic monologues remind us forcefully that the meaning of what is said depends on who says it.

An ordinary man, though, a man like me
eats and is full.
Only God is never satisfied.

These words change in tone when we locate them at the end of a poem called "The Good Shepherd: Atlanta, 1981."[8] To speak of "irony" is not sufficient. Print is both the most impersonal and the most intimate home of language. It belongs to nobody, is a thing; yet in reading it, with the imaginative and prosodic attention proper to poetry, we adopt it, as if we find ourselves speaking the words in order to understand them. Whether we read aloud or subvocalize or listen only to a voice in our minds, we somehow make the words ours before we can assign them to anyone else. To find the words of a child murderer in our mouths produces no simple revulsion, but a network of forces that includes the most intricate sympathy. Poems that are more purely lyric do not thrust but ease us into adopting an alien point of view, which we identify as belonging to the poet; dramatic monologues divide us more aggressively from ourselves.

To begin with, then, the poet must include among the opening strategies of a dramatic monologue some way both to raise and to solve the basic question of who is talking—to alert us that it is not the poet's own voice, and to give us a way to identify whose it is. Browning uses his titles: "Soliloquy in a Spanish Cloister" tells us most of what we need to know before we begin; "My Last Duchess" requires an extra deductive step; "Andrea del Sarto" and others give us the sop that most readily, if often meaninglessly, satisfies our curiosity: a name. This tradition of the packed, informative title is carried further by Eliot ("The Love Song of J. Alfred Prufrock") and Pound ("The River Merchant's Wife: A Letter").

Among contemporary poets, no one has more whole-heartedly embraced the dramatic monologue than Ai. Her fourth collection, *Sin*, is all monologues, though they vary widely in kind and method. In most of them, the titles still set the stage and name the player: "The Journalist," "The Death of Francisco Pizarro," "The Priest's Confession."

But some of Ai's poems enact a more delicate gambit. The title of the first poem in the book, "Two Brothers," sounds blandly generic. When we come in the sixth line to "Death, Bobby, hit me . . . ," the bell may or may not go off; even if we do leap to a name for the speaker at this first hint, we have already absorbed a certain amount of poetry ("You swim toward me out of sleep / like an eel") that quarrels with the image of him we bring with us out of history, because the intimacy of the language is so ahistorical. Seven lines later we get "Dallas. Dallas"; four lines after that, "John-John," and then "the White House." Though "Jack Kennedy" does not name himself until the third and last section of the six-page poem, we know him well before.

Our identification, while founded on piecemeal induction from fragmentary associations, is bound to come to us at one of these points suddenly, as a whole. In that respect it resembles our recognition of a human voice. Because it is delayed, it reaches us together with the shock of our *not* having recognized the voice. Even in the act of identifying the speaker, we are made conscious that the language is owned doubly, by the poet who makes it and by the character who belongs also to the independent world of history.

Nor is the language simply double. Reading a page, it is only by some kind of factual or stylistic analysis, conscious or subliminal, whose object is not a human gestalt but a poetic one, that we can identify anybody. This constraint seems quite dreadful in the abstract; but it becomes a condition of freedom, in which awareness can shift from one fictive self to another, the poet's own hypothesized self being perhaps not even the first among equals, but the most muted. While the natural condition in jazz is dialogue, and in song at most two or three voices can be split out from the sensory whole, poetry in its very silence tends (despite Bakhtin's opposition of it to the novel) toward dialogism.

The subtle uncertainty about ownership of the language in the first lines of "Two Brothers" (the subtitle, "A Fiction," helps to detach the voice in our minds from the poet, but not to settle it elsewhere) allows the words to hover among possible voices. This somewhat resembles our hearing both Waits and his character in "A Sight for Sore Eyes," or Mitchell and hers in "Michael from Mountains." But the second section of Ai's poem redoubles the ventriloquy: It is entirely quoted, by Jack, from Bobby (" 'I have this dream, Jack,' you say"). To quote the end of the section requires quite a bouquet of punctuation: " 'with nothing to say to anybody, / except, "My brother is the moon." ' " At this point we comprehend Jack, through Bobby's feeling about him in his dream, as he recounts it, as Jack understands it in quoting it, as we hear him speaking through several decades of our factual and mythic knowledge of Jack Kennedy, including our awareness that they are both dead. And this account does not include Ai's own intensity of selection and linguistic brilliance.

This layering is a kind of realism. Our consciousness is shaped by surrounding consciousnesses. (Bakhtin: "The ideological becoming of a human being . . . is the process of selectively assimilating the words of others."[9]) The ability to reenact this becoming, or at least to present its result without badly oversimplifying, is a strength of the dramatic monologue; and the distance and neutrality of print are its most efficient medium.

In these poems it is not Jack or Bobby Kennedy talking, or Pizarro or Joe McCarthy or Robert Oppenheimer; no one is talking; anyone might be. Identifying the speaker depends on facts, on statements we can somehow be sure the poet would not make, on names and other externals. All Ai's poems in *Sin* are marked by this dramatic externality. The speaker is always, whether a known historical figure or not, involved in named historical events (as in "The Journalist," "The Detective," "Elegy," "The Emigre"). Even the most anonymous speeches are carefully linked to history; the second stanza of "Immortality" begins with mention of the Great War. The one poem apparently spoken by the poet without the mediation of an invented character ("Conversation / For Robert Lowell") is addressed to the famous dead poet. (The following and matching poem, "More," is "For James Wright"; but it is apparently spoken *by* Wright, not to him.) But as I noted earlier, this historicity that Ai uses to anchor the poems is constantly undermined by the quality of her vividly metaphorical language, which adopts from surrealism an insistence on the untranslatable primacy of internal experience. The question of whose experience is enacted, in whose interior the language reverberates, remains in flux as we read:

> I stare at myself in the mirror:
> Jack Kennedy,
> thinner now, almost ascetic,
> wearing the exhaust fumes of L.A.
> like a sharkskin suit,
> while the quarter moon
> hangs from heaven,
> a swing on a gold chain. My throne.

No one is talking, including the poet, who is writing. Dramatic monologue creates tensions between our imagination of the speaker and our imagining of the poet's own speaking of the poem. When we seek, through the crowd, the poet's own "voice," we are "listening" for consistencies in the decisions of a writer who is attending, among other things, to "sound." If my quotation marks are to be denied at all—if the metaphor of voice in poetry is to have any sensory substance—we must not only assign the speech to a speaker, but imagine the sound of the words and assign the sound to an imagined mouth. If the sounds show consistencies from poem to poem, we assign them to the poet, and hear the other voices as *quoted* by her. Lifting written words into sound is the province of prosody, and we turn naturally to the details of versification in order to characterize the poet's voice.

Throughout *Sin*, Ai sticks close to a form depending on variable but fairly short lines, divided according to syntactical boundaries, so that the lines do not call much attention to themselves as lines:

> I lie on my daughter's body
> to hold her in the earth,
> but she won't stay;
> she rises, lifting me with her,
> as if she were air
> and not some remnant
> of failed reeducation
> in a Cambodian mass grave.

> ("*The Detective*")

But if one does stop to examine the lines, they reveal care. Each adds a measured gesture to the developing sentence, changing our understanding of the lines that precede it. Sometimes, most conventionally, the line breaks isolate a constellation of images ("baseball, hard work, beer halls"); sometimes a quasi-apothegm ("I gave up music for Justice"); sometimes a tune of phonemes ("a shoulder / death has whittled thin and sharp"); sometimes a common phrase shocked into intense puzzlement ("You know what I mean"—which suddenly seems logically impossible). We might be able to recognize the poet in an unidentified collection of such lines. A poet's particular verve in the making of lines can function as a kind of hallmark or signature—or voice. The rhythmic and phonetic orderings that we gather under the name of prosody constitute, once print has become the medium of poems, the remaining link between the poem and the human voice. This link may be seen as the characteristic that distinguishes poetic from nonpoetic writing; in any case, it is the closest thing to a literal "voice" in a poem.

Yet surely Ai's "voice" as a poet is characterized by larger choices: by the title of the book and the vision of historical existence it implies; by the violence of her images; above all, by what characters, what voices, she chooses to *do*. Several of her dramatic speakers are villains (like many of Browning's); many are victims—including some of the villains. These choices give the poems a moral or political point. The act of choice gives the poems their ethical character; and surely ethical character is a central feature of the speaking personality we seem to prize when we venerate "the poet's voice," an individual voice, a voice that demands to be heard. Ai's insistence on historicity is both a poetic device—the establishment of a common ground on which to know and distinguish speakers—and a framework for the political import of her book, part of what makes her an audible "voice" in contemporary poetry.

So the voice of the poet is both one and many. It comprises both sound (imaginatively reconstructed) and statement. It is both larger and smaller than the voices of her characters, to be found in both the grit they are made of and the stuff they breathe, as fish are composed largely of water.

The defining task of political poetry is to speak out against wrongs inflicted on ourselves or others. The task for white male middle-class poets in the United States after the Second World War is to speak for others: for those who have been silenced by governments, by imprisonment, by starvation, by death.

The rhetoric required by this kind of political poetry is different from the rhetoric natural to revolutionary poetry, poetry that seeks to liberate a group to which the poet herself or himself belongs. (Of course, liberating others is a way to liberate oneself; indeed, my point is that for people with no apparent need for liberation, that may be the *only* available way.) To speak for someone else is ventriloquy; and everything we have seen about the dramatic monologue makes it the obvious form for an other-directed political poem. The poet, for whom it is physically safe to do so, will project himself imaginatively into the situation of the oppressed person, using the poem to say what that other cannot say aloud. The poem will be called, for instance, by the name of a governmentally murdered Chilean songwriter, Victor Jara, who will be made to say ''I'' throughout.

But something will go wrong. Even if the North American poet (against rather steep odds) can construct a plausible speech for his Chilean counterpart, one that both captures Jara's individuality and treats him as representative, the poem still threatens to be condescending. After all, the indignity of being forcibly silenced is more aggravated than corrected by having someone else take over one's speaking, put words in one's mouth, publicize a hypothetical version of one's feelings.

Ai's poems (especially those spoken by victims, such as ''The Prisoner'') avoid this trap by means of their ambiguous relation to historical reality. The speaker's situation is historically defined, but the language is so internal that it seems to conduct its business of disclosure below or behind consciousness, like a kind of body language. The speaker gives herself or himself away as if unknowingly; the poet proceeds on another level entirely, arranging, enabling; and the relation between them—though richly complex in its ethical features—remains innocent. Yet one result of this successful strategy is that Ai's poems are only secondarily political. Individually they are, as it were, antipolitical, not directed toward the world of historical interactions at all; only when we take a number of them together do the poet's choices of speakers accumulate into a political declaration.

Philip Levine's seventh collection is called *The Names of the Lost*[10]—a title that announces his intention to rectify forced silences. The cover photograph shows an endless line of refugees, and the titles of many poems in the book insist on the same passion for recollective redemption: ''No One Remembers,'' ''Another Life,'' ''On the Murder of Lieutenant Jose del Castillo by the Falangist Bravo Martinez, July 12, 1936.'' Perhaps the most successful political poem in the book is called ''For the Poets of Chile'':

Today I called for you,
my death, like a cup
of creamy milk I
could drink in the cold dawn,
I called you to come
down soon. I woke up
thinking of the thousands
in the *futbol* stadium
of Santiago de Chile,
and I went cold, shaking   10
my head as though
I could shake it away.

I thought of the men
and women who sang
the songs of their people
for the last time, I
thought of the precise
architecture of a man's wrist
ground down to powder.
That night when I fell asleep   20
in my study, the false
deaths and the real blurred
in my dreams. I called
out to die, and calling
woke myself to the empty
beer can, the cup
of ashes, my children
gone in their cars,
the radio still moaning.
A year passes, two,   30
and still someone must
stand at the window
as the night takes hold
remembering how once
there were the voices
of play rising
from the street,
and a man or woman
came home from work
humming a little tune   40
the way a child does
as he muses over
his lessons. Someone
must remember it over
and over, must bring
it all home and rinse
each crushed cell
in the waters of our lives
the way a god would.
Victor, who died   50
on the third day—
his song of outrage
unfinished—and was strung
up as an example to all,
Victor left a child,

a little girl
who must waken each day
before her mother
beside her, and dress
herself in the clothes   60
laid out the night
before. The house sleeps
except for her, the floors
and cupboards cry out
like dreamers. She goes
to the table and sets out
two forks, two spoons, two knives,
white linen napkins gone
gray at the edges,
the bare plates,   70
and the tall glasses
for the milk they must
drink each morning.

What is peculiar about the opening of this poem is the apparent contradic-
tion between a project of ventriloquial advocacy and a preoccupation with the
poet's own self and situation. The title's "for" is ambiguous; the poem may
be a gift to the poets, or a speech on their behalf. The two ways of *speaking
for* someone are distinguishable by the meaning of the pronoun *I*, as a context
establishes it; and here, Levine begins by playing a shell game. "Today I
called for you"—this poet called (cried out) on behalf of those poets; or he is
speaking in the voice of someone who called for them (demanded their presence, as if by habeas corpus); or he is speaking in their voice to some still-
undefined "you." The line is ejected into vacancy, where all the meanings of
"call" and "call for" yearn to be realized. When "you" gets its appositive
in the next line—"my death"—the question seems settled. We can all too
easily imagine one of the poets, imprisoned and tortured beyond endurance,
calling for his death "to come / down soon." Yet the following sentence reverses our conviction by making it clear that this is the North American poet
himself. He is only "thinking of the thousands / in the *futbol* stadium"; he is
not one of them.

This opening seems to retreat drastically from the political purpose we deduce so readily from the title. It is just the gringo poet, calling melodramatically for his death, trumpeting his worldweariness, the thousands in the *futbol*
stadium merely examples for him of the world gone to hell. If we feel sensitive
to the possibility of his patronizing those he speaks for, this blatant egoism
strangely disarms our suspicion. He shows us exactly why he is in no position
to condescend. Of course, this strategy also entails the enormous risk that we

may have no faith at all in his advocacy, his ability to see beyond his own walls. How the poem triumphs over that risk is worth studying.

After the first, declamatory sentence, Levine offers just enough details of setting to help us imagine the poet, not only writing, but speaking. The phrases "I woke up" and "and I went cold" can both be taken to describe internal, spiritual events; but they are first of all consistent with a physical situation. The concretizing continuation of each phrase helps: "I woke up / thinking of . . ." (a grander or more abstract word—"aware of," "appalled by"—would destroy the drab realism of the scene); "I went cold, shaking / my head as though / I could shake it away." All of this language works both to describe the scene and to express an attitude. But both the description and the expression are reticent, each function of the language guarded by the other from becoming too fixed. We are not very sure where this is taking place, and the poet's commitment to outrage is not very definite.

In the next sentence the egoistic frame ("I thought of") pales in the company of the story which the sentence's last phrases, by their sequence, reenact: "the precise / architecture of a man's wrist / ground down to powder." Already, then, the poet's frank insistence on his own presence and his own feelings is becoming a foil, and so a vehicle, for the more vivid imaginative reality of Chile. The poet's sense of himself initiates our attention, but relinquishes control of it.

This beginning of detachment continues with an odd slip in time. Though the opening of the poem takes place "today," line 20 continues, "That night. . . ." At first—perhaps until we have finished this sentence and the next— we are not sure whether we have moved backward or forward in time. In fact, these sentences retrace the same ground as the opening of the poem: the waking, the calling, the poet's surroundings. He goes over the path in more detail this time ("in my study," "woke myself," "the empty / beer can," "the radio still moaning"), but also at a greater distance. In speaking of "the false / deaths and the real," he comes to judge the first sentence of the poem in the expanding context. Egoism becomes capable of its own limits.

This distancing movement accelerates in line 30: "A year passes, two. . . ." This middle section of the poem is notable for a kind of canny vagueness: "someone," "a man or woman." It culminates in a conditional prayer: "rinse / each crushed cell / in the waters of our lives / the way a god would." The vagueness of these twenty lines serves not only as evocative, not simply to pump up the level of usable emotion, but also to prevent us from feeling certain about whether the implied events take place *here* or *there*. Levine's balancing act between the North American and Chilean settings enables him to speak of human conditions in terms that feel genuinely universal without falling into the merely generic.

The chief device of this balancing act is the shifting use of the word *must*, which occurs five times in the poem. In the first instance ("and still someone

must / stand at the window . . . remembering'') it expresses imagined proba-
bility. A dozen lines later (''Someone / must remember it over / and over,
must bring / it all home . . .'') the word has begun to take on a new insistence:
This memorial action is obligatory; the alternative is not unlikely but unthink-
able. Though the verbs governed by the auxiliary ''must'' are almost the same
(''must / stand . . . remembering,'' ''must remember . . . , must bring / it all
home''), the reiterated but unresolved images effect a complete transition between lines 30 and 50. ''Must'' is the perfect word to mediate the different
selves that Levine needs to project for his poem to work: The man waking
among ashes in his study, gradually bringing the reality of Chile home to himself, imagines what ''must'' be happening in that distant place; the poet writing for the poets of Chile insists on what ''must'' happen for the struggle not
to have been in vain.

The final section begins by seizing firmly on ''Victor, who died / on the
third day''—the name, the day, and the preceding line about ''a god'' all
suggesting that the poem has reached an apotheosis. Instead of using Victor
Jara as a dramatic mouthpiece, Levine has chosen to set him up—in a way
that precisely subverts the junta's intention—''as an example to all,'' not denying that he has been silenced but insisting on it.

As if uncomfortable with the static presence of a martyr, though, the poem
does not rest on Victor, but instead discovers its real focus of feeling in his
surviving daughter. The problems of the living are what hold Levine's attention. He sets the ''little girl / who must waken each day / before her mother''
before us very plainly: The clarity of her presence dispels the indeterminacy
of the middle section of the poem; and the vision achieves this clarity by means
of a language of uncannily scrutinized detail (''the clothes / laid out the night
/ before''). The image pivots on yet another ''must,'' with the added implication of compulsion. By now, ''must'' has accumulated its full potential
weight, suggesting not only the certainty of the vision, but also the terrible
rightness of tragedy.

The sentence that introduces Jara's daughter is followed by a short one
about her surroundings. ''The house sleeps / except for her'' seems to be a
metonymy, ''the house'' standing for the people in the house (such as ''her
mother''). But in the next clause, ''the floors / and cupboards cry out / like
dreamers.'' This is not gratuitous surrealism, but a return to the beginning of
the poem, to the language of sleeping and crying out. Now, however, the poet
is projected into the animated house of the little girl; he has become her setting
and witness, not mute, but ''crying out'' like a Greek chorus. Then the poem
insists again on the image of the girl with a powerful anaphora, not three but
''two forks, two spoons, two knives,'' finally returning to the milk which was
a metaphor for the poet's imagined death and now, becoming literal, gathers
''the real'' death into itself under a final command:

and the tall glasses
for the milk they must
drink each morning.

The poem's movement is expansive, the spiral beginning with a tight rota-
tion around the poet's own dream and reaching centrifugally toward imaginative realization of the plight of another person. This ethical movement is shad-
owed by the prosodic one: The points where lines and sentences end together
(which in most free verse act as this kind of punctuation) define a sequence of
sections twelve lines long, seven, ten, twenty, and twenty-four. While each of
these sections works itself out, we feel ourselves in the midst of a stream of
language; and the stream lengthens its fall each time, the momentum carrying
us finally beyond ourselves.

The particular kind of expansive movement of "For the Poets of Chile"
depends on its *not* being a dramatic monologue. In a dramatic monologue, the
speaker seems to be improvising, while the poet stands silently behind the
speech with the special responsibilities of constructing and revising. What
Levine does instead can be called "lyric" as opposed to "dramatic," but the
point is certainly not that he avoids speaking through a persona, a personality.
The poem is not monologic in that narrow and perhaps impossible way.
Rather, Levine emphasizes the immediacy of his speaking by not beginning
with the premise of a voice complacent enough to be projected clear of itself.
In fact, the expectations and ambiguities of the opening throw us back with
special force on a sense of the poet talking directly, naturally for himself. This
disarming, almost ingenuous approach allies him with Antin, and with Williams in "The Yachts"; we see the poet as discovering, like a soloist, the
difficulty of what he needs to say in the act of saying it.[11]

The differentiation of the voice of the poem, its discovery of its own potential multiplicity, is a point arrived at, not begun from. Such a poem demonstrates how political consciousness arises out of, and is ultimately identical
with, imagination. The success of this political poem is finally located not in
the case that it advocates—"Poetry makes nothing happen," says Auden—
but in the advocate. It changes us not by giving us a completed model to
emulate or renounce, a hero or villain, but by playing out a pattern of realization that we accompany and so imitate. An advocate is literally one called to
speak. "For the Poets of Chile" incorporates the story of the calling into the
act of speaking. It is as if Levine spent the whole poem becoming ready to
write a dramatic monologue.

Unlike a monologue, where the voices move around a stage whose boundaries are static, his poem's voice is a movement of the self outward. "The
ideological becoming of a human being"—a process that need not cease with
childhood or adolescence—requires the human being to submit to dis-integra-
tion, to the risky business of admitting another voice into the senate of the
self.

On Closure _____

In his book on Amiri Baraka, William J. Harris says that jazz is "anti-Kantian": the aesthetic and the political are inseparable. That is, jazz players do not divide the world in a way that makes "art for art's sake" a meaningful proposition. Jazz is quite capable of adopting aestheticist ideals—formal perfection, density, and (to detach the work in greater self-sufficiency) irony. But something in at least the *history* of jazz keeps subverting those ideals, calling attention to their limitations, exhorting us to free ourselves from canons of taste that constrict as they age, reminding us of a state in which we care less about selecting notes or words than about making them, finding them, producing them in good time.

In a letter to the editor of *Science News* (November 1, 1986) Homer B. Clay, an engineer, remembers a computer program "in charge of ordering material for producing relays and transformers [that deduced needs] from production forecasts and lead times. When the lead time for copper wire crept up from several months to a year and a half, the order rate was dutifully increased until the weight of the copper, stored off in a corner of the first floor of a 10-story building, caused the foundation to fail."

A different view of art commands it to look always outside the shell of immediate aesthetic context it makes for itself.

Seven

Jackson Mac Low: Beyond Identity, or Objectively Hazardous Procedures

IN the 1980 *British Journal for the Philosophy of Science*, Kathleen V. Wilkes published an essay entitled "Multiple Personality and Personal Identity," scrutinizing "the principle that all persons are or should be in one-one relations to bodies" (vol. 32, p. 332). She takes as her main example the carefully documented turn-of-the-century case of one "Christine Beauchamp," who under the analysis of a Dr. Prince eventually revealed six strikingly different personalities. Dr. Prince named five of them *B*I, *B*Ia, *B*IV, *B*IVa, and *B*II, and one called herself Sally. Their mutual relations were somewhat strained: "It was infuriating for *B*IV and Sally to find themselves in church, distressing for *B*I to discover a cigarette in her hand; for all it was tiresome and time-consuming to take up to six baths a day (each personality wanted two, and if Sally had bathed first, neither *B*I nor *B*IV would know of it)" (p. 344). The article is often quite funny, except as one enters imaginatively into the plight of these young women. If it then becomes horrifying—if terror joins pity—the final effect is nevertheless oddly liberating.

Wilkes demonstrates meticulously that the value of this extreme case does not depend on the status of "multiple personality" as a medical concept.

> The primary question (a question difficult to frame in a way that is not grammatically suspect) is: how many people was Christine Beauchamp between 1893 and 1904? It should be clear that it matters not at all for this question whether the condition of multiple personality is or is not something that psychiatry should recognise as such, whether it is or is not an avoidable phenomenon unwisely encouraged by undue use of hypnotism; however it is produced, so long as we accept the general truth of the data provided by Prince, the question of personal identity arises urgently. (*P. 338*)

What is at stake is not diagnosis, but the social constitution of the idea of selfhood. "Our moral, social, legal, institutional, political and medical practices" are based on an ideal of individual unity. Because the matching of one person with one body is "almost exceptionless we, conservative in such matters, take it not merely as the norm but also as the ideal" (p. 343).[1] But in the Beauchamp case "the concept of a person breaks down completely; for powerful and intuitive considerations"—which Wilkes details with admirable precision—"militate for and against both plurality and unity" (p. 345).

Wilkes deduces from all this that "persons are, very centrally and significantly, what society thinks persons ought to be'' (p. 345). In conclusion, she suggests that ''were we to weaken our requirements on unity—in other words, were we to acknowledge that persons are or might be less well integrated than [the Lockean principle of] 'unity of consciousness' seems to require—there might be several advantages'' (p. 347)—for instance in the fields of theoretical and developmental psychology. But the course of her argument implies ethical advantages as well, in being less sure that we act either as or toward undivided selves. When we hear the apparently adult man whining in a child's voice, or the prejudices of the parents speaking through their grown-up modern daughter, we can respond with less confusion and more effect to *all* the persons present than to a too sharply defined individual personality. In a broader arena, we might grow suspicious of ideas like the vox populi, or of claims that an election yields a ''mandate'' rendering the winner (chosen, often for negative reasons, by perhaps 51 percent of the 40 percent of registered voters who actually vote) a consecrated Voice of the People. Too simple views of our own selves invite us to identify too simply with groups, conceived in too monolithic terms, that claim our allegiance. And certainly the whole doubtful puzzle of identity raises profound questions for anyone who wants to know the place of the self in the arts.[2]

The key word in this chapter's title, *identity*, has had an instructive career. The *Oxford English Dictionary*'s headnote on the word's formation suggests that late Latin felt the need for a term expressing ''sameness,'' to split the difference, or fill a gap, between the words for mere ''likeness'' on the one hand and complete ''oneness'' on the other. (Greek and classical Latin had not felt this want; languages, like people, develop by distinctions as much as by accretions.) In this original sense, ''identity'' can refer only to two things, not to one. Something is identical to something else. This is the primary, comfortable meaning of ''identity''—an indication that two things are very much alike, perhaps entirely alike, perhaps even the same thing. It corresponds to the first of the *OED*'s two classes of definitions for the word.

''Identity'' comes from the pronoun *idem*, ''the same,'' but *idem* has no combining stem. Though etymologists disagree, the favored explanation is that ''identi-'' was invented from the adverb *identidem*, ''over and over again.'' This begins to suggest the *OED*'s second and far more perplexing set of definitions: Identity is ''the sameness of a person or thing at all times or in all circumstances; the condition or fact that a person or thing is itself and not something else; individuality, personality.'' Am I the same at all times and in all circumstances? ''I is another,'' said Rimbaud. It may strike us that two things are much more likely to be *identical* than is one thing to have an *identity* by this demanding rule.

Still more insistent meanings were invented for the purposes of algebra and logic. These of course arose later; they do not predate the middle of the nineteenth century. Even that mature confidence, however, can be seen to stagger in the *OED*'s last recorded instance of the word, from the 1889 edition of Fowler's text in logic: ''Amongst the assumptions or pre-suppositions of reasoning, I have not included the so-called Law of Identity; as to say that all A is A, or a thing is the same as itself, appears to me to be an utterly unmeaning proposition.''

Though Wilkes helps to explain the simplifying power of the concept of individuality, her essay seconds my suggestion that no fully recognized voice is ever single. This is what liberates us from the strictures of the *OED*'s second class of definitions. Perhaps the fact that the self is irreducibly a collection of more or less realized persons is the saving grace that allows any of us to have an identity.[3]

''For the Poets of Chile'' acts successfully as a political poem because its method is dialogic. Instead of declaring the empty victory of ventriloquism, Levine lets the divisions within his own frank voice develop toward imaginative recognition of another's condition; at the same time we see her voice beginning to create itself from the cacophony around her. As the Talmud says, ''If I am not for myself, who will be for me? If I am only for myself, what am I?'' Both questioning and celebrating what it is to be a self, Levine's example points the way through some of the hardest questions about poetry in contemporary America.

Jazz, too, calls for dialogic understanding. Beyond the applications we have already seen, Bakhtin's idea can help us unravel a serious problem that jazz presents to performers, listeners, critics, and their society.

As part of the transition to what is sometimes called modern jazz, the players who had been entertainers (often black entertainers of white audiences) began insisting on the seriousness of their art.[4] Furthermore, they discovered an ability and responsibility to make political statements. From its outset the Bebop movement was linked with the new postwar articulation of black dissatisfaction and anger. Jazz since the forties has frequently been explicitly or implicitly political in import. Charlie Haden's Liberation Music Orchestra was an interesting example in the late sixties—the white bass player championing Latin American revolution. But the chief politics of jazz has always been black, related to the long growth of the civil rights movement. The view of jazz underlying William J. Harris's work on Amiri Baraka and ''the Jazz Aesthetic''—that jazz works by inverting the assumptions of white music—makes it an inherently political music. This is a post-Bebop outlook, shaped especially by the central presence of John Coltrane during the sixties. More than anyone else, Coltrane became not just a musician, but a black hero, a spiritual leader. His importance, beyond his personal charisma and the intensity of his musical explorations, had to do with jazz as a unique product of African-American culture.

But this sense of black uniqueness could mean either that jazz was black people's most obvious contribution to the mixture that is American culture, or that jazz was properly an exclusive black mode of expression, a refuge and protest against the hostile white society. It could emphasize the communal roots of jazz music and its socially binding function; or by a slight shift of view it could underwrite black separatism and charges of cultural imperialism. Haki Madhubuti (the poet earlier known as Don L. Lee) declared in 1972 that "we made the music and the enemy stole it!"[5] The same conviction underlay criticism of Joni Mitchell for her *Mingus* album at the end of that decade. Amiri Baraka has consistently articulated the same charge, from his 1963 essay "Jazz and the White Critic" to 1987 in "The Great Music Robbery."[6]

A recent example of this argument made the news (on PBS, anyway—the MacNeil/Lehrer hour on February 25, 1987).[7] Paul Simon had just won a Grammy Award for his album *Graceland*, on which he used musicians from South Africa, making black township music (*umbaqanga*) the basis for new songs of his own. When he spoke to students at Howard University in Washington, D.C., he was taken aback by angry criticism: "I do not understand this at all," one student said. "There is no automatic cultural diffusion. It's nothing but stealing." Another asked, "How can you justify going there, taking all of this music from this country, coming back here and coming to my school where I pay my money and just tell me, 'Look, I went to your country, and I stole this stuff.' Too long, artists have went and stolen African qualities in their music."

It is tempting to argue that this complaint conceives music in monetary terms.[8] One might like to counter that music is less like money than like love, or language—things undiminished by being shared. Yet this argument falters badly. Money is not the only thing that can be stolen. Museums are full of artifacts which in their original context sustained the spiritual and perhaps the physical life of the people who made them; and sometimes even if money has changed hands, the acquisition looks awfully like theft. The idea some peoples have about photographs provides another example: that the photographer steals the soul of the portrait subject, who will therefore die, or steals the pictured cattle, threatening their owners with starvation. This is not *our* idea of photographs; but neither idea is subject to proof or disproof, and we have no clear right to impose ours on anyone else. Despite Simon's dismay, the student (an American whose own identification with Africans governs his phrase "your country") has a complaint that cannot be simply refuted or denied.

Theft is only one possible model of the transaction by which a white person comes into possession of originally black music. A related model might be that of purchase, but it applies only in a sporadic and shabby way, since black jazz musicians have habitually been cheated by a production and distribution system overwhelmingly controlled by white people. Another model would treat the music as a gift; yet it is often much clearer that the dominant white culture has *taken* something than that it has been *given*—the "giver" is rarely consulted. Alternatively, we could speak of cultural dissemination; but though the vagueness of the term (no one is doing anything, the culture just spreads) seems to deflect the accusation, this model absurdly loses sight of the particular actions of particular people that must be involved. Still another popular model is that of cultural borrowing. Certainly American music grows—enriches itself—by additions from jazz, South African umbaqanga, spirituals, Yiddish song, ragas, polkas, and so on; but since the music, once "borrowed," can never be returned again to the "lender," this model too reveals itself as self-serving verbal slippage.

One source of confusion in this question is the complex relation between cultural and political views of artistic (and other) activity. Paul Simon notes that the students' "view of the world is essentially political," whereas "I come at the world from a cultural, sociological point of view." Of course he has the political leisure to do so. Amiri Baraka, on the other hand, insists that the "appropriation" of jazz by white players and listeners "is illegitimate to the degree that national oppression still exists in the U.S. and to the extent that any black anything can be appropriated without exact reciprocal social compensation!" (*GMR*, p. 329). From his specifically socialist perspective, music cannot be separated from economics, or culture from politics: "Black music cannot be just 'American music' until all Americans have equality and democracy. Otherwise such a term is just more racism" (*GMR*, p. 331). He sees the music "in danger of being forced into that junk pile of admirable objects and data the West knows as *culture*" (*Black Music*, p. 18).

Though I (like Paul Simon) of course prefer some ways of thinking about white Americans' use of black music to others, the fact is that I have no standing to choose among them. I have no authority to declare for the culture as a whole, or certainly for African-Americans, that one view is more true than the others. Stripped of all the ready rationalizations, my position with regard to this original black music is simply that I've got it, and couldn't give it back if I wanted to. This gives me no more justification than the receiver of stolen goods who has spent the money.

Yet this account is inaccurate. First, it ignores the power that African-American culture has over, or in, American culture—a power that shows up as pervasive influence on language, dress, political styles, and so on, and that makes the adoption of these things something other than a matter of conscious personal choice. Second, it ignores the way people are formed, their "ideological becoming." If I possess this black music, it also possesses me. I have been changed by jazz; and the self that results is something I do have a right to talk about, and to utter in poetry and in music. (I also have a responsibility toward it, and toward its sources—which though it is not my topic here does not go without saying.) Jazz has become for me, as for a great many white Americans, a Bakhtinian "internally persuasive word," not an "authoritative word" I repeat by rote, but one that participates in the internal dialogue with which I identify myself.

Jazz itself is the product of cultural dialogue, born of African and European musics. American culture too is dialogic, as Baraka notes: "By the time the Africans no longer thought of Africa as home and had become African-Americans, the culture of the United States itself was *brownish*" (*GMR*, p. 328). Furthermore, jazz is inherently dialogic in its performance, which is its existence. Even Konitz, the virtually solo musician, plays in the midst of a historical echo chamber. The more typical jazz performance by two or more sections (rhythm and lead instruments), each comprising two or more players, is literally a dialogue and an example of social creation.

The cutting-session view of the jazz player—the champion, the one who lasts longest—may contribute something to the idea of the jazz hero, and that would make cultural interchange appear as a loss of personal importance. I take that as an excrescence of jazz, not its essence. The heroism of a Charles Mingus (or John Coltrane or Miles Davis) lies not in his dominating other musicians, but in his refusal to be satisfied for long by given solutions. He hears around and within him a babble of musical possibilities, and in his career commands them all into a constantly evolving sequence of new wholes.

The dialogic nature of jazz places it at the American center. It does not solve the problems of cultural imperialism or endemic racism, but it overarches them. By the same token jazz suggests—if not a responsibility—a source of strength and fertility for all the contemporary American arts. Direct parallels between music and poetry (language) are not simple to make.[9] But the two arts are historically intertwined, socially linked, and, as this book has tried to show, mutually illuminating. Written poetry is in a state of yearning for its lost sound, for its voice—which it seeks directly in our reading, but which most poets also seek indirectly in the offshoot of voice which is music; poets listen and try to learn. Part of what makes the best contemporary poetry unique, and makes America a genuine center of poetry, is the availability of a music in which the sense of voice is paramount, a "fusion of voice and instrument" (Harris, *The Poetry and Poetics of Amiri Baraka*, p. 15). In the lives of many poets, jazz has been present at the turning point where something original begins to happen.[10]

In the realm of new American poetry—poetry whose affiliation with the grand and bitter history of modernism has thinned or broken—critics, teachers, and students would all welcome a dependable map with some clear lines of demarcation. Yet whatever tropics and latitudes one offered (and schemes are offered all the time for polemical or pedagogical purposes), Jackson Mac Low seems likely to escape the net.

Not that Mac Low's work is without contexts or precedents. In recent years the journal $L=A=N=G=U=A=G=E$ published his prose statement on the term "language-centred," and Ron Silliman reprinted it in his anthology of "language" poets, *In the American Tree* (Orono: National Poetry Foundation, 1986). There are longer-standing connections with the conceptual- and performance-art scene around New York; Meredith Monk, for instance, has participated in Mac Low's performance groups. He took an early and important influence from John Cage, and some of his first aleatory experiments were musical works. The metaphysics in and behind his poems is explicitly tied to Zen, which allies them with a long Western tradition of Eastern emulations.

But none of this background, even if a reader is aware of it, cancels the strangeness of any first encounter with Jackson Mac Low. Nor has there been (at least since the disappearance from print of the eighth issue of *Vort*) any single obvious place to begin the acquaintance. But recently he has published *Representative Works: 1938–1985*[11]—not "collected" or even "selected": In his introduction, Mac Low carefully explains how each work was chosen as "an example of one of the *kinds* of work I've made between 1938 and now."

For most poets, this would entail a pamphlet of perhaps three or four poems—or one. Mac Low's book comprises 336 pages, about fifty different pieces or groups of pieces. The number of "kinds" is so large because Mac Low's individual poems are characterized not by a topic or voice or figure of speech or any conventional genre, but by a *method*.

Consider the first poem from his series "The Presidents of the United States":

1789

George Washington never owned a camel
but he looked thru the eyes in his head
with a camel's calm and wary look.

Hooks that wd irritate an ox
held his teeth together
and he cd build a fence with his own hands
tho he preferred to go fishing
as anyone else wd
while others did the work *for* him
for tho he had no camels he had slaves enough
and probably made them toe the mark by keeping an eye on them
for *he* wd never have stood for anything fishy.

(RW, p. 154)

This seems straightforward enough—normal syntax, post–Black Mountain abbreviations, lineation clear and unemphatic. But the premise is zany (who suggested that George Washington might own a camel?), and the poem feels oddly calm; one expects a contemporary American poem about George Washington to be either enraged or Rabelaisian. On closer inspection the language becomes peculiarly stilted—why "eyes in his head"? Why the tame "keeping an eye on them" after the more vivid "made them toe the mark"? Plausible as the poem seems, the unprepared reader is likely to feel a growing suspiciousness toward it as an utterance.

The headnote to "The Presidents" substantiates the suspicion: "Each section is headed by the first inaugural year of a president. . . . And its structure of images is that of the Phoenician meanings of the successive letters of the president's name"—in this case, "camel," "look!," "eye," "head," "camel" and "look" again, "hooks," "ox," and so on.

Mac Low's emphasis on method means that he is often explaining himself, in a prose that presents him as a sober, even pedantically rational man—an instructive contrast to the apparently nutty texts he produces and the apparently nutty mechanisms he chooses to produce them.

The "Presidents" poems contain a great deal of *made* material connecting the given key words. In the majority of Mac Low's poems, the method is given more complete control. The prose-like "Pattern Recognition by Machine" hints at a method that is not specified, the hints again being identifiable in our displaced relation to the poem's language:

> *Perceive. As letters.* Think? Think? Elusive, relations, now met most of the classic criteria of intelligence that skeptics have proposed.
>
> Relations, elusive, *can* outperform their designers: original: group from the Carnegie Institute of Technology and the Rand Corporation (now met most of the classic criteria of intelligence that skeptics have proposed). In *Principia Mathematica*, think? In *Principia Mathematica*, original: now met most of the classic criteria of intelligence that skeptics have proposed.
>
> Bertrand Russell. In *Principia Mathematica*.
>
> More elegant than the Whitehead-Russell version. *As letters. Can* outperform their designers: His ability to solve problems, in *Principia Mathematica*, now met most of the classic criteria of intelligence that skeptics have proposed. Elusive. (RW, *p. 96*)

The result of what is obviously a mechanical process is weirdly incantatory. Repetitions and syntactical discontinuities make the language unfamiliar in a way oddly similar to rhyme and meter.

In many of Jackson Mac Low's works, no single word or syntactical structure can be attributed directly to Jackson Mac Low. He creates rules for some transformation of a prior text; *choice* means selecting the text and making up the rules. How peculiar is this? Is it just a question of degree? Poets (except nonsense poets) use words we can all find in the dictionary; new poems always bear a complex relation to old poems and other texts; poetry has always helped poets limit their choices through formal rules or by narrowing and intensifying a diction. Mac Low's process of drawing all a poem's words out of a single name (as in the "Vocabulary Gathas") does not differ absolutely from "the exclusions of a rhyme," which may be one reason why we often find ourselves responding to Mac Low's unconventional poems in disorientingly familiar ways.

Yet the difference in degree is striking. *The Virginia Woolf Poems* closes with an explanation of the "genesis" of the book's first sequence, "Ridiculous in Piccadilly." The explanation includes the sort of data librarians gather: specifications of the manuscript book in which the poem was composed, meticulous records of dates and times. But as usual it centers on the rules of procedure:

> "Ridiculous in Piccadilly." comprises 11 poems drawn from Virginia Woolf's novel *The Waves* by what I call the "diastic" (on analogy with "acrostic") or "spelling-thru" method, which I began using to make poems from source texts in January 1963.
>
> After finding the title phrase in line 4, p. 88, of the first American edition (New York: Harcourt Brace, 1931), I drew one word for each of its letters. Beginning with the phrase itself, I culled only words in which the letters occupied corresponding positions (I disregarded hyphens). . . . Having spelled the phrase out once, I began again, & did so repeatedly till I'd drawn the first word of "9"—'pillarbox."—from p. 292. Then, finding no word with "u" in the 9th place, as in "ridiculous," from there thru the last page (297), I began reading the book again.[12]

Here is the first of the eleven poems:

ridiculous
Piccadilly.

end stain
bookcase,
reassuring brutally
eating-house.

eating-house.

waitresses,
in and plates right
included.

prick contains forged
companion
pale-yellow

smooth-polished melancholy
rooted,
Rippling side.

hesitating consciousness
treasures ridicule sensations,
mysteriously eating-house
imbue entirely phrase with
pictures,
thick.

Whether this is stranger than many other contemporary poems (Merwin at his most surreal, Ashbery at his most abstract, and so on) depends partly on how one reads it. Implicit in the explanation is an invitation to trace the seed phrase through the words of the poem—or, more thoroughly, to follow simultaneously Mac Low's double text and *The Waves*. We begin to scrutinize diction with a new intensity. The predominance of relatively long words, we notice, is due to the same predominance in the title-and-seed phrase, and of course to potentialities in Woolf's novel. Her dialogic language embraces possibilities like "reassuring" and "brutally," which the poem's special forgery ("forged / companion") links on one line. In the following one-word line, the usual French "restaurant" is replaced by its insistently Anglo-Saxon doublet "eating-house," which is called forth three times by three different letters it shares, position by position, with "ridiculous." "Ridiculous in Piccadilly" can provide a rich experience because it encourages a reading of so many "levels" at once—not the critical cliché of Deep Meanings, but the levels of magnitude in the text itself: phrase, word, sentence, letter, paragraph, stanza. After that, *everything* one reads becomes strange for a time.

We can also hear an invitation to emulate his method, which after all can be applied to any text. (Does this hark back to an old ideal of poetry as offering heroes for emulation?) For the sake of thoroughness, the free choice of the seed phrase (did encountering the words "ridiculous in Piccadilly" inspire Mac Low's whole labor?) can be eliminated as well by adding one more rule: Make the text its own seed. The only question then would be when to stop.

Consider a poem made from *Ulysses*. The first word's first letter is "s," and we use that word ("Stately") as ours. Because "Stately" is followed in Joyce's text by a comma, we add the comma to our poem and begin a new line after it; following Mac Low's rules, we will also use capital letters as cues to start new lines. The second letter is *t*; the next word of which that is the second letter is "stairhead"; we add that to our poem, with its comma and consequent line break. Proceeding through the *a* and *t* of "Stately," we get "bearing sustained" as our next line. Next, "Halted" shares its fifth letter with "Stately," and its capital and following comma make it a line by itself.

Finally, the line "gravely country" completes the "spelling-thru" of the first word of *Ulysses*.

The seed here might be the whole opening phrase of the novel: "Stately, plump Buck Mulligan." We might even go on past that—say, through the book's first sentence:[13]

Stately,
stairhead,
bearing sustained
Halted,
gravely country pale blood
Shut calm.

plump broke quietly mockery neck.

Mulligan's
Mulligan,
Hellenic
Will jesuit.

Mulligan,
Mulligan
Mulligan
cried came him wiped for Irish snotgreen.

them the
Thalatta!

She sweet
Stephen
Leaning sinister tolerant breath,
skyline razorblade.

contentedly,
bowsy left wear wear
Mulligan
Norman.

curling and bard.

forward always
Mulligan of if laughter,
table,
with with scared answered.

of anxiety went
What?

said,
which death,
asked,
mother's die.

for your doctor buttercups and into had am round walked gazing
Loyola,
staircase,
level day,
bay chords.

crying those fans,
beads laughed *circumdet*:

Beyond this loom other, larger works. An important one results from continuing the diastic process until it has run once through *Ulysses*. This would be a long poem—perhaps fifty pages.[14] In constructing it, I would be reading *Ulysses* with extreme care, engaged in as intense a relation to the precedent text as T. S. Eliot ("tradition and the individual talent") or Harold Bloom ("the anxiety of influence") could ask. My reading, though obviously idiosyncratic, would in fact be difficult to distinguish in terms of pure diligence from some kinds of literary critical readings.

Or is "idiosyncratic" just the wrong word? What have *I* to do with it? The course of my work would not be arbitrary in the slightest; this poem is the *only* poem that (beginning from the beginning and using these rules) can be constructed from *Ulysses*. It has inevitability, which we have been taught to expect of the greatest art.

Beyond this once-through-the-book poem, we may intuit a far vaster one: the poem that results from diastically applying the whole novel to itself, building stanzas from every single word in Joyce's text—in the process, reading through *Ulysses* five to ten thousand times.[15] Even this gigantic work would not include all the poems that could be "spelled-thru" from *Ulysses* using seeds it contains—starting points could differ. Still, though it is not certain that every word in *Ulysses* would appear directly as a word in the poem, from the poem one could reconstruct Joyce's whole book.

This suggests that my diastic poem adds no information to its precedent text. In this it differs importantly from Mac Low's "Ridiculous in Piccadilly." However silently, he embeds Woolf's text in a new context. Rules create redundancies, which introduce information and urge the resulting text toward new meaning. But rules alone are not enough to surmount the threshold of meaning; we need to perceive them as intention, invention. Mac Low accomplishes this partly by *not* pursuing the method to its logical conclusion. Mac Low's transformation presents him to us, and Woolf in his act of reading her book, and the moment of his discovering the title phrase and deciding to perform the operation of this poem, and his relishing the result ("friends splendid footballs; / disorderly continuity?"), and the moment of his deciding ("possibly cued by the coincidence of elevens") to stop. In his text we hear a dialogue among hers, her authorship, and his own.

Whether the diastic process is applied mechanically or with the luck of genius, it is impossible to *predict* how long it will take, though the procedure itself is completely deterministic. Consider the spelling through of "dressing-gown" in the second sentence of *Ulysses*. "Crouching" (*g* in the ninth position) appears on page 13, "affirmation" (*o* in the tenth) not until page 21; yet "corpsestrewn" (an improbable *w* in the eleventh position) occurs just three pages later. The book may well contain a long word whose final letter is duplicated in that position only in that word itself; its consequent repetition in the poem logically requires a complete and thorough rereading of the novel.

So the diastic poem resembles what physicists call a "chaotic" system: an incalculably complicated situation arising from the action of a simple set of motions that are completely predetermined. No true randomness is involved; the diastic method is not a chance operation. What makes Mac Low's procedures, whether random or arbitrary, seem so peculiar when we consider their results as poetry, is that once the work is begun the poet exercises no choice. In this sense his process is the opposite of improvisation, though, as we will see, he finds a way around this opposition.

Why eliminate free choice? To quote the whole two-page explanation of "Ridiculous in Piccadilly" would involve an interesting problem in copyright law: It would be (with one or two minor additions) a formula for the poem itself; anyone could reproduce it. As in other conceptual art, the *art* is partly displaced from the work of the hand or voice back into its generative idea; and in the mind it becomes anonymous, common property, like language.[16] Mac Low acts like a kind of opposite of Antin, whose deceptively plain method (go somewhere and talk) requires a unique mind and kind of mind. Mac Low is an avowed Taoist-turned-Zen-Buddhist, for whom the ego and its anxieties of identity and ownership are, if not illusory, burdensome. (This is Zen, not the "pop Zen" that, as Andrei Codrescu has remarked, is the majority religion of young Americans whether they know it or not.) Though he never really eliminates himself from the poems—fortunately—his methods push the act of making poetry in that direction.

Transcendence of the ego makes art deeply problematic, as long as art is defined by a very popular set of assumptions about lyric self-expression. Quite modern post- or anti-Romantic people find themselves implacably ruffled by the idea of computer poetry, or any other challenge to the poet's egoistic control of the work. Yet if the poet is one who selects the right words in the right order by something that more or less closely resembles divine inspiration, why should this not operate through dice or cards or yarrow stalks or some version of the *sortes Virgilianae*, all of which have been consulted for the Word of

God at one time or another? Mac Low sometimes appeals to Jung's idea of synchronicity, of meaningful simultaneity; his poetic goal is to make himself, in Alan Watts's phrase, "a source of marvelous accidents." "At one point," he remembers, "I began to think it was all bullshit: the next words I drew were 'Bear up, mule'!—so I did, and continued the work."[17] Things happening together around us mean something even when we are not aware of having meant it. His work embodies a theory about the Universe.

Some of Mac Low's poems are extravagantly formalist. The rules by which the text of "Asymmetry from Sayings of Gurdjieff" was derived are not stated; but the poem is observably self-acrostic in two dimensions, the text repeating itself both horizontally by the first letters of words and vertically in the initials of lines:

There Humanity earth's received Everything
has us masters are not 'I' there You
empty aim rule, to hundred small
river experiences; create evokes in vibrations
   Everything 'directors'
each voluntary, externals. Reach yes their
   highly illusion. Not God,
has and speak
unconsciously suffering
man and simply talk. External rule, surrounding
and real, experiences;
nothingness only that
is
the Hope English Russians East
yourself only universe . . .

                                                  (RW, *p. 104*)

But while traditional hypertrophies of formalism—including some late modernist ones—emphasize the virtuosity of the poet's control, Mac Low's redundant rescripting of his text seems instead ritualistic. It too may be traditional, but the tradition implied is an enthusiastic or ecstatic one, not aesthetic.

So it is logical that a majority of Mac Low's methods (unlike the ones examined here) are what he calls "objectively hazardous" procedures. His phrase appreciates—characteristically—how words buckle into vividness when recombined: "Hazard" means chance; he asks us, Do you feel chance to be dangerous?[18] More specifically, when the words of a poem are chosen by an elaborate method of throwing dice or referring to a table of a million random digits, is our sense of "poetry" threatened? Is the threat more or less than what we may feel in the face of Antin's quite different subversion?

When we hear any of Jackson Mac Low himself in the poems—in the chosen texts and seeds, in the "President" poems, in the gorgeous "Early Light

Poems'' that proceed by naming different kinds of light, in some poems from the eighties (such as ''Central America'') that are more direct than most mainstream poetry—his voice is charming, energetic, untrammeled, and intelligent. But he wants the poems to be more, and less, than that. Chance, as a way of defeating the ego's control, entails giving up the authority of authorship. Ego is not self, but the insistence that self be unitary. When its control over the poem is sufficiently complete, it will shut out any experience or impulse, internal or external, that threatens to be destabilizing or alien or simply unfamiliar to the ruling party. For Mac Low, chance not only allows life back into the poem, but restores life to itself as well:

> And chance—what else can I call it?—has opened
>   my life now again
> Again again again beautiful life opening up and
>   blossoming when it seems to have died to the roots
> Nothing but rotting at the roots . . .

> (RW, *p. 62*)

''Why,'' Mac Low asks in the introduction to *Representative Works*, ''did I begin to view *performance* as central and texts as primarily notations for performance (if only by a silent reader)?'' We have seen the beginnings of the answer. For a poet with Mac Low's convictions, the poem cannot stand alone on the page, either as a self-sustaining perfection or as a monument to its author. The poem needs its audience.[19]

Since the beginning of the sixties, a majority of Mac Low's poems have been meant, if not exclusively then optionally, to be spoken or sung or danced or acted out by groups of people. The performers' actions are scripted to some extent, but he leaves plenty of room both for chance operations at the time of performance and for the performers' own spontaneous choices.[20] They may decide which word to speak next, how loud, how long a silence to leave after it. (The dancers receive a text including lines like ''Pretty soon everyone's giving gold cushions or seeming to do so''; what they do next constitutes the dance. Their interpretive work is a kind of critical reading defined by his phrase ''finding concrete meanings as actions for every phrase.'')[21] Mac Low's instructions for his ''simultaneities,'' though often very elaborate, always acknowledge that his only fundamental rule is that the people performing should *listen* to each other. He calls for virtuosity, but not competition: ''Sensitivity, tact, and courtesy must be exercised in order to make every detail of one's performance contribute toward a total sound sequence that is as similar as possible to what the performer would choose to hear. While egoistic overpowering of the total sound should never occur, the exercise of virtuosity is strongly encouraged when it is carried out with as much consciousness as possible of the total situation'' (*RW*, p. 115).

Though he urges his performers to subordinate their exclusivist egos to the group, it would be perverse to hear the whisper of fascism here. The group itself is conceived not in terms of unity, but of diversity or harmony. Certainly there is no question of a leader, even when (as is usually the case) Mac Low is one of the performers. He does not much function as a playwright, much less a puppeteer. (Nor is he a bandleader.) The works for group performance complete his abnegation of authorship.

The performance pieces survive surprisingly well on the page. This may be because they are so word-centered, so attentive to the life of words in living situations—that is, against all odds, so well *written*. The ubiquitous explanations help too, and the speed of page-reading produces a rhythmic effect supplementary to anything available on a stage. But in an important way they resemble the texts of plays, or Antin's talk poems; the life of the script depends on our imaginative reconstructive ability as readers.

Yet though Mac Low has written some short plays, his work is not really dramatic in any usual sense. What Mac Low is after in these works is indicated by the "stylistic considerations" for performance that he proposes. Besides "sensitivity," they include "clarity," "seriousness," "straightness," and "audibility" (*RW*, p. 84). These are not quite what one would ask of actors. For instance, he stresses that though "loud speech may sometimes be needed for audibility—the point is not to give the effect of violent feelings" (*RW*, p. 258). "As much as possible, these emphasized words should be spoken loudly *without seeming to express anger or other violent feelings*. The effect should be that of 'turning up the volume'—a relatively 'objective' kind of loudness" (*RW*, p. 108). In part this recalls the fundamental Buddhist principle that the passions anchor one to the wheel of karma; as engagements in action, they hamper the development of the self toward the perfect disengagement of nirvana. More directly, however, the instruction to avoid overtly emotional expression is aimed at sustaining the balance of events within the performing group. Emotion, which within the self gives the whole floor to one feeling, tends in the same way to dominate a group of people.[22]

The ideal, instead, is as rich as possible a multiplicity of awareness: "Performers must become acutely conscious of both the sounds they themselves are producing and those arising from other performers, the audience, and/or the environment. It is essential to the realization of [the poems] that all performers choose as many aspects and details as possible of their individual realizations within the context of as clear an awareness of the total aural situation at each moment as performance circumstances allow" (*RW*, p. 106). Though he speaks here of the performers, Mac Low also clearly implies the experience he means the audience to have. So massive a call on our sensory attention can be overwhelming, and it can make us shut down; but as long as we balance between hysteria and boredom, the effect is exhilarating. Danny Kaye used to repeat the words of someone talking to him, a split second later; some people got mad, most found it hilarious, and almost none could keep going for more than a few seconds. Closer to the point, this is how we listen to jazz when we are listening best, hearing the response of each player to all the others. Keeping the channels open—both for performers and for the audience—can be thought of (in the terms we explored earlier) as acknowledging the multiplicity of one's own voices.

So perhaps it is not ultimately surprising that Mac Low turns out to be a consistently and intensely political poet: "My attitude toward politics is somewhat different than that of most 'committed' or 'engaged' writers and artists. I don't think that any artist *has* to 'be politically or socially conscious.' I simply feel that politics is an important aspect of life and art and that it is natural for me to incorporate political statements or attitudes or choices in my work" (Private correspondence, October 8, 1987). For Mac Low, "All's political that takes breath" (*RW*, p. 129). If this seems an improbable stance for a poet fascinated with closed linguistic systems, it is worth remembering that all linguistic systems are closed; if meaningful political discourse is possible at all, why not here? David Antin (quoted by Rothenberg in his preface) recalls Mac Low "at Bryant Park, where we had been expressly forbidden to read 'sexual or political poetry,' reading his 'non-political poem,' which he explained 'expressed no attitudes or opinions or ideas of a political nature' and nearly causing a riot with a simple litany of names."

Mac Low's most intense political statement, however, is implicit in the structure of the works for group performance.[23] In several statements over the years, he has made explicit the vision of society that this kind of project embodies, declaring himself a pacifist and an anarchist: "An 'anarchist' does not believe, as some wrongly have put it, in social chaos. He or she believes in a state of society wherein there is no frozen power structure, where all persons may make significant initiatory choices in regard to matters affecting their own lives. In such a society coercion is at a minimum & lethal violence practically nonexistent."[24] His works act out these dauntingly simple commitments, giving the performers, and to some extent the audience, a sense of what such a "state of society" would feel like. The inspiration is not only noble, but interesting. Anarchism has had as rough a time of it from the disillusioned left as from the long-dominant reactionary regimes. To hear someone unsentimentally espouse it is refreshing; to see him act it out is invigorating; to take it as seriously as he does his work could be transforming.

When Mac Low uses the word *improvise* in a performance note, he places it in quotation marks, "since each individual's choices are circumscribed by the procedural rules" that constitute the written poem (*RW*, p. 296). Spontaneous group performance that centers on words—if only because words subside into ordinary semiconsciousness so readily—probably needs that much of a given structure. But what if the performers in a group piece brought with them a whole complex of learned, invented, and imitated structures, small and large—tropes, phrases, feelings for the size of a temporal unit—all full of information in the sense that they would render significant utterances both possible and improbable enough to engage interest?

At the beginning of the sixties—at just the time when Mac Low was creating his first important performance works—Ornette Coleman gathered a "double quartet" (his own group and another with similar instrumentation) in a recording studio, and got eight people to improvise for about forty minutes. The result was *Free Jazz*. Later John Coltrane did much the same in *Ascension*. In both, one soloist after another comes to the fore while the others continue to play freely. Cecil Taylor did similar things. So did other musicians. Now, after three decades, we may be more ready to hear.

Notes

Introduction

1. Michael Harper, "Brother John," the opening poem in *Dear John, Dear Coltrane* (Pittsburgh: University of Pittsburgh Press, 1970).

2. I take my capsule definitions of the less familiar terms from Richard A. Lanham's mesmerizing *Handlist of Rhetorical Terms: A Guide for Students of English Literature* (Berkeley: University of California Press, 1968).

3. Another name for antistrophe, pretty nearly, is epistrophe. "Epistrophy" is also the name of an important Bebop tune written by Kenny Clarke and Thelonious Monk. Its melody is constructed almost entirely from variations and inversions of a single four-note theme.

Chapter 1
Lee Konitz

1. African music is not one thing, of course, despite our long-distance tendency to think so. Some of it ("particularly historical songs") keeps close to a preestablished pattern; but "the latitude for variations as well as for extemporaneous expressions gets wider and wider as one moves from such musical types to those which provide a basis for expressions of social values or social interaction," such as "songs of insult, songs of contest or boasting" and so on (Joseph H. Kwabena Nketia, *The Music of Africa* [New York: Norton, 1974], p. 237).

2. At least in what is, from a European viewpoint, the characterizing case. "The performance of music in such contexts [as sports, ceremonies and festivals] assumes a multiple role in relation to the community; it provides at once an opportunity for sharing in creative experience, for participating in music as a form of community experience, and for using music as an avenue for the expression of group sentiments" (Nketia, *Music of Africa*, p. 22).

3. "It is," for instance, "not usual to provide names for individual items of a musical type" (ibid., p. 25).

4. See Frank Kermode's enlightening essay *The Sense of an Ending* (London: Oxford University Press, 1966).

5. See Walter J. Ong, *Orality and Literacy* (London: Methuen, 1982), especially pp. 132–35 and 147–51.

6. A few of the chords indicated differ from those of published texts such as that in *The Jerome Kern Songbook* (New York: Simon & Schuster, 1953), in the direction of the usual jazz versions. The lyrics of the song are by Oscar Hammerstein, Jr.

7. Alec Wilder, in *American Popular Song* (London: Oxford University Press, 1972), calls it "not only very ingenious, but very daring. I am as surprised as Kern is alleged to have been that it became a hit" (p. 79). Wilder also retails the allegation: "There is a story to the effect that Kern was convinced that a song so complex could

never be a hit, but that a moment after voicing this fear to a friend he heard a passing pedestrian whistling it'' (p. 78).

8. The title of a blues by Desmond (on a record from the early fifties), ''Sacre Blues,'' would seem merely a weak pun on the mild French oath, except that it takes its theme from the opening bassoon solo of Stravinsky's *Sacre du printemps*. Desmond was one of the very few really verbal jazz musicians, and anecdotes of his wit are common and charming.

9. An alternative version of this relation between artist and material, especially relevant in an art born of African-American vernacular traditions, is embodied in the idea of ''Signifyin(g)'' as expounded by Henry Louis Gates, Jr., in *The Signifying Monkey: A Theory of African-American Literary Criticism* (New York: Oxford University Press, 1988). Gates's book appeared when *Jazz Text* was nearly complete. His path and mine, though origins and destinations differ, cross at important points—appreciation of jazz as culturally central, identification of Mikhail Bakhtin's ''dialogic'' criticism as a fruitful theory of ''double-voicedness,'' and so on.

10. The Konitz/Mulligan performance has been available recently on a Blue Note reissue, *Revelation* (Blue Note BN-LA-532-H2). The original, long out of print, was a ten-inch extended play disk from World Pacific records; the same company reissued *Konitz Meets Mulligan* (ST-20142), now also out of print. The session was recorded some time during 1953.

11. This technique became a West Coast jazz cliche, and Desmond and Dave Brubeck popularized it. It had roots in the Third Stream interest in classical models, to be discussed later; but Martin Williams among others points out that it also represented a revival of the relation among improvisers that prevails in Dixieland jazz—a relation radically different from that between successive soloists.

12. Eric Dolphy's bass-clarinet meditation on ''God Bless the Child'' comes to mind, along with a dozen *almost*-solo pieces by various players, such as Sonny Rollins's trios with bass and drums recorded at the Village Vanguard in 1957. It requires not only a daring horn player, but one whose native mode is *copia*, plenitude and redundancy, to undertake the reduction of jazz to a sequence of single notes. John Coltrane would do it; Miles Davis would not.

13. The various styles of jazz transcription are half-answers to the basic impossibility of accurately notating jazz (especially its rhythm, but also aspects of pitch). Notation was invented to guide performance, not to reproduce it. (This note, therefore, applies to Konitz's version of the tune, not to Kern's.) In transcription's reversal of priority, I incline less toward Gunther Schuller's pursuit of always elusive exactitude, and more toward Lewis Porter's ideal of readability. (See the Bibliography.) The most pervasive decision is whether to notate ''swung'' eighth notes as eighth notes, or to approximate the performance a little more closely with quarter-note and eighth-note triplet groups. Like Porter, I see transcription's function as better fulfilled by the former. Schuller may be too professional a musician to perceive the problem. The general problem of transcription, to which Porter's pp. 9–19 are a good introduction, will continue to concern us in later chapters.

14. Some of the names for these groups are particularly telling: the Renaissance ''consort'' suggests the concerted efforts of the players; the ''ensemble'' specializes in playing together, with maximum synchronization, which discourages improvisation.

On a different tack, the "orchestra" (from the Greek *orchesthai*, to dance), though they sit in chairs on a stage, are wont to sway and bob "with the music." Pound remarks in *The ABC of Reading* (1934; rpt. New York: New Directions, 1960) that "music begins to atrophy when it departs too far from the dance. . . . Bach and Mozart are never too far from physical movement" (p. 14).

15. Naturally jazz presents many defensible starting points. Histories sometimes begin with blues, or with the musics from which jazz took its essential elements. My concerns here lead me to accept a more usual view of jazz as a twentieth-century music. Jelly Roll Morton claimed to have invented jazz; and the audacity of the claim does not render it wholly inaccurate. Morton began very close to ragtime, as is made clear in his recording of "Maple Leaf Rag," set parallel to Scott Joplin's original piano-roll version in *The Smithsonian Collection of Classic Jazz*. This collection, compiled by Martin Williams, is certainly the best introduction to jazz available in one box.

16. This procedure finds its European musical parallel no longer in Mozart's kind of theme and variations, but in Bach's *Goldberg Variations*.

17. In the Hawkins recording, by the same token, the soloist is all; the other players merely support the extended improvisation which begins, ends and constitutes the performance. The Konitz (and Mulligan) "All the Things You Are" resembles the "Body and Soul" very closely in this respect.

18. The harmonic basis did not stay quite the same; one of Parker's chief innovations was to extend the conception of each chord to include more high and altered notes—that is, to count more notes as belonging to the chord. (This development parallels the harmonic history of European tonal music.) Again, however, the fundamental revolution of Bebop concerned the rhythmic basis of the music.

19. Besides Davis, the personnel included John Coltrane, Bill Evans, and Cannonball Adderley, as well as Wynton Kelly, Paul Chambers, and Philly Joe Jones. Recorded on February 2, 1959, the session remains dependably available—for instance, as Columbia KCS 8163.

20. The rise of free verse provides an obvious literary example. See my *Free Verse: An Essay on Prosody* (Princeton: Princeton University Press, 1981).

21. Coleman's album was in fact preceded by two brief atonal recordings (May 1949) by the Lennie Tristano group that included Lee Konitz, though those recordings were not released at the time.

22. Rather than the A of the orchestra. In general, wind instruments home on $B\flat$ more characteristically than strings. The reversal of dominance between horns and strings is another characteristic of jazz.

23. And *less* as well; a justified but unexpected "wrong" note is the heart of many of the best phrases jazz players play.

24. I leave aside the difficult question of whether tropes distinguish themselves from ordinary language, or constitute it. There is no "ordinary music"; but Stanley Fish has effectively questioned the idea of "ordinary language" as well. In any case the analogy will not run on all fours; music and language are very perplexing, though enticing, to compare. My point in commandeering the term *trope* is simply that within the general run of notes in a piece of music, a certain kind of attention leads us to pick out (and even categorize) certain moves or gestures that seem to bear a special proportion of the weight of meaning.

25. A tabulation:

Once-repeated notes: A–3; A–10/11; A–23/24; A–33; B–8/9; B–12; C–22; C–34 (?); D–15; D–
26/31 (variation); D–34; E–27/28 (simplification); E–33/34 (augmentation); F–1/4; F–12/13;
F–19/20 (augmentation); F–24; F–26/27.

Sequences: A–22/25; B–24/25; B–27/28; C–2/4; C–13/14; C–16/20; C–24/25; D–13/14; E–10/
11; E–20/22; F–16/18.

The "teetering" pattern: B–36; C–29; C–30; D–33; E–9; E–27/28; F–21/22.

26. A link with Saussure's notion of language as a structure of differences seems at
least possible, though misleadingly puristic.

27. Nor does the mining stop there. Eight years after the Mulligan recording, during
a session of August 29, 1961, released as *Motion* (Verve, reissue UMV 2563)—again
a small, loose group (Elvin Jones and Sonny Dallas on drums and bass) improvising
together for the first time—on "I'll Remember April" (third chorus, measures 25–28)
Konitz slightly revises four bars from his "All the Things You Are" (D–16/19). The
harmonic situation is the same (ii-V-I in the key of G) in the two tunes. This reuse of
material—a very far cry from the early jazz habit of working out solos and repeating
them more or less uniformly—suggests a kind of formulaic underpinning to the improvisational process, which will concern us in later chapters.

The December 1985 *down beat* magazine (pp. 54–56) provides an informative footnote on Konitz's process: In an interview, Konitz presents a sequence of ten variations
on the opening strain of "All the Things You Are," graded by increasing distance from
the tune.

28. James McCalla has suggested to me that the analogue in European music to the
structure of Konitz's solo is what Schoenberg calls the "developing variation," and
cites the second movement of Beethoven's E♭ quartet, op. 127, as an example.

Chapter 2
Robert Creeley

1. *Singing in the Rain*, another backstage musical of around the same time, and
again with a book by Comden and Green, exchanges for this stage/screen dichotomy
the watershed between silent and sound films. Again, the issue is whether the performers can survive, and capitalize on, a change of medium that is motivated by historical
pressures compounded of the artistic, the technological, and the commercial.

2. Halliwell's *Filmgoer's Companion* has this to say about Eugene O'Neill: "His
gloominess led Hollywood to regard his works as art, which killed many of the film
versions stone dead."

3. This is the same classicism parodied by Mel Brooks in *Young Frankenstein*,
when the monster and its creator shuffle and grin their way through "Puttin' on the
Ritz"—originally an Astaire number.

4. "Discourse in the Novel," from *The Dialogic Imagination*, trans. Caryl Emerson
and Michael Holquist (Austin: University of Texas Press, 1981), pp. 296–97.

5. The poem, first published in 1955, is most readily available in Creeley's *Selected
Poems* (New York: Scribner's, 1976) or the *Collected Poems* (Berkeley: University of
California Press, 1982). Donald Hall first anthologized it in *Contemporary American
Poetry* (New York: Penguin, 1962); many others have followed suit.

6. See Hugh Kenner on "stories people tell themselves" in Joyce's work, in *The Pound Era* (Berkeley: University of California Press, 1971), pp. 32–40.

7. Elsewhere I have suggested that this version is implicit in the critical ideas of Eliot and of the New Critics after him. See "Condensation: The Critical Vocabulary of Pound and Eliot," *College English* 39, no. 2 (October 1977), pp. 179–90.

8. Bakhtin, though in examining novels as dialogic economies he by no means subscribes to the New Critical reification of works of art, expresses this one shared conviction well: "The semantic structure of an internally persuasive discourse is *not finite*, it is *open*; in each of the new contexts that dialogize it, this discourse is able to reveal ever newer *ways to mean*" ("Discourse in the Novel," p. 346).

9. Preface (printed on the dust-jacket flap), *All That Is Lovely in Men* (Asheville, N.C.: Jonathan Williams, 1955), with drawings by Dan Rice. This rare book has as its cover a photo, by Jonathan Williams, of the windshield of a car of the time, through which two men can be discerned. The passenger is mostly obscured by the bright reflection of clouds and tall trees; the driver's face is also undistinguishable, but his hands grip the steering wheel tightly at the top.

10. Just so, the most common complaint against nonmetrical verse, at the beginning of its vogue in our century, was that it was prose cut arbitrarily into lines. See my *Free Verse*, especially chapter 3.

11. The finality of the last line, "out where yr going," is aided by its imitating the conclusion of a Sapphic stanza. A distant echo of the Greek form is audible throughout the poem.

12. Quoted by Trilling, *Sincerity and Authenticity* (Cambridge: Harvard University Press, 1972), p. 103.

13. Edward Storer, "Form in Free Verse," *New Republic* 6 (March 11, 1916), p. 154.

14. This is one burden of the essay, "A Backward Glance O'er Travel'd Roads." Even more to the point is Whitman's claim in the first preface to *Leaves of Grass*: "What I experience or portray shall go from my composition without a shred of my composition. You shall stand by my side and look in the mirror with me" (ll.290–92).

15. "Tradition and the Individual Talent," *Selected Prose of T. S. Eliot*, ed. Frank Kermode (New York: Harcourt Brace, 1975), p. 38.

16. See "Condensation: The Critical Vocabulary of Pound and Eliot."

17. I have examined some of the issues of Williams's prosody in *Free Verse*.

18. Quoted, from Williams's letter to the *New English Review* of November 10, 1932, by Paul Mariani, *William Carlos Williams: A New World Naked* (New York: McGraw-Hill, 1981), p. 332.

19. Quoted by Elinor Langer, *Josephine Herbst: The Story She Could Never Tell* (Boston: Little, Brown, 1984), p. 10. Langer, following Herbst, rightly narrows the phase in question to the era of the Cold War and after; but studies like Trilling's suggest that the crisis of debilitating confusion has been building up for some time.

20. From an unpublished presentation, "The Writer's Voice and Other Voices: A Dialogic Perspective" (1984). Bialostosky has extensively enlisted Bakhtin's terminology in *Making Tales: The Poetics of Wordsworth's Narrative Experiments* (Chicago: University of Chicago Press, 1984); and I am grateful to him for introducing me to its possibilities.

21. The publishing history of *Kora in Hell* is appalling. After a hiatus of fifty years, this and other early improvisational prose works have at last been available since 1970 (Williams died in 1963) in *Imaginations* (New York: New Directions, 1970). An edition by City Lights Books was in print some time previously.

22. *I Wanted to Write a Poem*, ed. Edith Heal (Boston: Beacon Press, 1958), p. 27.

23. Rather, it directly spurns the artistic traditions Williams felt Europe had imposed. Yeats had said in "Adam's Curse": "A line will take us hours maybe; / Yet if it does not seem a moment's thought, / Our stitching and unstitching has been naught." One does not miss the admonition that it had better not *be* a moment's thought.

24. "De Improvisatione: An Essay on *Kora in Hell*," in *Inventions: Writing, Textuality, and Understanding in Literary History* (New Haven: Yale University Press, 1982), p. 146.

25. *Spring and All* (1923), reprinted in *Imaginations*, p. 107.

26. This resembles the *vers libéré* characteristic of Williams's nemesis, Eliot. I have discussed the opposed methods of *vers libre* and *vers libéré* in *Free Verse*. Briefly, the latter kind of "freed verse" maintains a variable but conscious relationship with meter, while verse like most of Williams's begins and remains definitely free from the iambic repetitions of English poetic tradition.

27. Hugh Kenner is especially enlightening on this aspect of poetic language in the modern era. See *The Pound Era*, pp. 96ff.

28. Robert Frost: "It is but a trick poem and no poem at all if the best of it was thought of first and saved for the last." "The Figure a Poem Makes," *Selected Prose of Robert Frost*, ed. Hyde Cox and Edward Connery Lathem (New York: Collier, 1968), p. 19.

29. The link between religious meditation and English Metaphysical poetry is outlined by Louis Martz in his introduction to volume 1 of *The Anchor Anthology of Seventeenth Century Verse* (published in 1963 as *The Meditative Poem*; rpt. New York: Anchor, 1969), and at length in *The Poetry of Meditation* (New Haven: Yale University Press, 1954). It makes a connection with modern poetry that recalls Donne's importance to Eliot—and in fact, Eliot's to Donne.

30. First published in a book of the same name in 1953. Currently available in the *Collected Poems*, p. 125.

31. Markedly out of place in the context implied by Creeley's other rhythms and his associations within poetic history, this metrical intrusion must strike us as ironic. The iambic pentameter is there to seduce us by its sound, by its appeal to literary nostalgia; it offers us an "immoral proposition" of auditory luxury. In short, the rhythm is quoted (though here the words, their abstraction so much more mysterious than that of the first sentence, do not feel quoted). For the rhythm to feel quoted, it must be heard as double, as dialogic; and it invites comparison with the cross-rhythms that define jazz in our ears. (We do not need to hear the whole structure of a jazz performance, or even identify the tune, to know it as jazz within seconds.)

32. Pound came to center his ideas about language on a dichotomy between the Chinese, "ideogramic" method of concrete juxtapositions, and a Western scholasticism: "In Europe, if you ask a man to define anything, his definition always moves away from the simple things that he knows perfectly well, it recedes into an unknown

region, that is a region of remoter and progressively remoter abstraction. Thus if you ask him what red is, he says it is a 'colour.' If you ask him what a colour is, he tells you it is a vibration or a refraction of light, or a division of the spectrum. And if you ask him what vibration is, he tells you it is a mode of energy, or something of that sort, until you arrive at a modality of being, or non-being, or at any rate you get in beyond your depth, and beyond his depth'' (*ABC of Reading*, p. 19).

33. Ashbery, a much more broadly rhetorical poet than Creeley, has made this connection also: ''What I like about music is its ability of being convincing, of carrying an argument through successfully to the finish, though the terms of this argument remain unknown quantities. What remains is the structure, the architecture of the argument, scene or story. I would like to do this in poetry.'' Quoted by Richard Howard, *Alone with America* (New York: Atheneum, 1969), p. 29.

34. In the ''Author's Introduction (1944)'' to the *Collected Later Poems* (New York: New Directions, 1950, 1963).

35. As Auden says in the seventh sonnet of ''In Time of War'': ''. . . till he mistook for song / the little tremors of his mind and heart. . . .''

Chapter 3
Ornette Coleman

1. Whitney Balliett, ''Ornette,'' *New Yorker*, August 30, 1982, p. 63.

2. Ross Russell, *Bird Lives!* (London: Quartet Books, 1976), p. 87.

3. *Miles Davis and the Modern Jazz Giants*, Prestige PR 7650, recorded December 24, 1954.

4. See Jan Mukarovsky, *Aesthetic Form, Function, and Value as Social Facts*, trans. Mark E. Suino, Michigan Slavic Contributions (Ann Arbor: University of Michigan, 1970).

5. It begins Coleman's first record for a major label, *The Shape of Jazz to Come*, Atlantic 1317, released in 1960, with Donald Cherry on trumpet, Charlie Haden on bass, and Billy Higgins on drums.

6. Here is Michael J. Budds's review of the available literature, as of 1978: ''Because the scholarly study of jazz is a relatively recent development, the musicological literature on the topic is by no means considerable. What does exist is focused primarily on the music and musicians of the earliest periods in the history of jazz. Gunther Schuller's *Early Jazz* (New York: Oxford University Press, 1968) until recently was the only grand scale, fully documented study of jazz to date. (Frank Tirro's *Jazz: A History* [New York: Norton, 1977] was not available when this was written.) The only scholarly journals devoted to this music are *Jazzforschung* (founded 1969) and the *Journal of Jazz Studies* (founded 1974).'' Budds's own *Jazz in the Sixties* (Iowa City: University of Iowa Press, 1978), the beginning of whose preface I am quoting, is a useful though somewhat pedestrian study. The situation is changing as jazz becomes a more widely accepted area of academic specialization.

7. Gunther Schuller, ''Sonny Rollins and Thematic Improvisation,'' *Jazz Panorama*, ed. Martin Williams (New York: Da Capo, 1979), p. 241.

8. This attitude is common among critics who have leaped the gap to jazz from European concert music. Thus Budds: ''Because jazz is primarily an improviser's art, the role of the arranger has never been as prominent as that of the player'' (p. 6). More

extremely (p. 71): "The one requisite consideration for the musical structure of jazz compositions is the accommodation of the improviser."

9. Walter J. Ong, *Orality and Literacy: The Technologizing of the Word* (London: Methuen, 1982), p. 9.

10. The melody choruses take about 168 seconds, as opposed to 66 seconds of improvised solo. The introduction and coda (bass and drums only) take another 54 seconds.

11. See Ong, *Orality and Literacy*, pp. 142–43 especially, on narrative structure in Homer's oral epics, as opposed to the later Aristotelian and Virgilian artfulness.

12. (New York: MJQ Music, 1968), p. 21.

13. I have already mentioned that Lennie Tristano's group, including Lee Konitz, recorded two atonal improvisations in 1949; but also that these brief recordings were not released until much later. A few experiments in serial jazz, mostly orchestral and heavy-handed, were tried during the fifties. Bill Evans's "Twelve Tone Tune" is a charming result, but serial principles apply only to the construction of the tune itself, not to the performances built on it.

14. Budds suggests that the popularity of the Dorian in jazz is due to its affinities with the "blues scale" (Budds, *Jazz in the Sixties*, p. 47). More generally, he is perceptive about the different uses of modes in jazz and in "art music": "The use of anachronistic modal scales in both twentieth-century fine-art music and jazz . . . was not a rejection of functional harmony, but an attempt to obscure it without denying the presence of a tonal center. The use of modal scales in twentieth-century fine-art music is characterized by the use of modal scales for melodic construction, the avoidance of the leading tone, unconventional voice-leading, and the use of retrogressive or unorthodox chord progressions. In jazz the introduction of modal scales served primarily to create a static harmonic situation. Whereas earlier jazz pieces had depended upon chord progression to define key center, modal pieces depended upon the establishment of a drone or pedal point to establish tonal center. The leading tone, the dominant-tonic relationship, and other cliches of traditional harmonic practice were avoided" (pp. 44–45).

15. Most of Coleman's compositions display this kind of angularity, as Balliett points out: "His melodies are in odd lengths and shapes, and are distinguished for their lyrical beauty, which is often dirgelike, and for their sheer graceful irregularity. Clear in all he writes is the influence of Thelonious Monk, who admired Duke Ellington" ("Ornette," p. 65). Balliett's perception that the asymmetry and the lyricism are connected is acute, as is the association with Monk—the other great outsider in modern jazz.

16. "Lonely Woman" is distinguished from typical Bebop tunes also by its harmonic structure, which is either simpler (considering only the implied root movements among tonic, subdominant, and dominant) or freer, depending on one's point of view. Whereas Bebop melodies depend on and usually derive from harmonic structures, this one appears to precede any harmony imposed on it. The distinction will become clearer when we compare Coleman's version with another.

17. Though not notated in the *Collection*, Coleman's bridge actually has a quite consistent melody, moving (like the bridges of many jazz standards) into the subdominant. On the evidence of sound, this section has as *composed* a melody as any of the

rest. The MJQ version does not use it—additional evidence that they began with the transcription more in mind than the recording.

18. Budds (*Jazz in the Sixties*, pp. 71–79) gives a brief and sympathetic history of the Third Stream movement.

19. It is at first surprising to realize that the same characteristics also link this performance with ragtime music. But in fact the piano rags, at the beginning of written and recorded jazz history, were the first examples of confrontation between an oral music growing out of blues and a literate European musical tradition. Notation again represents the battle ground. The Third Stream movement, then, was not the first attempt at ecumenism, nor the last. Recordings on the ECM label (from Germany) since the early seventies represent a more recent style uniting a number of different musics; so-called ''New Age'' music is the bland descendant.

20. *Jazz Abstractions* (Atlantic 1365, 1961). The first—one might almost say the other—important Third Stream record was *Third Stream Music* (Atlantic 1345), released a year earlier, not long after *The Shape of Jazz to Come*.

21. What *are* we to call non-jazz music? Here I am calling it ''European'' in the interest of suggesting some distinctive characteristics of American art; but of course Europe has its folk musics as well, and the history of European music offers enormous variety, recently including some excellent jazz. Nor are American contributions to ''classical'' music negligible. There are only nonce solutions to this problem.

22. I am indebted to Michael Carnes, composer and computer programmer, for this observation.

23. To put it another way, as Lewis Porter suggests, notation represents a mental model of a piece of music, not a performance of the piece. Having helped shape the composer's whole understanding of music, it has a natural accuracy in representing his or her intentions. But in jazz transcription the problem is twofold: First, the mental model behind the performed music is being deduced by a listener and reproduced at second hand; and second, the improviser may be far less governed than the composer by the European post-Renaissance written-music tradition.

24. Budds, following Schuller, sees this as a derivation from African music: ''The first African retention [in jazz] was the matter of role assignment or the distribution of labor within the musical ensemble. In African music, such assignments are mainly concerned with rhythmic functions. In jazz, a harmonic consideration is also present. Each instrument was assigned to either a rhythm group or a melody group. The rhythm group, known in jazz as the 'rhythm section,' was responsible for presenting the essence of the model by providing its meter, by setting forth its harmonic architecture, and by keeping time. Members of the rhythm group usually included the drums, a bass instrument (tuba or string bass), and a 'chording' instrument (banjo, guitar, or piano). The melody group, comprised of melody instruments, was responsible for delivering melodies and counter-melodies within the harmonic context and for providing layers of rhythmic interest above the fixed foundation'' (*Jazz in the Sixties*, p. 2).

25. Coleman, quoted in Joe Goldberg, *Jazz Masters of the Fifties* (New York: Macmillan, 1965), p. 239; quoted in turn by Budds, *Jazz in the Sixties*, p. 69.

26. Cecil Taylor, quoted by Nat Hentoff in *down beat* 32 (February 25, 1965), 17; quoted in turn by Budds, *Jazz in the Sixties*, p. 80.

27. Quoted in liner notes on *The Shape of Jazz to Come*.

28. In European culture, by the same token, the performing arts have long been socially inferior to the more contemplative arts cultivated by the upper classes. At a time when musicians were servants and actors were on a social par with prostitutes, poetry was an acceptable hobby for a gentleman. A composer, then, though involved with the performing art of music, was a writer and the superior of those who realized his works in performance.

29. At the same time, Holiday's relation to the commercial songs she was given should be seen in Gates's terms as one in which she "Signified" upon the material, on the musical environment, and indeed on the whole worldview these songs underwrote. This is not to say that she parodied them. Parody means to reduce its object. Signi-fyin(g) celebrates the Signifier—perhaps at the expense of the Signified (upon), but even when insult is the ostensible purpose it remains subordinate to the boast that is the celebratory essence of Signification. In this sense, Billie Holiday did not merely conquer her inferior material, but transformed it into her own.

30. Budds is one who speaks of tone in African languages—"the vital relationship between melodic inflection and the spoken word" (*Jazz in the Sixties*, p. 18)—and goes on to quote Leroi Jones (*Blues People* [New York, Morrow, 1963], p. 227): "These young musicians . . . rely to a great extent on a closeness of vocal refer-ence. . . . Players like Coleman, Coltrane, and Rollins literally scream and rant in imitation of the human voice, sounding many times like the unfettered primitive shouter. Charlie Parker also had to restore this quality of jazz timbre after the legiti-mizing of commercial swing."

31. It is worth noting that the history of jazz—quite unlike European music—is almost coextensive with the history of its capture on disk. The first jazz records ap-peared around the end of the First World War; only the first decade or so of the music went wholly unrecorded.

Chapter 4
David Antin

1. Michael Davidson, "Writing at the Boundaries," *New York Times Book Review*, February 24, 1985, p. 1. *talking at the boundaries* was published in 1976 by New Directions—the press founded by James Laughlin at Ezra Pound's instigation to pub-lish the modernists—which released a second volume of talk-poems, *tuning*, in 1984. Further references to the first collection will be to *boundaries*.

2. George Economou, "Some Notes Towards Finding a View of the New Oral Po-etry," *Boundary2* 3, no. 2 (Spring 1975), p. 655. This special issue of *Boundary2* entitled "The Oral Impulse in Contemporary American Poetry" is one of the main repositories of critical response to Antin's work. Further references to this issue will be to *Boundary2*.

3. It is the urgency of saying something that radically distinguishes Antin's pieces from earlier experiments like the "word jazz" that Ken Nordine did for many years on Chicago radio.

4. "Antin, Cats, &c," *Vort* #7 (vol. 3, no. 1, 1975), p. 87. Half of this issue of *Vort* is devoted to Antin, and while it was available in print it provided the best array of work by and about him. Further references to this issue will be to *Vort*.

5. " 'No More Margins': John Cage, David Antin, and the Poetry of Perfor-

mance,'' the final chapter of *The Poetics of Indeterminacy* (Princeton: Princeton University Press, 1981), p. 335. Perloff gives an excellent introduction to Antin's work.

6. This dissertation, totaling over 850 pages of words and music in two volumes—surely among the best bargains available from University Microfilms International—includes almost two hundred complete transcriptions and an extensive analysis of the principles of choice and connection by which motives are linked in solos. Owens's analytic approach cannot tell us how Parker derived the motives, or how his combinations of them manage to define his unmistakable ''voice''; but the catalogue provides an indispensable basis for exploring those broader questions. Thomas Owens, ''Charlie Parker: Techniques of Improvisation,'' Ph.D. diss., UCLA, 1974. The University Microfilms order number is 75-1992; the legibility is fair.

7. ''Notes on Antin,'' *Vort* #7, p. 66. Later in this chapter we will examine the limits of the comparison between Antin's work and oral epics. Note also that ''riff,'' though suggestive, is not quite accurate; a riff is a melodic figure repeated *consecutively*, usually to provide a consistent but harmonically responsive background for a soloist.

8. David Bromige in *Vort* #7, p. 68. Perloff (*Poetics of Indeterminacy*, pp. 292–93) indicates deftly how far Antin is from doing the easiest kind of thing available in the domain of contemporary poetry. Note that the point here is not the same as Cage's defense of his silent piano piece, *4'53''*—that even if anybody *can* do it, nobody else *has*. Antin has revised some concepts of his chosen art, but he is not a conceptual artist.

9. I draw the distinction from Elaine Morgan's *The Descent of Woman*, in which she contrasts baboons, who establish troop dominance by threat and violence, and our closer relatives the chimpanzees, who vie by showing off. This distinction has some whimsical promise as a theory of art.

10. ''talking at pomona.'' This piece appeared in Antin's final book before the better-distributed New Directions volumes, called *Talking*, published in 1972 by Kulchur Press and now scarce.

11. ''The Postmodernism of David Antin's *Tuning*,'' *College English* 48, no. 1 (January 1986), p. 13. Altieri's essay is the most lucid and detailed account to date of what Antin has to say and the strategies by which he gets it said.

12. Paul quotes Perloff's letter in *So to Speak: Rereading David Antin* (London: Binnacle Press, 1982), p. 50. This pamphlet uses a journal format to respond to Antin's work in something a little like his own terms. Perloff herself, in her early review of *talking at the boundaries*, steps gingerly around the question of ''whether 'poetry' is the best term for the sort of 'improved talk' Antin gives us.'' (*New Republic*, March 5, 1977. This review includes useful close readings that do not much overlap the analyses in *The Poetics of Indeterminacy*.) She offers (like Stephen Fredman before her [*Vort* #7, p. 66]) Levi-Strauss's term *bricolage*.

13. Here Antin quotes himself in the introduction to the first piece in *talking at the boundaries*. This is not simple bad-boyism. Antin's objections to Lowell, especially, as presented in his important essay ''Modernism and Postmodernism: Approaching the Present in American Poetry'' in the first issue of *Boundary2* (Fall 1972), are as closely reasoned, persuasive, and angry as Pound's rejection of the late Victorians.

14. Antin, ''meditation 15,'' *Meditations* (Los Angeles: Black Sparrow Press, 1971), p. 36.

15. *Vort #7* interview with Barry Alpert, p. 32. I am paraphrasing for the sake of speed; Antin makes the argument at length, in some detail, and with great fervor.

16. Altieri, p. 17. The talk Altieri analyzes in detail, "the currency of the country," from *tuning*, is centered on the grandest of Antin's narrative inventions—a kind of instantaneous science-fiction invention.

17. *tuning*, p. 140. See Altieri, "Postmodernism," pp. 14–15, for a fuller analysis of this project.

18. *Vort #7*, p. 18. See also p. 12, on Antin's disaffection from the Deep Image school of poetry in the early sixties. On p. 80 (in his answer to Michael Davidson), Antin elaborates: "I'm not attacking or supporting *emotion*. I'm hostile to the vocabulary of 'emotion' and its role in social discourse. It is almost always introduced as an alibi for something else."

19. References to Frye's distinction (which occurs in *The Well-Tempered Critic*) are scattered throughout Perloff's book. Her historical literary context encourages her to make it a link between Antin and the "free prose" of Sterne, Beckett, Stein, and Ashbery. A more horizontal contemporary cross-section suggests jazz and visual performance artists as closer relations.

20. One way to improvise poetry would be to treat words primarily as sounds; one might learn to extemporize something like Edith Sitwell's poems. (Sitwell felt her work to be close to Stein's; the intervening decades have demonstrated in dozens of ways how wrong that assessment was.) Antin rejects that alternative, and indeed the whole conventional idea of "musicality" in poetry, in favor of continuous discourse—though I am arguing that in another sense music provides a good model for what he does.

21. A partial exception is Sherman Paul, who notes that the printed form is "what in fact may first 'trouble' us on opening the book" (*So to Speak*, p. 8); but he has little specific to say about it. Charles Altieri, while professing to ignore this "important issue," devotes a long footnote to the "substantial differences between the performances as spoken and what Antin calls the scores which we get as printed texts" ("Postmodernism," p. 12n.). Altieri's most pertinent observation is that anyone trying to type out Antin's texts discovers "the importance of copying his lines exactly. Very different senses of the material weight of speech emerge if we let our attention lapse, and we lose an intriguing formal game of interpreting the choices in spacing." Barry Alpert, too, notices that "Transcribing isn't merely a mechanical act for Antin—a secretary couldn't produce the final form. Intuitive artistic decisions are made. . . . The process by which Antin transcribes is certainly analogous to the way he 'writes' poems or prose" (*Boundary2*, p. 677).

22. The first books were: *Definitions* (New York: Caterpillar imprint, but self-published, 1967); *Autobiography* (New York: Something Else Press, 1967); *Code of Flag Behavior* (Los Angeles: Black Sparrow Press, 1968); and *Meditations* (Los Angeles: Black Sparrow Press, 1971). The essays in *Vort #7* contain some useful comments on these books. A collection of Antin's early work has been advertised as forthcoming by Sun and Moon Press.

23. See especially pp. 631–32 in *Boundary2*, where Antin analyzes shrewdly the implications of prose as a form and its allegiance to the kind of exclusive rationalism he associates with Kant, Descartes, and the Royal Society.

24. Richard Buckley, *The Best of Lord Buckley*, Elektra EKS-74047 (originally re-

corded in Los Angeles in 1951 and released on two disks from Vaya Records). The reader who has not heard Buckley may have a hard time doing so; his recorded performances were not many, and are usually out of print. Frank Zappa produced some of the best, from old homemade tapes, on *A Most Immaculately Hip Aristocrat* in the early seventies. Buckley was born in Stockton, California, early in the century; he was white, but spoke most often in a personal idiom compounded of black slang and stage British. His performing career encompassed mining camps and Chicago Prohibition night clubs. His talks included set pieces obviously worked out over many performances and perhaps even written down (jive biographies of Gandhi, Christ, Einstein, and the Marquis de Sade; a jive version of "The Raven" surprisingly congenial to the original), and raps that are almost certainly purely improvised. "Jonah and the Whale," by my guess, falls somewhere between the two. Buckley's most continuous project—the translation of texts (Poe, the Bible, biographies) into talk—bears an interesting relation to Antin's.

25. I am grateful to Preston McClanahan—a visual and conceptual artist more attuned than I to *opsis*—for pointing out Antin's informative though probably unconscious choreography.

26. In conversation. He has released only the two cassettes listed in the discography.

27. Howard Nemerov, noting the oversimplified belief that "a photograph never lies," helps explain how the *least* translation of an experience may be the most misleading (in conversation).

28. On "address," see the interview with Barry Alpert in *Vort* #7, and the first pages of "talking at the boundaries," where the talks' freedom of "address" is specifically opposed to the "unnatural language act" of "going into a closet   so to speak   sitting in front of a typewriter." See also *tuning*, p. 88. The phrase "uninterruptible discourse" recurs throughout Antin's and others' talk about him in *Vort* #7 and elsewhere.

29. Antin's comparison of Homer and Socrates as improvisers is worth examining; it occurs in *Boundary2*, p. 643. He and Socrates do share some purposes; both deconstruct linguistic assumptions prevalent in their societies which contribute to what can be seen either as the society's stability or its stultification. Also in *Boundary2* (p. 672), see Barry Alpert on Antin and interactive art.

30. The performance—the audible aspect of it—is available on "Diminuendo and Crescendo in Blue," *Ellington at Newport*, Columbia CS 8648.

31. Perloff comments about "whos listening out there," the last piece in *talking at the boundaries*, that "confronted by the anonymous radio audience, he cannot quite interweave his arguments and plots as he does in a live performance" (*Poetics of Indeterminacy*, p. 330).

32. William Spanos, one of the editors of the *Boundary2* issue on orality, and George Economou, in that issue, are the most forthright advocates of Antin as a truly oral poet. Even Barry Alpert sees Antin as trying to disprove Albert Lord's thesis that it is "impossible for a literate individual who expressed himself in writing to become an oral poet" (*Boundary2*, p. 675). Perloff notes that "such enthusiasm is misleading" (*Poetics of Indeterminacy*, p. 291), and Donald Wesling remarks that Antin and others "show to what degree the oral must always remain a fiction in our era" ("Difficulties

of the Bardic: Literature and the Human Voice,'' *Critical Inquiry*, Autumn 1981, p.70).

Chapter 5
Joni Mitchell

1. Joni Mitchell, *Song to a Seagull*, Reprise RS 6293, about 1968.
2. *ABC of Reading*, p. 54. Also quoted by Hugh Kenner in *The Pound Era*, p. 87, in connection with Marianne Moore's poem ''Bird-Witted.''
3. My discussion in this chapter of the special critical problems presented by songs consumes material from two essays printed in the *Centennial Review*: ''The Criticism of Song'' (vol. 19, no. 2 [Spring 1975]), and ''Analysis of a Song: Joni Mitchell's 'Michael from Mountains' '' (vol. 21, no. 4 [Fall 1977]). Mark Booth presents a different perspective on these issues—concentrating less on the interaction between words and music, more on the effect of words in the special contexts defined by song's various subgenres—in his thoughtful and urbane *The Experience of Songs* (New Haven: Yale University Press, 1981). Another excellent examination of words-with-music is James Anderson Winn's *Unsuspected Eloquence: A History of the Relations between Poetry and Music* (New Haven: Yale University Press, 1980); and every student of the subject must be indebted to John Hollander's *The Untuning of the Sky: Ideas of Music in English Poetry, 1500-1700* (Princeton: Princeton University Press, 1961).
4. One clue that more than simple transcription is involved: The distribution of words between lines 5 and 6 in the third verse breaks the syllabic pattern established in previous verses. The effect is a visual representation of an audible fact—that the caesura in line 5 in the first two verses becomes a sharper syntactical disjunction in the third.
5. John Hollander, *Vision and Resonance* (New York: Oxford University Press, 1975), p. 10.
6. In *The Philosophy of Literary Form* (1941; rpt. New York: Vintage, 1957), pp. 296–304.
7. For the distinction, see Leonard B. Meyer, *Emotion and Meaning in Music* (Chicago: University of Chicago Press, 1956), pp. 102–3, and the comments on that passage by W. K. Wimsatt, Jr., and Monroe C. Beardsley in ''The Concept of Meter: An Exercise in Abstraction,'' *PMLA* 74 (Dec. 1959), p. 589.
8. Of course, as the name reminds us, the familiar poetic ''feet'' were originally just such musical *metra*, rhythms to which a singing group could dance. But the history of poetic meter parallels the history of European concert music (and one version of the history of jazz) as a gradual process of abstraction from the physical dance toward what Pound in another context called ''the dance of the intellect among syllables.''
9. In a sense, music is speech whose pitch features are overdetermined and systematized. This is the truth and absurdity of the line from *The Music Man*: ''Singing is only *sustained talking*.'' For more on pitch in speech, see for example Kenneth L. Pike, *The Intonation of American English* (Ann Arbor: University of Michigan Press, 1956).
10. *The Roches*, Warner Brothers BSK 3298, released in 1979.
11. Thus, later verses of the song do not obey the syllabic pattern of the first with anything like Mitchell's strictness.
12. Compare, for a similar technique with a range of results: the witty cross-rhythm

of a single phrase repeated at several different points relative to the measure in Paul Desmond's solo on "How High the Moon" (*Dave Brubeck: The Fantasy Years*); the rhythmic shift that a subliminal meter creates in Eliot's "Burnt Norton"—words "Decay with imprecision, *will* not stay in place, / Will *not* stay still"; the obsessive song printed at the end of Beckett's *Watt*, with its multiple readjustments of a single falling melodic phrase.

13. Dylan too has used "enjambement," even over the break between verses in a song, to deepen an ironic tone. See "Fourth Time Around," from *Blonde on Blonde*:

> I waited in the hallway, she went to get it
> And I tried to make sense
> Out of that picture of you in your wheelchair
> And leaned up against
>   [four-measure break]
> Her Jamaican rum;
> And when she did come
> I asked her for some . . . .

14. Elektra Musician 60366-1-E. The album was recorded in 1984 at various concerts in Germany.

15. Finally, perhaps one should add what might be McFerrin's own—as opposed to a recording company's—reason for giving his album its title: "On July 11, 1977, I distinctly heard a voice inside my mind telling me to be a singer" (liner notes to *The Voice*).

16. Brian Priestley, in *Mingus: A Critical Biography* (London: Quartet, 1982) recounts this history. He sniffs at Mitchell, Mingus's "last and most unlikely collaborator," in the predictable way of many jazz aficionados: "Her singing is almost good enough to make one think of Sheila Jordan or Annie Ross" (p. 220). Mingus himself, who believed passionately in the continuity of various musics, would have been the last to share this trite disdain.

17. "Although the Joni Mitchell recordings can hardly be considered part of the Mingus canon, it is worth noting that her lyrics for *Goodbye Pork Pie Hat* are far superior to those recorded by Rahsaan Roland Kirk." Priestley, *Mingus*, p. 220.

18. The phrase "classical American music" has gained increasing currency among historically conscious (and often academically employed) jazz musicians. It is a debatable term—"Romantic" might be more apt, for instance—and one that is often used merely for its honorific force to assure the dignity of an art that (as the universal folklore has it) began in whorehouses. But the phrase does suggest some characteristics of jazz that are too rarely included in the popular view: the length of its heritage (on at least three continents), its difficulty (the theoretical and technical expectations of modern jazz players rival those of any other musical discipline), the richness of its variety, and the intensity of its mutual involvement with American culture.

19. In these respects she sounds much more like Sarah Vaughan, the consummate "instrumentalist" among jazz vocalists, than like the singers Priestley names, though her voice does not have the weight of Vaughan's.

20. On *Mingus Ah Um*, Columbia CS 8171, recorded in about 1959.

21. This is a species of jazz that would be utterly improbable if it were not for records.

Chapter 6
Jazz, Song, Poetry

1. *Together* (Concord Jazz CJ-289, 1985). Concord Jazz is Remler's home company rather than Coryell's.

I suppose this is the place to add the gloomy note that Emily Remler died—at 32, of a heart attack—early in 1990. I have kept references to her in the present tense in which they were written.

2. Larry Coryell has since confirmed my identification. Note that my experience suggests that this skill of recognition benefits from *un*consciousness, like many other skills discussed by Julian Jaynes in *The Origin of Consciousness in the Breakdown of the Bicameral Mind* (Boston: Houghton Mifflin, 1976).

3. Another realm in which the ability to recognize voices sometimes comes under scrutiny is the courtroom. An article from the *Providence Journal* (July 16, 1986) bears these headlines: ''Judge faults fairness of 'voice line-up,' blocks its use as evidence; Police told to use more similar voices when making tape.''

4. A more elaborate example is the recording by Art Garfunkel, Paul Simon, and James Taylor of Sam Cooke's ''What a Wonderful World It Could Be.'' Our practiced ears are asked to identify not only the quick changes among lead singers, but also the three possible pairs of singers. It is a delightful example of complex, instant nostalgia.

5. Asylum 7E-1117, released in 1977.

6. I have taken all quotations from the printed version of the lyrics on the record sleeve inside the liner. As usual, there is no guarantee that Waits approved the lineation, spelling (''payed for''), punctuation, or layout. But printed lyrics are at best an aid to listening anyway, and attempts at correction would simply introduce more mediation of debatable value.

7. ''Barber Shop,'' on the same album, carries the method still further, giving us a mélange of all the customers in the shop as well as the barber himself. The characters are not very clearly delineated, of course; but the experiment is fascinating.

8. Ai, *Sin* (Boston: Houghton Mifflin, 1986), pp. 27-29.

9. Bakhtin, *The Dialogic Imagination*, p. 341.

10. Philip Levine, *The Names of the Lost* (New York: Atheneum, 1978).

11. Few poets are as disarmingly aware of the problem of a first person as Levine. At a reading at Washington University in 1972, he told the following improbable story on himself: that when his first book was in press the printer called him at night with ''a terrible emergency—we've run out of capital I's!''

Chapter 7
Jackson Mac Low

1. On the same page Wilkes gives offhand an example that shows how deeply our ideas about identity are embedded in the logical structure of language. After remarking that ''we are simply unaccustomed to individuals . . . who want to smoke and do not want to smoke,'' she points out in a footnote that ''we are of course familiar with the fact that millions of people want to smoke while wanting *not* to smoke.''

2. It also provides an unexpected common ground for theories of the constitution of human mentality as different as those of Freud (ego, superego, and id, with a submerged part of mind inaccessible to consciousness), Herman Hesse (in *Steppenwolf*),

Julian Jaynes (*The Origin of Consciousness in the Breakdown of the Bicameral Mind*), and indeed Bakhtin in his suggestion of the self's internal heteroglossia.

3. All the words that denote selfhood are subject to similar critiques. An "individual" is that which cannot be divided from itself, and "individuality" embodies all the logical conundrums that entails. "Person" and "personality," from *persona*, presume at least the doubleness of the actor's face and mask. Even "self" arises from a pronoun meaning "same" by a very slow growth of self-consciousness, not becoming the familiar philosophical substantive "Self" until late in the seventeenth century. As this modern construct has arisen, it has inexorably displaced the one really unequivocal term, "soul."

4. The jazz journalism of Philip Larkin, collected in *All What Jazz: A Record Diary, 1961–1971* (New York: Farrar, Straus, 1985), gives a clear but quite perverse view of this historical shift.

5. Introduction to *Black Spirits: A Festival of New Black Poets in America* (New York: Random House, 1972), p. xxi.

6. "Jazz and the White Critic" was reprinted as the lead essay in Leroi Jones, *Black Music* (New York: Morrow, 1973). "The Great Music Robbery" ends Baraka's 1987 collection (with Amina Baraka), *The Music: Reflections on Jazz and Blues* by the same publisher; later references to this essay will be to *GMR*.

7. A transcript of the program—number 2978—is available from Box 345, New York, N.Y. 10101.

8. To clarify: Simon invited a number of black South African musicians to the United States to record with him, paying them three times the New York union rates. The theft, then, cannot be seen as monetary in a *literal* way.

9. On this point, see especially the painstaking work of Fred Lerdahl and Ray Jackendoff, *A Generative Theory of Tonal Music* (Cambridge: MIT Press, 1983). An early chapter entitled "The Connection with Linguistics" carefully clears away the grand tempting oversimplifications (summarized by the cliché of "music as a universal language"); a late chapter entitled "A Deep Parallel Between Music and Language" tries to establish a much narrower bridge with a more solid foundation.

10. Levine, Creeley, and Antin have all mentioned in conversation—always with a certain intensity—the personal importance of jazz early in their careers.

11. New York: Roof Books, 1986. Further references will be to *RW*.

12. *The Virginia Woolf Poems* (Providence: Burning Deck, 1986).

13. Mac Low does not state the grounds for dividing stanzas, but inspection of "The Virginia Woolf Poems" indicates that any terminal punctuation mark ("."," "!", "?") dictates a following blank line. This principle is actually rather important to the sense of continuity—the mad, evocative sense of near-sense—that the method produces.

14. It is very difficult—for reasons to be outlined in a moment—to estimate from a relatively small sample what the dimensions of a longer operation would be. The guesses given here are plausible statistically; but nonstatistical flukes can alter results grossly.

15. Doubling the size of the input text more or less doubles the size of the output text (larger than input by a factor of roughly six), but increases re-entrances (points where we have read through the text and must return to "Stately, plump Buck Mulligan" again) by only about 20 percent. *Ulysses* contains about 1½ million characters. It is possible to extrapolate an output text of perhaps nine million, with about six thousand re-entrances; but these estimates are necessarily very tentative.

16. Some of Creeley's smallest poems—

Here I
am. There
you are.

(a section from "I cannot see you" in *Pieces* [*Collected Poems*, p. 389])—seem like conceptual art in just this sense. Their medium is not really the page or even the ear (they are over almost as soon as one begins reading), but in the mind that instantly memorizes them and can turn them over and over like odd, clear pebbles. It is the sense of this release that makes Creeley seem, not the latest master in the Whitman-Williams-Olson line, but the first master of postmodernist poetry.

17. *Vort* #8 (vol. 3, no. 2, 1975), p. 4.

18. Mac Low must have derived the phrase from the Surrealist motto "le hasard objectif," though the array of puns is absent in French. Jerome Rothenberg, in his preface to *Representative Works*, is especially clear on the difficulties and achievements that Mac Low's use of chance creates.

19. Such a poetry—as much as performed jazz—makes the position taken by Wimsatt and Beardsley in their essay "The Affective Fallacy" irrelevant; it is not a matter of "confusing the poem with its effects," but of recognizing that it is impossible to understand the poem separately from the audience's active, receptive work with it. At the same time, as we have seen, jazz (and much of the poetry in close historical relation to it) obviates the principle of their earlier essay, "The Intentional Fallacy"; we can hardly separate jazz from its "cause," the jazz musician. At least to this extent, these contemporary arts place the New Critical tradition based on those Fallacies irrevocably in the past.

20. There is a potential point of contact here with Antin's dedication to improvised poetry. In the interview with Barry Alpert in *Vort* #7, while discussing the constrained improvisational nature of "The London March" and "In Place of a Lecture," which immediately preceded his discovery of the pure talk poem, Antin said, "I'd even thought at that time of getting together an improvisatory group and working as a kind of director" (p. 29). Some closer but more complex parallels emerge from Antin's descriptions of various kinds of *sortes* and *skimming* poems that he tried during the sixties; see *Vort*, pp. 22–23 and 27.

21. "Some Remarks to the Dancers (How the Dances Are to Be Performed & How They Were Made)," *The Pronouns: A Collection of Forty Dances for the Dancers* (Barrytown, N.Y.: Station Hill, 1979), p. 67.

22. It is probably relevant to recall Antin's rejection of a "vocabulary of emotion" as obscuring the clear perception of "the real."

23. It is interesting to compare Mac Low's work in this respect with that of Steve Reich, the "minimalist" composer. Both use deterministic methods as the basis for works; both are interested in the intricacies of arranging multiple performers in concert with one another; and Reich insists that even the most apparently mechanistic piece—such as "Clapping Music"—has political content.

24. This is the beginning of a statement originally published in *A Controversy of Poets* (ed. Kelly and Leary; Garden City: Doubleday/Anchor, 1965); Mac Low quotes himself in the "Reflections on the Occasion of the DANCE SCOPE Issue" in *The Pronouns*, his most remarkable performance work to date.

Bibliography

Ai. *Sin*. Boston: Houghton Mifflin, 1986.

Alpert, Barry. "Post-Modern Oral Poetry: Buckminster Fuller, John Cage, and David Antin." *Boundary2* 3, no. 3 (Spring 1985), p. 665.

Altieri, Charles. "The Postmodernism of David Antin's *Tuning*." *College English* 48, no. 1 (January 1986), p. 13.

Antin, David. "Modernism and Postmodernism: Approaching the Present in American Poetry." *Boundary2* 1, no. 1 (Fall 1972), p. 98.

————. *Autobiography*. New York: Something Else Press, 1967.

————. *Code of Flag Behavior*. Los Angeles: Black Sparrow Press, 1968.

————. *Definitions*. New York: Caterpillar, 1967.

————. Interview with Barry Alpert. *Vort* #7, vol. 3, no. 1 (1975), p. 3.

————. *Meditations*. Los Angeles: Black Sparrow Press, 1971.

————. *Talking*. New York: Kulchur, 1972.

————. *talking at the boundaries*. New York: New Directions, 1976.

————. *tuning*. New York: New Directions, 1984.

Bakhtin, Mikhail. *The Dialogic Imagination*. Trans. Caryl Emerson and Michael Holquist. Austin: University of Texas Press, 1981.

Balliett, Whitney. "Ornette." *The New Yorker*, August 30, 1982, p. 63.

Baraka, Amiri (Leroi Jones). *Black Music*. New York: Morrow, 1973.

————. *Blues People*. New York, Morrow, 1963.

————. *The Music: Reflections on Jazz and Blues*. New York: Morrow, 1987.

Bialostosky, Don H. "The Writer's Voice and Other Voices: A Dialogic Perspective." Unpublished presentation to New England Modern Language Association, 1984.

————. *Making Tales: The Poetics of Wordsworth's Narrative Experiments*. Chicago: University of Chicago Press, 1984.

Booth, Mark W. *The Experience of Songs*. New Haven: Yale University Press, 1981.

Bromige, David. "Talking Antin as Writing." *Vort* #7, vol. 3, no. 1 (1975), p. 68.

Bruns, Gerald. *Inventions: Writing, Textuality, and Understanding in Literary History*. New Haven: Yale University Press, 1982.

Budds, Michael J. *Jazz in the Sixties*. Iowa City: University of Iowa Press, 1978.

Burke, Kenneth. "On Musicality in Verse." *The Philosophy of Literary Form*. 1941; rpt. New York: Vintage, 1957, p. 296.

Coleman, Ornette. *A Collection of Twenty-six Ornette Coleman Compositions*. New York: MJQ Music, 1968.

Creeley, Robert. *All That Is Lovely in Men*. Asheville, N.C.: Jonathan Williams, 1955.

————. *Collected Poems*. Berkeley: University of California Press, 1982.

Davidson, Michael. "Writing at the Boundaries." Review of David Antin's *Talking at the Boundaries*. *The New York Times Book Review*, February 24, 1985, p. 1.

Economou, George. "Some Notes Towards Finding a View of the New Oral Poetry." *Boundary2* 3, no. 3 (Spring 1975), p. 655.

Eliot, T. S. "Tradition and the Individual Talent." *Selected Prose of T. S. Eliot*. Ed. Frank Kermode. New York: Harcourt, Brace, 1975.

Fredman, Stephen. "Notes on Antin." *Vort #7*, vol. 3, no. 1 (1975), p. 66.

Frost, Robert. "The Figure a Poem Makes." *Selected Prose of Robert Frost*. Ed. Hyde Cox and Edward Connery Lathem. New York: Collier, 1968.

Frye, Northrop. *The Well-Tempered Critic*. Bloomington: Indiana University Press, 1963.

Gates, Henry Louis, Jr. *The Signifying Monkey: A Theory of African-American Literary Criticism*. New York: Oxford University Press, 1988.

Goldberg, Joe. *Jazz Masters of the Fifties*. New York: Macmillan, 1965.

Harris, William J. *The Poetry and Poetics of Amiri Baraka: The Jazz Aesthetic*. Columbia: University of Missouri Press, 1985.

Hartman, Charles O. "Analysis of a Song: Joni Mitchell's 'Michael from Mountains'." *The Centennial Review* 21, no. 4 (Fall 1977), p. 401.

————. "Condensation: The Critical Vocabulary of Pound and Eliot." *College English* 39, no. 2 (October 1977), p. 179.

————. "The Criticism of Song." *The Centennial Review* 19, no. 2 (Spring 1975), p. 96.

————. *Free Verse: An Essay on Prosody*. Princeton: Princeton University Press, 1981.

Hollander, John. *Vision and Resonance*. New York: Oxford University Press, 1975.

Howard, Richard. *Alone with America*. New York: Atheneum, 1969.

Jaynes, Julian. *The Origin of Consciousness in the Breakdown of the Bicameral Mind*. Boston: Houghton Mifflin, 1976.

Jones, Leroi. *See* Baraka, Amiri.

Kenner, Hugh. "Antin, Cats, &c." *Vort #7*, vol. 3, no. 1 (1975), p. 87.

————. *The Pound Era*. Berkeley: University of California Press, 1971.

Kermode, Frank. *The Sense of an Ending*. London: Oxford University Press, 1966.

Kern, Jerome. *The Jerome Kern Songbook*. New York: Simon & Schuster, 1953.

Konitz, Lee. "Lee Konitz: Back to Basics." Interview with David Kastin. *down beat*, December 1985, p. 54.

Langer, Elinor. *Josephine Herbst: The Story She Could Never Tell*. Boston: Little, Brown, 1984.

Larkin, Philip. *All What Jazz: A Record Diary, 1961–1971*. New York: Farrar, Straus, 1985.

Lee, Don L. *See* Madhubuti, Haki.

Lerdahl, Fred, and Ray Jackendoff. *A Generative Theory of Tonal Music*. Cambridge: MIT Press, 1983.

Levine, Philip. *The Names of the Lost*. New York: Atheneum, 1978.

Mac Low, Jackson. *Representative Works: 1938–1985*. New York: Roof Books, 1986.

————. *The Pronouns: A Collection of Forty Dances for the Dancers*. Barrytown, N.Y.: Station Hill, 1979.

————. *The Virginia Woolf Poems*. Providence: Burning Deck, 1986.

MacNeil/Lehrer News Hour. Transcript no. 2978 (February 25, 1987).

Madhubuti, Haki (Don L. Lee). Introduction to *Black Spirits: A Festival of New Black Poets in America*. New York: Random House, 1972, p. xxi.

Mariani, Paul. *William Carlos Williams: A New World Naked*. New York: McGraw-Hill, 1981.

Martz, Louis. Introduction to vol. 1 of *The Anchor Anthology of Seventeenth Century Verse*. Published in 1963 as *The Meditative Poem*. Rpt. New York: Anchor, 1969.

————. *The Poetry of Meditation*. New Haven: Yale University Press, 1954.

Meyer, Leonard B. *Emotion and Meaning in Music*. Chicago: University of Chicago Press, 1956.

Morgan, Elaine. *The Descent of Woman*. New York: Stein and Day, 1972.

Mukarovsky, Jan. *Aesthetic Form, Function, and Value as Social Facts*. Trans. Mark E. Suino. Michigan Slavic Contributions. Ann Arbor: University of Michigan, 1970.

Nketia, Joseph H. Kwabena. *The Music of Africa*. New York: Norton, 1974.

Ong, Walter J. *Orality and Literacy: The Technologizing of the Word*. London: Methuen, 1982.

Owens, Thomas. "Charlie Parker: Techniques of Improvisation." Ph.D. diss., UCLA, 1974.

Paul, Sherman. *So to Speak: Rereading David Antin*. London: Binnacle Press, 1982.

Perloff, Marjorie. Review of David Antin's *talking at the boundaries*. *The New Republic*, March 5, 1977.

————. *The Poetics of Indeterminacy*. Princeton: Princeton University Press, 1981.

Pike, Kenneth L. *The Intonation of American English*. Ann Arbor: University of Michigan Press, 1956.

Porter, Lewis R. "John Coltrane's Music of 1960 through 1967: Jazz Improvisation as Composition." Ph.D. diss., Brandeis University, 1983.

Pound, Ezra. *The ABC of Reading*. 1934; rpt. New York: New Directions, 1960.

Priestley, Brian. *Mingus: A Critical Biography*. London: Quartet Books, 1982.

Russell, Ross. *Bird Lives!* London: Quartet Books, 1976.

Saussure, Ferdinand de. *Course in General Linguistics*. Ed. Charles Bally and Albert Sechehaye with Albert Riedlinger. Trans. Wade Baskin. New York: McGraw-Hill, 1966.

Schuller, Gunther. "Sonny Rollins and Thematic Improvisation." In *Jazz Panorama*. Ed. Martin Williams. New York: Da Capo, 1979.

————. *Early Jazz: Its Roots and Musical Development*. New York: Oxford University Press, 1968.

————. *The Swing Era: The Development of Jazz, 1930–1945*. New York: Oxford University Press, 1988.

Silliman, Ron. *In the American Tree*. Orono: National Poetry Foundation, 1986.

Storer, Edward. "Form in Free Verse." *The New Republic* 6 (March 11, 1916), p. 154.

Taylor, Cecil. Interview with Nat Hentoff. *down beat* 32 (February 25, 1965), p. 17.

Trilling, Lionel. *Sincerity and Authenticity*. Cambridge: Harvard University Press, 1972.

Wesling, Donald. "Difficulties of the Bardic: Literature and the Human Voice." *Critical Inquiry*, Autumn 1981, p. 69.

Whitman, Walt. "A Backward Glance O'er Travel'd Roads." In *Leaves of Grass*. Ed. Sculley Bradley and Harold W. Blodgett. New York: Norton, 1973. P. 561.

Whitman, Walt. Preface to 1855 edition of *Leaves of Grass*. Ed. Sculley Bradley and Harold W. Blodgett. New York: Norton, 1973. P. 711.

Wilder, Alec. *American Popular Song*. London: Oxford University Press, 1972.

Wilkes, Kathleen V. ''Multiple Personality and Personal Identity.'' *British Journal for the Philosophy of Science* 32 (1980), p. 331.

Williams, Martin, ed. *Jazz Panorama*. New York: Da Capo, 1979.

Williams, William Carlos. ''Author's Introduction (1944).'' *Collected Later Poems*. New York: New Directions, 1950, 1963.

———. *I Wanted to Write a Poem*. Ed. Edith Heal. Boston: Beacon Press, 1958.

———. *Imaginations*. New York: New Directions, 1970.

Wimsatt, W. K., Jr., and Monroe C. Beardsley. ''The Concept of Meter: An Exercise in Abstraction.'' *PMLA* 74 (December 1959), p. 589.

Winn, James Anderson. *Unsuspected Eloquence: A History of the Relations between Poetry and Music*. New Haven: Yale University Press, 1980.

Yeats, W. B. ''Adam's Curse.'' In *Collected Poems*. New York: Macmillan, 1956.

Discography ———————————————————————

Antin, David. *The Archaeology of Home & Lemons*. High Performance Audio HP014, 1987.

———. *The Principle of Fit, II*. Watershed Tapes C-145, 1980.

Buckley, [Richard] Lord. *The Best of Lord Buckley*. 1951; reissue Elektra EKS-74047.

Coleman, Ornette. *The Shape of Jazz to Come*. Atlantic 1317.

Coryell, Larry, and Emily Remler. *Together*. Concord Jazz CJ-289, 1985.

Davis, Miles. *Kind of Blue*. Columbia KCS 8163, 1959.

———. *Miles Davis and the Modern Jazz Giants*. Prestige PR 7650, December 24, 1954.

Dylan, Bob. "Fourth Time Around." *Blonde on Blonde*. Columbia C2S 841, 1966.

Ellington, Duke. "Diminuendo and Crescendo in Blue." *Ellington at Newport*. Columbia CS 8648.

Garfunkel, Art, with James Taylor and Paul Simon. "What a Wonderful World It Could Be." *Watermark*. Columbia JC 34875, 1978.

Konitz, Lee. *Lone-Lee*. Inner City 2035, 1974.

McFerrin, Bobby. *Bobby McFerrin*. Elektra Musician EI-60023, 1982.

———. *The Voice*. Elektra Musician 60366-1-E.

Mingus, Charles. *Mingus Ah Um*. Columbia CS 8171.

Mitchell, Joni. *Song to a Seagull*. Reprise RS 6293.

Modern Jazz Quartet. "Lonely Woman." *The Art of the Modern Jazz Quartet: The Atlantic Years*. Atlantic SD2-301.

———. *John Lewis Presents Contemporary Music: Jazz Abstractions: Compositions by Gunther Schuller and Jim Hall*. Atlantic 1365, 1961.

Modern Jazz Quartet and guests. *Third Stream Music*. Atlantic 1345, 1960.

Mulligan, Gerry, and Lee Konitz. *Revelation* (Blue Note BN-LA-532-H2).

Roche Sisters. *The Roches*. Warner Brothers BSK 3298, 1979.

Tristano, Lennie. *Crosscurrents*. Capitol Jazz Classics, vol. 14. Capitol M-11060.

Waits, Tom. *Foreign Affairs*. Asylum 7E-1117, 1977.

Williams, Martin, comp. *The Smithsonian Collection of Classic Jazz*. Smithsonian P6 11891, in collaboration with Columbia Special Products.

Index